ZWINGLI'S THEOCRACY

ZWINGLI'S THEOCRACY

Robert C. Walton

UNIVERSITY OF TORONTO PRESS

© University of Toronto Press 1967

Printed in Canada

To
My
Parents

Preface

PROFESSOR ROLAND H. BAINTON PROPOSED THE GENERAL
theme of this study and guided the research. Thanks to his good offices,
Professor Fritz Blanke, of the University of Zurich, was kind enough
to show the author how to begin to work with the Zwingli material. The
object of the study was to discover what Zwingli's conception of the
role and relationship between the magistracy and the clergy in the
government of society was during his early years as a reformer. Professor
Blanke's suggestion that the best way to begin was to consult Zwingli's
later writings on the subject opened a new perspective. When the conclusions reached in these treatises, composed between 1528 and 1531,
were compared with Zwingli's earlier works, those dating from his
humanist phase and his first four years at Zurich, a marked continuity
in Zwingli's thought became apparent.

Subsequent research also revealed a close connection between the
actual development of the relationship of the clergy and the secular
magistracy at Zurich, both before and during the Reformation, and
Zwingli's conception of what it should be. The key to Zwingli's success
at Zurich appeared to be that the theory, which he had begun to elaborate
before his arrival in the city, conformed to the pattern which had already
been established by the city magistracy before 1519.

The evidence revealed a discrepancy between the findings reached by
secondary works on the subject, especially those written by Mennonite
Historians, and what Zwingli himself had said and done. Few of the
authors consulted agreed upon what Zwingli's conception of the two
offices was, but all insisted that Zwingli was the advocate of "theocratic"
government at Zurich. The material drawn from the primary sources
indicated that, although Zwingli was the defender of a theory of government which envisaged the co-operation between the spiritual and secular
authority in a Christian society, he was not the proponent of a "theocracy" as the term is understood by modern writers.

The book was long in writing. Now that it is ready to go to press the
author wishes to express his appreciation to a former teacher, Professor
George H. Williams, of Harvard Divinity School, who tried to teach a

none too promising divinity student to respect a document and to read it with care. As the study slowly took form Professor Bainton was ever generous in his advice and comment. At a crucial moment, Dr. Charles Garside gave the encouragement needed to complete the study and flattered the writer by making use of it before its completion. Dr. John Headley, of the University of North Carolina, read and criticized the manuscript, and saved it from some of its many failings. Father James Hanrahan, C.S.B., of the University of British Columbia ever gently corrected the author's unfortunate Latin translations. Where they are correct his hand can be seen, but sad to say he could not always be present. An unknown reader for the University of Toronto Press also helped a great deal, more in fact than he can know. Dr. Richard Marius, of the University of Tennessee, was always ready for a talk which helped the most. Mr. Emerson Ford, of the Duke University Library, found the books which were needed and was invariably patient with a young instructor. Professor Margaret Ormsby, of the University of British Columbia, found the money which paid for the final typing of the manuscript. Miss Francess Halpenny, of the University of Toronto Press, kindly consented to read the finished product and had it referred to the Humanities Research Council of Canada. This work has been published with the help of a grant from the Humanities Research Council of Canada using funds provided by the Canada Council. The author alone is responsible for the errors of omission and commission which are surely present.

Finally, I can only thank Professor Leonhard von Muralt, of the University of Zurich, for giving me a copy of his article "Zum Problem der Theokratie bei Zwingli," which is soon to be published in the *Bonjour Festschrift*. Unfortunately, this book was in page proofs before I received the article and it was not possible to make use of Professor von Muralt's discussion of "theocracy" and his extremely revealing remarks concerning the actual composition and function of the Secret Council, and Zwingli's relationship to it.

Contents

Abbreviations

PRIMARY SOURCES

E.A. Egli, E. (ed.), *Actensammlung zur Geschichte der Zürcher Reformation in den Jahren 1519–1533.*
ECP Erasmus, *The Education of a Christian Prince.* Ed. L. K. Born.
PF Erasmus, *The Praise of Folly.* Ed. H. H. Hudson.
L Dr. *Martin Luthers Werke, Kritische Gesammtausgabe.* Ed. P. Pietsch.
   Vol. XI.
M *Philipi Melanthonis Opera Quae Supersunt Omnia.* Ed. C. G.
   Bretschneider. Vol. I.
Q *Quellen Zur Geschichte der Täufer in der Schweiz.* Ed. L. von Muralt,
   W. Schmid. Vol. I.
LCC *Library of Christian Classics.* Ed. J. Baillie, J. T. McNeill, H. P. Van
   Dusen, Vol. XIV.
Z *Huldreich Zwinglis Sämtliche Werke.* Ed. E. Egli, G. Finsler, Vols.
   I-XIV.

ARTICLES AND PERIODICALS

ARG *Archiv für Reformationsgeschichte*
ASR *Archives de Sociologie des Religions*
DTC *Dictionnaire de Théologie Catholique*
JES *Journal of Ecumenical Studies*
JSG *Jahrbuch für Schweizerische Geschichte*
GR *The Germanic Review*
MQR *Mennonite Quarterly Review*
NB *Neujahrsblatt zum Besten des Waisenhauses in Zürich für 1921*
NJKA *Neue Jahrbücher für das Klassische Altertum, Geschichte und*
   Deutsche Literatur und für Pädagogik
TSK *Theologische Studien und Kritiken*
ZSK *Zeitschrift für Schweizerische Kirchengeschichte*
ZWI *Zwingliana*

Introduction

THE PURPOSE OF THIS BOOK IS TO CLARIFY THE RELATIONSHIP between the clergy and the magistracy which grew out of Zwingli's reforming work at Zurich. After a careful examination of the material, I have concluded that Zwingli had evolved the substance of his political theory by the end of 1523; and consequently the main focus of the study is upon the early stages of Zwingli's career at Zurich. The developments which took place after 1523 are only briefly discussed as a preface to the concluding chapters.

This examination of Zwingli's first years at Zurich rests upon one major assumption. Speaking of the middle ages as a whole, Gierke has said that this period was dominated by a theocratic ideal.[1] Men thought of society as a single Christian body, a *corpus christianum*, whose government and purpose had been established by God. The spiritual and secular power formed the framework for the Christian society and the policies of both were oriented towards the realization of God's plan for the world. Locher has maintained that during the sixteenth century the reformers, including Zwingli, still lived and thought in terms of the *corpus christianum* ideal, while Wolf has argued that local traditions caused Zwingli to place a marked emphasis upon the unity of Zurich's Christian society.[2] The ensuing study accepts the assumption that Zwingli believed in a Christian society ruled by two God-ordained officers, the magistrate and the pastor, and asks "What place did Zwingli assign to the magistrate and the clergy in order to realize the rule of God?"

It does not ask "Did Zwingli really attempt to set up a theocracy?" According to modern usage, the word "theocracy" assumes that a state which desires to realize the rule of God is governed by God's representatives, the clergy. Zwingli certainly did wish to realize the rule of God at Zurich, but this does not mean that he endeavoured to subordinate the city government to the power and influence of the clergy. If anything, Zwingli sought to deprive the clergy of the secular authority and wealth

1. Gierke, III, 514.
2. Locher, "Die evangelische Stellung der Reformatoren zum offentlichen Leben," *Kirchliche Zeitfragen*, Heft 26 (1950), 11–12; Wolf, "Die Sozialtheologie Zwinglis," *Festschrift Guido Kisch*, 168, 174.

it had gained since the end of the eleventh century, because he believed that these secular concerns had diverted the clergy from its God-given function, which was to preach the Gospel. The clergy's failure to preach the Gospel deprived society's civil rulers of the guidance necessary for them to play their part in God's plan for the orderly government of the world. Only if the contemporary definition of a theocracy which identifies the aim of society, the realization of the rule of God, with a government dominated by the clergy, is set aside and the term is used merely to designate the God-oriented aim of a society, is it proper to refer to Zurich in the sixteenth century as a theocracy and to Zwingli as the advocate of a theocracy.

The phrasing of the question "What place did Zwingli assign to the magistrate and the clergy in order to realize the rule of God?" avoids the use of the terms church and state, for Zwingli would not have understood them as we do. Although he thought and wrote a great deal about civil authority, the secular magistrate, and the government, he never mentioned the state. The modern secular state which justifies itself in non-religious terms and sets its own goals had only barely begun to take form in the sixteenth century and would have been incomprehensible to Zwingli. In discussing Zwingli's views on civil authority the term state will be employed, but its use in this context is an anachronism.

Zwingli did speak often of the church, but even here his conception rested upon assumptions which are unfamiliar to the contemporary reader. To him, the civic community provided the external framework of the visible church and all the citizens belonged to it. In order to answer the question asked above, the past tradition of government control over the local church at Zurich and elsewhere in Europe must be considered in connection with the intellectual climate that influenced Zwingli's attitude toward spiritual and temporal authority. Finally, the domestic and foreign situation within which Zwingli worked out his solution to the problem has to be explained.

Much of the confusion that surrounds the discussion of this aspect of Zwingli's achievement is the result of the last seventy-five years of scholarship. Because the term "theocracy" has not been used consistently, Zwingli's work has been given a variety of explanations under that heading and the description of the origins of the "theocracy" created at Zurich has been as varied as the discussion of its function. The interpretation of the origins falls into two general schools: those who assume that Zwingli began with a church separate from civil society, and then was driven to fuse the two, and those who are less influenced by modern definitions of church and state, and see Zwingli's idea of a Christian

Zurich as the natural product of local traditions in which sharp distinctions between church and secular society were never present. The latter group admits that Zwingli's position was hardened by threats to it offered by the Baptists,[3] as well as Zwingli's conservative opponents, but still insist that Zwingli's work maintained a logical continuity until his death. Within the two general interpretations of the reform movement at Zurich two major views of the nature of Zwingli's theocracy have emerged. Some have depicted it as an Anglican-style polity which subjected the church to civil authority, while others have termed it an example of Gelasianism, i.e., the parallelism of clergy and ruler.

A closer look at the secondary works on the question reveals the lack of clarity which has resulted from the diverse use of the term "theocracy". Even when the recent work of Mennonite scholars such as Yoder and Bender is taken into account, those who have maintained that Zwingli abandoned his initial view of the church as an independent body and allowed it to be subordinated to the power of the civil magistrate which led to the creation of a theocracy have been in the minority. The assumption of this group that state control of the church produced a theocratic society represents a reversal of the current definition of the term which pictures a theocracy as a society dominated by the clergy.

Rudolph Staehelin, writing in 1897, subscribed to this opinion: he depicted Zurich as a theocracy in which the government exercised an unhealthy amount of control over the church. According to Staehelin, Zwingli gave up his original conception of the magistrate's role in the affairs of the church and replaced it with a theocratic ideal parallel in its purpose to the Israel of the Old Testament. The task of the secular authority, as Zwingli had originally defined it, was to permit the preaching of the Word, so that all of society would be permeated with the spirit of the Gospel. However, the government, which had already gained a great deal of control over the church before the Reformation era, did not remain content with the role to which it had been assigned. It took over the complete direction of the church. Staehelin contends that this usurpation of authority, which went unopposed by Zwingli, led to the creation of a state church. The establishment of a state church was disastrous, for the faith of the majority became the law of the community, religion and worship being part of the legally required and enforced duty of the citizen.[4]

---

3. The term Baptist refers to those who in the sixteenth century were called Anabaptists, i.e., rebaptizers. Anabaptist was a pejorative term used by those opposed to the movement. Scholars now agree that Baptist is the proper term.

4. Staehelin, II, 149; I, 328–9; I, 121; 142–3.

Alfred Farner, whose book, *Die Lehre von Kirche und Staat bei Zwingli*, appeared in 1930, took a similar position. He interpreted the emergence of a theocratic state at Zurich as a departure from the original Zwinglian ideal that the church and government were two independent though God-ordained orders. His picture of the development of state control over Zurich appears to be heavily influenced by the example of the Lutheran churches in Germany. Zwingli is said to have used the same reasoning that Luther first employed to justify the prince's regulation of church affairs, and the Zurich church is described as suffering the same fate as the Lutheran churches.

According to Farner, Zwingli accepted this development because the Anabaptists had caused him to change his doctrine of the church. Zwingli ceased to distinguish between the church congregation, the instrument of spiritual affairs, and the city assembly, the vehicle for secular activity. He justified a union of the two with the argument that the state, as a defender of the weak and a supporter of order, also served God and had a place in the realization of his Kingdom.

For Farner, the final stage in the creation of a "prophetic theocracy" was reached in 1528 when Zwingli, by assuming a position of leadership in the Secret Council, merged the prophetic office with the magisterial. At this point, Farmer argued, the religious and political assemblies were finally merged and Zwingli began to view the Christian city as nothing more than the visible church.[5]

J. V. M. Pollet's article, "Zwinglianisme," which appeared in the *Dictionnaire de Théologie Catholique* in 1950, represents a scholarly Catholic approach to Zwingli. His account of the changes in Zwingli's doctrine of the church reveals his dependence upon Alfred Farner and makes him a member of the Staehelin "fall of the church" school. Pollet's interpretation of the interpenetration of the political and ecclesiastical bodies is borrowed from Köhler's work, which will be discussed later. It is the fusion of the two originally separate institutions under a single administrative office, which he designates as a theocracy.

According to Pollet, the Anabaptists caused Zwingli to give up his original view of the church as a mystical body. In its place Zwingli presented an ecclesiology which stressed the physical body and externals of the church. Communion served to support the external solidarity of the structure, while baptism became a right of initiation into the visible church. Threats from without and within then led to the absorption of the ecclesiastical community by the city. In the process, as Pollet interpreted it, the city modeled its own internal structure to conform with the

5. A. Farner, 76–8, 83, 85–6, 95, 106, 109–10, 9, 41–2, 44, 123–4, 132.

doctrine and cult of the church. At the same time, the political and the prophetic offices, represented by the Council and by Zwingli, were fused in the Secret Council.[6]

The most cogent proponents of the "fall of the church" school are found among Mennonite scholars. Anxious to rectify the wrongs done to their Baptist forebears by the polemics of the more conservative reformers, they have been not so much concerned with calling Zwingli a theocrat as they have been eager to prove that he was the father of the Baptist (*Täufer*) church. At the crucial moment, they claim, Zwingli denied his initial biblical concept of the separate church and compromised with the state.

Harold S. Bender and John H. Yoder have made the most important recent contribution to this interpretation of the Zwinglian Reformation. In his life of Conrad Grebel, published in 1950, Bender portrayed Zwingli as the originator of the "free church" ideal and then attempted to explain his conversion to the principle of the state church. According to Bender, until the end of the Second Disputation of October, 1523, Zwingli, who believed in the necessity of co-operation with the Council, had been sure that the magistrates would act according to his interpretation of the scriptures. After the Second Disputation the Council decided not to follow Zwingli's plan for immediate action against the Mass and the images, because it wished to wait for a more propitious time. This decision put Zwingli on the horns of a dilemma: he had to choose between his more enthusiastic followers, who favoured the original policy of immediate action against the Catholic abuses, and the dictates of the Council. Despite his own sympathy for the enthusiasts, he gave in to the policy of the government. At this point, Bender argues, Zwingli gave up his original conception of the "believers' church" and adopted in its place the "principle of the state church."[7]

An important article reflecting a similar line of argument was printed in the April, 1958, issue of the *Mennonite Quarterly Review* by John H. Yoder. In the "Turning Point in the Zwinglian Reformation" Yoder argued that Zwingli originally intended to introduce the Lord's Supper in December of 1523. When he bowed to the Council's wishes and failed to celebrate the Lord's Supper, he gave up the true church for the sake of uniform religious observance in Zurich.[8] Yoder's position bears close resemblance to Staehelin's claim that when the state began to legislate religion and to number right faith among the duties of the citizen, the

6. Pollet, "Zwinglianisme," *DTC*, XV, Part II, 3852–3, 3842, 3882.
7. Bender, 91–2.
8. Yoder, *MQR*, XXXII, 137, 138–9.

original Zwinglian church was set aside. For Staehelin, as for Yoder and Bender, the Zwinglian church of 1531 was a church fallen from grace, a product of compromise.

A more detailed version of this argument appeared in 1962 in Yoder's book *Täufertum und Reformation in der Schweiz*. He contended that Zwingli's original conception of the congregation as a persecuted remnant made up of faithful believers was transformed by his success at Zurich. Zwingli began to identify the congregation of the church with the people of Zurich and was willing to accept the competence of the people's elected representatives, the magistrates, to govern the affairs of the church. Thus, Yoder argued, the consequences of Zwingli's new attitude led to a break between him and Grebel. Grebel and his followers went on to develop their church along the lines originally laid out by the Zurich reformer himself.[9] The remainder of the book gives a clear definition of what the Baptist church was and how it developed its Zwinglian heritage to offer an alternative to the state churches championed by Zwingli and his allies in German Switzerland.

The majority of historians who have considered Zwingli's achievement at Zurich see it as a natural synthesis of mediaeval tradition, local constitutional structure, and his reformed theology. A few of them do not refer to Zurich as a theocracy, but the remainder identify the result of Zwingli's work at Zurich as a theocracy because, as a result of Zwingli's influence, a conscious effort was made to orient the city's government towards the realization of God's will on earth. Except for Oskar Farner none of them define a theocracy as the product of state control over the church.

Emil Egli, whose *Schweizerische Reformationsgeschichte* appeared posthumously in 1910, stressed the magistracy's central role in the Zwinglian reform, but saw nothing wrong with the part which the government played in the whole affair. The peaceful introduction of reform at Zurich was possible because it was carried out according to Swiss tradition, under the direction of the magistracy and with the approval of the guilds and village assemblies in the countryside. Egli attributed Zwingli's willing acceptance of the Zurich Council's place in the programme of Christian renewal to his belief that external order was necessary and useful to religious life.[10]

Karl Dändliker, writing in 1908, assumed that the product of Zwingli's work was a state church in which the civil authority issued the laws for both worldly and spiritual affairs. Since the policy of the civil authority

9. Yoder, *Taufertum und Reformation*, 164–5, 167–9, 162.
10. Egli, 342–3.

was ultimately oriented towards the norm of scripture, as expounded by the clergy, Dändliker argued that Zwingli's Zurich was also in fact a theocracy. The dominant position of the magistrate in the affairs of the church, Dändliker noted, was already established before the Reformation. It was essential for the success of the reform movement which brought to a culmination developments already well under way. As Dändliker saw the problem, Zwingli succeeded because he was willing to accept the precedents of the past and to give wise advice for future policy. Dändliker stressed the fact that the policy of the magistracy was influenced by the preaching of the prophet, in this case Zwingli, who had no official function in the government.[11]

One of the most incisive studies of Zwingli appeared in the fifth number of the 1938 *Breslauer historische Forschungen*. Written by Brigitte Brockelmann, it was entitled "Das Corpus Christianum bei Zwingli." Brockelmann attempted to put Zwingli's work at Zurich into the context of the mediaeval *corpus christianum* ideal and denied that Zwingli sought to establish a state-dominated church. She saw the way in which Zwingli defined and separated the spiritual and secular functions carried on within the Christian society at Zurich as a return to the Gelasian theory of the early middle ages. If one accepts the assumption that Zwingli thought in terms of the *corpus christianum* ideal, then her conclusion appears as a most plausible explanation for Zwingli's attitude towards the two realms.

Although Zwingli rejected the possibility of gaining salvation through good conduct, nevertheless he assumed that God had assigned man a purpose in keeping with his limited capabilities. This purpose was, Brockelmann claimed, to live peacefully in society. Since the elect were known only to God, external behaviour was the only standard of judgment which Zwingli's doctrine offered to men in the world. For the purpose of this life, Brockelmann added, those who kept the external standard were accepted as the "elect." This was necessarily the standard of the church as well as of the society and led naturally to a theocracy, since, in Zwingli's eyes, God's will for men in the world, peaceful behaviour, was best served when all men belonged to a society in which community and church were identical.

Brockelmann rejected Alfred Farner's thesis that Zwingli altered his doctrine of the church. Although she admitted that his full definition of the visible church appeared in Zwingli's later writings, she argued that from the first his doctrine of the church was based upon human

11. Dändliker, *Geschichte der Stadt und des Kantons Zürich*, II, 379, 286–7, 288, 348, 352.

righteousness, external good behaviour. Zwingli's aim, she insisted, was not to realize the kingdom of God on earth but only to encourage the inner man and to control his external desires. To achieve this Zwingli believed that God had provided the Word to be administered by the clergy and the sword to be used by the ruler. Since both institutions served the same end, the fulfilment of God's will, it was possible for Zwingli to enforce a strict division of function between church and magistracy, while still viewing them as part of a single whole. Brockelmann asserted that the way Zwingli separated the two functions led to a return to the Gelasian theory of the middle ages.

Zwingli's entire conception, as Brockelmann described it, was based upon the presupposition that politics and religion interacted and supported each other in the service of a common goal. The common goal, in this case, was the kingdom of God, which though unattainable through human effort, served as an ultimated norm for church and government striving to realize the purpose assigned to them by God on earth.[12] Brockelmann's picture of Zwingli's theocracy organized around an almost Kantian principle of "as if" behaviour, in which men adhere to external good conduct as if they were elect, is unique.

Walther Köhler's biography of Zwingli, which he published in 1943, also dealt with the question of theocracy at Zurich. Although Köhler gave greater weight to the importance of the corporate tradition which dominated life and thought at Zurich, his conclusions were similar to those reached by Brockelmann. To begin with, Köhler noted, the creation of a Christian magistracy was a common, conscious aim among the reformed reformers. A Christian magistracy expressed for these reformers the close union of government and church which was common to the city state. Although the organic view of society known in the city states was foreign to Luther, who knew only the empire with its territorial divisions, both he and Zwingli, according to Köhler, accepted the idea of a Christian society divided between the spheres of the kingdom of God and the kingdom of this world. While Luther failed to bridge the gap between the two realms and left the magistrate almost unlimited authority in this world, Zwingli, working within the city state's corporate structure and drawing heavily upon the Old Testament models of a Godly commonwealth and the mediaeval ideal of the Christian body, bridged the gap between the two worlds with his concept of the Christian magistracy. A similar religious function linked the representatives of both realms. The magistrate guaranteed order, while the prophet directed the spiritual sphere; together they formed a

12. Brockelmann, 56, 34–5, 37–9, 40–1, 49, 51, 60–1, 21.

perpetual unity of two which sought to function in harmony with God's commands. Köhler interpreted the "perpetual unity of two" as the foundation of the Zurich theocracy.

As long as Zwingli was alive, Köhler maintains, his conception of the magistrate as a servant of God prevented the creation of a church dominated by state policy. This development came only after his death. On the other hand, Köhler was quick to stress that neither Zwingli nor the Zurich councillors desired the creation of an independent church structure. The council had had enough of an independent church before the Zwinglian reform. Zwingli made no distinction between the church congregation and the city assembly, which left very little practical possibility for the development of a self-governing ecclesiastical body possessing its own rights. Zwingli, as the prophet, was able to control both spheres in the commonwealth.[13] Köhler's analysis emphasized, as did Dändliker's, the continuity of development at Zurich and denied that Zwingli departed from his original doctrine of the church. Köhler's suggestion that the city assembly did not absorb the church congregation but instead adopted its aims was an important contribution.

Helmut Kressner's work, *Schweizer Ursprünge des anglikanischen Staatskirchentums*, though written during the early years of World War II, was first published in 1953. Kressner, like Brockelmann, argued that Zwingli achieved a unique balance between church and government which was used, after his death, to lay the foundations for the theory of a state church. Zwingli's primary aim, as Kressner saw it, was to set up a *respublica christiana*, whose geographical limits coincided with the extent to which the new faith had spread. Zwingli achieved his wish because he did not attempt, as Calvin did later, to endow the church with independent organs of administration. Zwingli left the administrative control of the church in the hands of the magistracy and justified his action on the grounds that the city councillors were the duly delegated representatives of the Zurich citizenry.

Officially, Kressner added, the Reformation was carried out in the name of a church assembly considered capable of independent action. The corporate nature of Zurich's constitution made it possible to consider the magistrate's action the realization of the believers' wishes.[14] Kressner's analysis assumed, as did Köhler's, that Zwingli viewed the city state as a Christian body which could have but one aim, to serve God and that the clergy and the magistracy should work together to achieve that end.

13. Köhler, 98, 132–5, 273, 124.
14. Kressner, 25–7, 30, 32–3.

Siegfrid Rother, in *Die religiösen und geistigen Grundlagen der Politik Huldrych Zwinglis* (1956), never mentioned the term theocracy at all, but his description of Zwingli's desire to subordinate all elements of society to the divine will as the product of the reformer's political theology provides ample grounds for stating that his conception of the purpose of society was theocratic. The important point which Rother made was that Zwingli's practical activity was the logical consequence of his doctrine of God. What resulted was neither accidental, nor the child of compromise; it was the product of Zwingli's theology.

Zwingli's aim, in Rother's view, was the restoration of the life of the early church in the form of a people's church upheld by the Christian state. The Christian state, as Zwingli understood it, was a combination of the Old Testament idea of cultic unity within the community and the Greek view that politics and ethics were inseparable. The Christian state was a true state. Its task was to protect God's honour, to secure the salvation of the people, and to uphold the republic. Zwingli sought to secure first Zurich, then the Confederacy, and finally the world for the ideal of the Christian state. Zwingli, Rother concluded, sought to use all elements in society for the realization of God's kingdom. For Zwingli, church and state were one in the service of the divine will.[15]

Oskar Farner, in the fourth volume of his monumental biography of Zwingli, published posthumously in 1960, recognized the unique balance between the sphere of the magistrate and that of the clergy which Brockelmann and Kressner had seen in Zwingli's Zurich, but he denied that what Zwingli achieved could be termed a theocracy because the distinctions that he made between the two spheres were always maintained. According to Farner, neither Zwingli's activities in the Secret Council, nor the Morality Ordinance of 1530, which reflected a sizeable increase of magisterial control over the church, prove that Zwingli intended to set up a theocracy. There was never a confusion or fusion of the two powers. The prophet preached the standard of God's absolute righteousness, while the magistrate administered justice on the basis of human righteousness. The most Farner was willing to admit was that in response to the pressure of Zwingli's various opponents, the authority of the magistrates was enhanced, thus causing the city to incline towards a theocracy.[16] Farner's conclusions rest upon the assumption that the relationship between church and state determines whether or not a society can be called a theocracy. Brockelmann, Kressner, and Köhler

15. Rother, 19, 24, 51, 74, 38, 42, 75, 99, 100–2, 113, 149.
16. O. Farner, IV, 387–9.

refer to the balance of powers at Zurich as a theocracy because their definition of "theocracy" is determined by the purpose which the two powers who govern society seek to achieve. In the case of Zurich there was no doubt that both authorities sought to realize the will of God for men.

Bernd Moeller's *Reichsstadt und Reformation*, which appeared in 1962, considered the nature and significance of Zwingli's work at Zurich. Moeller incorporated and developed further the insights of many of the scholars who have been considered above. His work represents a coherent and convincing attempt to clarify the historical circumstances which conditioned Zwingli's work at Zurich. He described the product of Zwingli's labours in Zurich as a theocracy: "a spiritually led church-civic commonwealth."

Moeller based his conclusions upon a careful study of the imperial cities of both upper and lower Germany before the Reformation. He claimed that the corporate theory of city government was most fully realized in the upper German cities, where the guilds had achieved a predominance in the direction of public affairs which gave even the lower strata of the citizenry a certain say in government. Under the influence of the corporate idea the distinction between the secular and religious sphere was obscured, and the city assembly became identified with the church congregation. The chosen representatives of the assembly, the magistrates, naturally took responsibility for the affairs of the church and as a result, Moeller argued, the cities came to see themselves as small-scale embodiments of the *corpus christianum*.

The reformed Reformation in the towns of upper Germany succeeded because it found popular support, especially in the guilds, who often played a crucial role in gaining constitutional recognition for it. Once recognized, the Reformation was supported by the councils, who justified their suppression of traditional religious practices in terms of their responsibility to God for the well-being of the people. Moeller cited this as an example of the continuity between late-mediaeval attitudes toward the function of city government and those of the Reformation.

Zwingli, whose work as a reformer was intimately connected with his activity as a citizen, accepted the *corpus christianum* ideal and identified the visible church at Zurich with the political assembly of the city. Though he carefully distinguished between the functions of the clerical and civil officers within the Christian society, Moeller claimed that it was natural for Zwingli to assume that the government's support of true religion was essential for the Reformation. This assumption prevented him from making common cause with the Baptists. Until after Zwingli's death, Moeller contended, no clear division between the ecclesiastical and the civic sphere was made at Zurich.[17]

If anything, the way in which the term theocracy has been used by the authors considered reveals how varied its definition can be, and how little it helps to clarify the roles which Zwingli assigned to the magistracy and the clergy at Zurich. Without desiring to confuse the issue further I intend to refer to Zwingli's conception of government at Zurich as theocratic. When this is done, the word will describe the purpose which Zwingli believed the magistrate and the pastor, working together, fulfilled: the realization of the rule of God. At no time will its use imply that Zwingli sought either to subordinate the magistracy to the authority of the clergy, or to allow the state to dominate the church.

17. Moeller, 43, 55, 67, 63–4, 12–13, 15, 25, 62–3, 28–9, 32, 52–3, 39–41, 42–3, 53.

ZWINGLI'S THEOCRACY

1　The Zurich Magistracy and the Local Church before the Reformation

THE STORY OF THE ZURICH MAGISTRACY'S RELATIONSHIP TO the church within its territories before the Reformation is part of the history of the creation of strong central government in the canton. This development, which was paralleled in the other major Swiss and south German cities and fits the general pattern of European affairs in the fifteenth century, stands in sharp contrast to the failure of the Confederacy as a whole to evolve a powerful central administration.[1] The Confederacy, which Zurich joined in 1351, remained based upon a series of parallel agreements of varying terms which left each member free to pursue independent action even in the face of majority decisions.[2] Zurich had played an important role among the Swiss cities in advocating a uniform alliance for the Confederates in order to permit the formation of a stronger central government. The rural cantons, fearful that centralization would favour the cities and threaten their more democratic institutions, had resisted the idea, and, rather than to risk civil war over the question, Zurich and the other cities had signed the Stanser Agreement of 1481 which maintained the decentralized structure of the federation.[3] The freedom of action left to the individual members of the Confederacy helps to explain how Zurich, despite the hostility of the majority of the Confederates, was able to support Zwingli's programme of reform.

The weakness of the federal constitution prevented the Swiss from using the power which the prowess of their soldiers had won for them during the late fifteenth and early sixteenth centuries. Because of internal disagreements, the policy of expansion at the expense of the Duchy of

1. von Muralt, 352–3; Guggenbühl, I, 316, 322–3.
2. Heusler, 116–7, 208–9.
3. Largiadèr, I, 237–8; Guggenbühl, I, 322–3, 332–3. For the sake of clarity the term "canton" has been used throughout this study to refer to the various regions which made up the Swiss Confederacy. However, it should be noted that this term was not generally used by the German Swiss to refer to the individual parts of the Confederacy until after the collapse of the old Confederacy in 1798. Therefore the use of canton in this study is an anachronism.

Milan ended in disaster at the Battle of Marignano in 1515, and the position of authority among the European states which the Swiss had gained in the preceding decades was lost forever.[4]

The fact that the supporters of centralism had to confine their attention to their native regions may also explain the successful assertion of territorial sovereignty in the city states of the Confederacy. Speaking of Zurich, Largiadèr sums up the result by saying that the city and territory were identical; the country people did not enjoy political equality with the inhabitants of the city whose representatives governed the whole of the canton.[5] This does not mean that the control of the city government over its territories was accepted without question. The country districts fought hard for their traditional local freedoms and, due to internal conflicts within Zurich itself, were able to check the expanding authority of the city from time to time.[6] The fall of Burgomaster Waldmann in 1489, as well as the reaction which took place after the death of Zwingli in the Second Kappel War, and the peasants' unrest of 1525, provide examples of the countrymen's attempt to defend their local freedoms and to claim some say in the government of the canton.[7]

However, despite periodic checks to its policy, the Zurich government steadily increased the extent of its control over the countryside. Local political assemblies (*Gemeinde*) continued to function throughout Zurich's territories, but the presiding officers were under the direction of the Zurich magistracy.[8] This fact, which has sometimes been ignored, is of crucial importance for an understanding of Zwingli's view of the magistracy's role in the affairs of the church and must be kept in mind when the claim that Zwingli championed "congregational autonomy" is considered.

The two councils which governed Zurich won far-reaching administrative control over the territorial church long before Zwingli arrived in the city.[9] As was the case in many cities, the Zurich Council's efforts to subordinate the church to its authority were aided by a number of general factors. The Council avoided an ideological struggle with ecclesi-

---

4. Guggenbühl, I, 312, 316.
5. Largiadèr, I, 185.
6. Birnbaum, "The Zwinglian Reformation in Zurich," *ASR*, IV, 17.
7. Largiadèr, I, 245–51, 329–31, 319–21.
8. Steinemann, 122–4.
9. The Small Council, originally the Council of 26, formed part of the membership of the Great Council (212 members). The constitutional reform of 1498 fixed the final form of the two councils. By this time the Small Council consisted of fifty members (Largiadèr, I, 248; Guggenbühl, I, 352). The two councils will be referred to collectively as the Council, except where clarity demands a separate reference.

astical authority and concentrated instead upon attacking the immunities of the clergy. The corporate theory of government and society which dominated the south German and Swiss cities assumed that church and state were one and recognized neither a distinction betwen the political assembly of the city and the church congregation, nor any limit to the magistracy's authority. As the delegated representatives of a Christian people, the city's rulers were far stronger than the church within the town.[10]

Aside from the Council's desire to control all aspects of local life, the magistrates believed that as the people's representatives they must serve the "common good." Since the Christian religion was regarded by all as a necessary element in the healthy life of the city, the city fathers had to make sure that the faith and its services were maintained. To achieve this end, the councillors claimed a right of guardianship over the ecclesiastical foundations within its domain.

This attitude was not confined to Zurich. The most striking example of it is found in a statement issued by the Basel City Council in 1450:

Above all, the government of each city is to be established for this: to increase and to consolidate the honour of God and to repulse all evil and especially gross sin and misdeed, according to the regulation of the Holy Christian World.[11]

Such opinions were expressed by the rulers of the cities to justify the exercise of a *jus reformandi,* a right of reforming the church, long before the Reformation. However, the power which the magistracy claimed and exercised over the church was not utilized to alter doctrine or liturgy. Zwingli was the first man to gain the support of the magistracy to reform the church's dogma and cult. He was able to do this because his conception of the function of the magistrate and the pastor fitted the constitutional traditions of the city and pre-supposed the authority which the government already exercised over the churches of the canton.[12]

The nature of the Zurich Council's relations with the clergy before 1519 provides the key for a clear understanding of the situation upon which Zwingli based his achievement. In the process of asserting its

10. Schultze, "Stadtgemeinde und Kirche im Mittelalter," *Festgabe für Rudolf Sohm,* 106–8; Schultze, "Stadtgemeinde und Reformation," *Recht und Staat in Geschichte und Gegenwart,* 11–12, 30–1; Moeller, 12–15; von Muralt, 350, 352–3; Steffen-Zehnder, 12.

11. Wackernagel, II, Part II, 871.

12. Moeller argues that the theology of both Zwingli and Bucer was deeply influenced by an urban environment and fitted the "corporate spirit" of the upper German cities. This fact, he claims, explains the success of the "reformed Reformation" in the cities (Moeller, 52, 66–7).

sovereignty over the church, the Zurich Council was favoured by a series of fortunate circumstances. An imperial city since 1262, Zurich was able to use the struggle between the empire and the papacy to win concessions from both sides.[13]

A series of constitutional reforms, beginning with those instituted by Burgomaster Rudolf Brun, broadened the basis of representation within the city and strengthened the hand of the government in dealing with the church. The major beneficiaries of these reforms were the guilds, who took predominance in the government of the city away from the merchant and noble families of the *Constafel*. They gained equal representation with the *Constafel* in the Small Council of 26, which later became the Council of 50, the majority of whose members were recruited from the guilds. They also dominated the Great Council of 212, which emerged from obscurity after 1370.[14] The guilds were the driving force behind the development of Zurich's territorial sovereignty and, during the Reformation, the Great Council's support for Zwingli was a result of his popularity with the guilds.[15]

The corruption of the clergy gave the Council frequent opportunity to concern itself with clerical matters. The Council's dealings with the most important religious foundation in the city, the Fraumünster Nunnery, offer a good illustration of what took place. The combined rights, including the secular privileges of a bishop, which the papacy and the empire had conferred upon the Abbess of the Fraumünster, left the establishment she ruled in a position to dominate the affairs of the city.

13. Steffen-Zehnder, 20.
14. Bluntschli, Bk., 3, 320–3, 330, 336. References to Bluntschli refer to book three, unless specifically cited as book two. Heusler, 94, 192–3.
15. Dändliker, *Geschichte der Schweiz*, II, 265–6, 269; Largiadèr, I, 215. Birnbaum's careful study of Zurich's social structure necessitates a qualified acceptance of this statement. During the fifteenth century there was a power struggle between a group of newly wealthy guildmasters and the old ruling elite. The aristocracy made common cause with both the artisans and the peasantry to check the advance of the guildmasters. Though the new constitution which was framed after the fall of Burgomaster Waldmann in 1489 put the control of the city in the hands of the artisans, their victory was thwarted by a "partial *rapprochement*" between the guildmasters and the old aristocracy. Between 1490 and 1519 these two groups controlled the city. The Reformation reopened the conflict between the patricians and the *novi homines*. The new men, whose fortunes were based upon "mercantile and entrepreneurial activity," used the Reformation to replace complete the old patriciate. By 1529 the political status of the *Constafel* had been reduced to that of another guild, and the new elite were firmly established as the governors of the city. Birnbaum asserts that the interests of artisans as a whole were not served by this change and notes that the patricians who favoured the old church had the support of artisan groups from the more "traditional" sectors of the economy (Birnbaum, "The Zwinglian Reformation in Zurich," *ASR*, IV, 17, 18, 25–6, 28).

She had control of the mayor's court, the mayor's (*Schultheiss*) court, which served as the city court and had jurisdiction over the regulation of ground rents due to the Nunnery. Her other rights included the right of coinage for the city, as well as the control of customs and the market.[16] However, although the Abbess and her nuns were under the protection of the German emperors, they found no real support from them and still less help from the imperial administrator (*Reichsvogt*) who, from the beginning of the fifteenth century, was appointed by the Council. The control of the imperial administrator provided the Council with a firm basis for the assertion of its sovereignty, for it gave the magistracy immediate supervision over high justice and strengthened the whole apparatus of city government. Appeals from both the lower courts in the city and the country districts now came to a judge chosen by the Council.[17] The city eventually purchased the imperial administrator's right to collect imperial taxes, and his authority to levy troops for imperial service also passed to the Council.[18]

The papacy did not afford any greater protection to the Nunnery from the growing power of the Zurich government than did the emperor; nor did the Bishop of Constance, the immediate spiritual overlord of the city, whose belated attempts to reform the cloister in 1470 were thwarted by the Council. Deprived of outside support and lacking local military strength, the nuns were compelled to call upon the city for aid, which was always given at a price.[19]

The Fraumünster was beset by other difficulties. As the number and importance of the nobility in the area decreased, the community of nuns, recruited exclusively from this class, grew smaller and less able to maintain its independence.[20] Not all of the few who were recruited proved to be willing servants of the faith. A series of abbesses who were personally immoral, and incompetent financial managers, invited the attention of the Zurich magistrates. Burgomaster Rudolf Brun put the mayor's court under the supervision of three representatives from the Small Council. Although in theory the Abbess retained the right to appoint the court judge until 1524, from early in the fourteenth century the Council in fact controlled the court and its functions. Brun also placed the financial affairs of the Nunnery under the supervision of the

16. Steffen-Zehnder, 19–21. The Council of 26, the first governing body of the city, was drawn originally from the *ministeriales* of the Fraumünster (Steffen-Zehnder, 21).
17. Bluntschli, 386; Heusler, 93.
18. Steffen-Zehnder, 24.
19. *Ibid.*, 20, 48–9.
20. Largiadèr, I, 277–8.

Council as a temporary measure. At the end of the century (1397), the Zurich magistracy placed the Fraumünster under the permanent direction of guardians (*Pfleger*) appointed by the Council.[21]

Brun's interim measure had set a never-to-be-forgotten precedent. Until the coming of the Reformation, the Council, with ever-increasing frequency, used the maladministration of the religious houses as an excuse to intervene in their affairs and to place them under its control.[22] An administrative technique was developed, and a certain class of administrators were trained by the city. The existence of men familiar with the management of church finances guaranteed the magistracy the means to expand its hold over the temporal affairs of the church. This was not merely the result of an ambitious secular authority's aggrandizement; it was also the result of the church's inability to keep its house in order.

The other major religious foundation in the city was the Cathedral Chapter, the *Grossmünsterstift*. Although the evidence indicates that the city Council never devoted as much attention to the supervision of the canons, who were the leaders of the city's clergy and more difficult to control than the nuns, they did not remain untouched by the persistent efforts of the magistracy to supervise the church.[23] Through direct negotiation with the Holy See, Zurich enhanced its power over the canons. Martin V (1417) limited the absence of the canons or the Provost of the Chapter from Zurich to a period of two months.[24] By enforcing residence, the Pope's decree limited the worst abuses of absenteeism and secured for the faithful at Zurich resident canons to perform the offices to worship.

The second privilege, gained from Sixtus IV in 1479, was a recognition of powers already exercised by the government, and it applied to the Fraumünster, Grossmünster, and the monastery at Embrach. It granted the magistrates at Zurich the right of presentation (*jus praesentationis*) to certain prebends of these foundations, which fell open during the "papal months."[25] Next to the two privileges, the Council's most important gain was the right to subject the canons to regular taxation. The canon law and imperial immunities guaranteed the clergy exemption from taxation except in times of emergency. After a long struggle, in

---

21. Steffen-Zehnder, 46.
22. Egli claims that by the fifteenth century a *jus reformandi* was vested in the magistracy (Egli, "Die zürcherische Kirchenpolitik von Waldmann bis Zwingli," *JSG*, XXI, 5).
23. Steffen-Zehnder, 23–4.
24. Egli, *JSG*, XXI, 21; Rohrer, "Das sogenannte Waldmannische Konkordat," *JSG*, IV, 18–19.
25. Largiadèr, I, 282; Steffen-Zehnder, 56–7.

1389 the canons of the Grossmünster agreed to pay voluntary taxes at the request of the city. It took until the end of the next century for the town councillors to replace voluntary payments with a regular imposition.[26]

Maladministration and immorality in the Chapter led to further intervention in the Grossmünster's affairs. During the era of Burgomaster Hans Waldmann (1477–89), there were complaints that the income of the Chapter was used by the clergy for private purposes. An ordinance calling for improved administration of finances was issued by the magistracy, but it had little effect.[27] The immorality of the canons led to the ordinances of 1485 and 1487/88, which sought to improve the conduct of the clergy and to ensure the proper performance of the cult.[28] The ordinances issued under Waldmann's leadership increased the power of the Council over the canons and caused the latter to complain that they were forced to accept the rule of laymen.[29] Although the Chapter completely abandoned its claims to legal and financial immunity and its rights of presentation to a large number of prebends only with the coming of the Reformation, it was already dominated by the city fathers before the sixteenth century began.

The ecclesiastical foundations in the outlying territories suffered the same fate as those within the city. During the Great Schism the Cistercian cloister at Kappel was beset both by internal feuds over the question of allegiance to the proper pope and by economic difficulties. The Abbot himself put the administration of the secular affairs of the monastery in the hands of the Zurich government for a period of six years.[30] By the beginning of the sixteenth century, representatives of the Council supervised the financial and legal affairs, as well as the appointment of prebendaries for all the foundations within its domains. In addition, the Council taxed not only the cloisters in the canton but also those in other regions which held land in Zurich's domain.[31]

The nullification of the Bishop of Constance's authority was a gradual process. The curia at Constance claimed legal jurisdiction at Zurich over

26. Steffen-Zehnder, 25–7.
27. Rohrer, *JSG*, IV, 18. Since the ordinance, and those which followed, offered no plan for a reorganization of the Chapter, Pestalozzi claims that they were not ordinances, but rather warnings to the Chapter to reform itself (Pestalozzi, *Die Gegner Zwinglis am Grossmünsterstift in Zürich*, 19, 23–4). In view of the past activities of the Council this seems doubtful. Steffen-Zehnder's account notes a greater amount of supervision than Pestalozzi is willing to admit.
28. Rohrer, *JSG*, IV, 21, 22.
29. Egli, *JSG*, XXI, 12–13; Largiadèr, I, 242.
30. Largiadèr, I, 171.
31. *Ibid.*, I, 286.

church property, interest and tithes due to the church, probate of clerical wills, marriage questions, and civil offences committed by clerics. These prerogatives restricted the Zurich magistracy's taxing power and civil authority, and the Council tried to limit such clerical privileges. As early as 1304 an agreement was reached which established joint jurisdiction over legal cases involving priests and laymen. Clerics were tried before three judges who were priests (*Pfaffenrichter*), while laymen were charged and heard before the Council. Fines resulting from the decisions of the judges were split between the church and the government, and in cases where the judgment of the *Pfaffenrichter* was not respected by priests the church had the right to call upon the secular authority for help. At about the same time an apparatus for the arbitration of disputes between high ecclesiastical personages and the laity was set up. Judges, *Scheiderichter*, whose decisions would be acceptable to both sides were to be chosen by city officials. The desire of the Council to settle legal disputes at home was again revealed in 1333, when the government forbade citizens to cite each other before the Bishop of Constance's court without the express consent of the magistracy.[32]

Joint action with Luzern, Zug, Uri, Schwyz, and Unterwalden led to a further restriction of the Bishop's legal competence. While visiting Zurich, the major of Luzern, Peter von Gundoldingen, became involved in a dispute with the two sons of Rudolf Brun. In violation of Zurich's market peace, the Bruns arrested Peter and his companions. This abuse of custom outraged the citizenry of Zurich, and they instituted legal proceedings against the Bruns. Bruno Brun, who was provost of the Cathedral Chapter, refused to accept the judicial authority of the Zurich Council and claimed the right as a cleric to be tried in a church court.[33] Brun was expelled from the city by the Council and Zurich joined with the other cantons to end unlimited clerical immunity. The result was the *Pfaffenbrief*, Priests' Letter, of 1370. The Letter required an oath of loyalty to the Confederacy from all its inhabitants and made it illegal for citizens of the allied cantons to be called before a foreign court. Justice had to be sought in local courts, save in marriage questions, or in spiritual matters, which were left to the Bishops' courts.[34] The *Pfaffenbrief* limited clerical immunity and also served as a foundation for the enforcement of public order in the individual cantons by making the

32. Bluntschli, Bk. 2, 177–9.
33. Heusler, 122–3.
34. Gagliardi, II, 529. There is no better illustration of the loose nature of the Swiss Confederacy than the fact that not all of the cantons took part in the framing of the *Pfaffenbrief*. Only Zurich, Luzern, Zug, Uri, Schwyz, and Unterwalden took part (Heusler, 120).

citizens subject to the jurisdiction of the region in which they lived.[35] The events of 1370 demonstrate that the development of local control over the church and its representatives was not confined to Zurich. Another example illustrates this. The villages of the forest cantons gained the right to appoint their own priests long before the Reformation began.[36] Only during the Reformation when the Zurich government used its authority to sanction the reform of the dogma and the cult of the church did the conservative cantons react negatively.

The conflict with the Bishop of Constance over jurisdiction continued for another century. Finally in 1506 an attempt was made to settle the matter. The city fathers and the Bishop agreed that the Council was to have full competence in cases of mixed jurisdiction, except when the matter involved high justice or excommunication. When high justice (crimes involving the death penalties) was required, jurisdiction was divided, laymen being subject to the judgment of the Council and clergy to the Bishop's justice. The magistracy also obtained the right to investigate cases involving the clergy and the laity, even if no complaint had been made.[37] The Council even began to fine citizens who sought the arbitration of the episcopal curia in marriage questions. In this matter, as in so many others, the marriage court, established in 1525 by the Council in co-operation with the clergy to supervise marriage questions, completed what had been begun long before Zwingli arrived in Zurich.

The government's desire to prevent the concentration of tax-free land holdings in the hands of the church compelled it to challenge the church's jurisdiction over the probate of wills. As early as 1280 the Zurich clergy were forbidden to buy property in the city and were obliged to sell property willed to it within a year and a day.[38] Late in the fifteenth century the Council successfully asserted its right to probe all wills granting donations to the church. The Council also took control of litigation pertaining to interest and tithes due the church (1460) and appointed an interest judge, *Zinsrichter*, to consider these cases. This judge favoured the claims of the citizenry against the clergy and soon began to arbitrate disagreements which arose between clergymen. Once again the Bishop, who was the legally competent agent, found himself excluded by action of the magistracy.[39] The Council's ability to extend its authority was the natural product of the city's corporate tradition of government.

35. Largiadèr, I, 231; Heusler, 121–3.
36. Heusler, 216.
37. Rohrer, *JSG*, IV, 20, 30.
38. Steffen-Zehnder, 29.   39. *Ibid.*, 30–1, 37.

The governors of Zurich did not confine themselves to economic and legal issues. They expanded their police powers and began to intervene in questions of morality, an heretofore undisputed province of the church. In 1370 they issued the first of a series of *Sittenmandate*, morality ordinances, which attacked excessive luxury, raucous conduct, and immorality, and in 1415 they made adultery a civil offence. The ruler's interference in moral questions became so frequent that the Bishop of Constance registered a series of fruitless complaints.[40]

The privileges granted the city by Martin V and Sixtus IV weakened the Bishop's hold upon the lower clergy. The control exercised through the *Pfleger* over the policies of the ecclesiastical foundations in the canton gave the Council a voice in the distribution of their prebends. Clergy desiring an appointment began to rely upon the Council rather than the Bishop for help. Rudolf Brun had not hesitated to deprive priests of their prebends and to appoint others in their place when they disobeyed the orders of the city government. The need to control the local clergy and to prevent the abuses of pluralism and absenteeism were an inducement for the Council to extend its own patronage rights. The bulk of local patronage was in the hands of the monastic houses and subject to the influence of the government, but this influence was not, in the Council's view, sufficient to reform abuses of clerical privileges. It therefore increased its direction of patronage through lease and purchase. It obtained patronage rights to the prebends of the town and castle of Greifensee in 1402, when Duke Frederich of Toggenburg leased them to the Council for 6,000 gulden. An important acquisition came in 1467, when the city received the right of patronage over the city of Winterthur, the largest city in Zurich's territory. Another method which the magistrates found successful was to detach filial churches from their mother church. Once this was done, the councillors encouraged the assembly of the separate parish to elect a candidate chosen by their representatives.[41] Since the candidates chosen were always those favoured by the city, the patronage was theirs.

The patronage right was of limited value. It allowed the holder to present a qualified candidate to the church authorities in charge of the prebend. Although candidates thus presented were rarely refused, the

40. *Ibid.*, 40–1; Bluntschli, 427.
41. Steffen-Zehnder, 14, 61–3. Steffen-Zehnder terms this practice an application of the *Gemeindeprinzip* (congregational principle), and it may be the type of local action which Zwingli thought of when he discussed the role of the local assembly in the reform of the church. However, the influence and authority of government in the congregation's proceedings is clear enough to prevent the conclusion that in such a case true autonomy was exercised by the local assembly.

patronage right implied no power of supervision for the possessor. A means of directing the prebendary's conduct came from the principle of trusteeship which was evolved during the fourteenth and fifteenth centuries. Individual citizens willed altar prebends or other endowments to the church and left the city Council as the trustee.[42] Normally the supervision of bequests belonged to the Bishop, but the city bourgeoisie showed a marked lack of faith in clerical trustees. As the trustee, the Council presented the candidate, supervised his activities, administered his income, and, if necessary, deprived him of his holding.[43]

The combination of papal privileges, patronage rights, and trusteeship made the city a more important factor in the life of the lower cleric than was the Bishop. The city, directly or indirectly, provided for him, decided his fate, and, as time went on, it was also the city who tried and fined him. This loss of authority over the lower clergy by the Bishop helps to explain the ease with which Zurich was later able to break away from the old church.[44]

Centralization of power in the hands of the Zurich magistrates was slow and steady. Burgomaster Hans Waldmann increased the tempo but brought no striking change in the pattern of government supervision of ecclesiastical affairs. Waldmann's major contribution was the further extension of the city's control over the clergy in the countryside.[45] Waldmann was indeed the key figure behind the negotiation with Sixtus IV which resulted in the jurisdictional privileges granted to the city in 1479, but this success was as much the first fruits of the Swiss military supremacy as it was the product of Waldmann's work. Waldmann was responsible for the reforming ordinances directed against the Grossmünster Chapter.[46] The moral and financial corruption of the nuns in the Fraumünster aroused him to action. He had the seals of office and the keys to the Nunnery forcibly removed from the Abbess, Sybilla von Helfenstein (1485).[47] The main theme of his church policy was to prevent the exploitation of church property by the clergy for its own selfish ends. The conservative reaction after his fall was not accompanied by any lessening of the Council's interest in this aim and generally in the affairs of the church.[48] The petition of the canons for the return of their old freedom was ignored.[49]

---

42. Schultze, *Festgabe für Rudolf Sohm*, 123–5, 127–9; Schultze, *Recht und Staat in Geschichte und Gegenwart*, 15.
43. Steffen-Zehnder, 59–60.
44. *Ibid.*, 59.   45. *Ibid.*, 30, 56–7.
46. Rohrer, *JSG*, IV, 18, 21–2.   47. Egli, *JSG*, XXI, 12.
48. Dändliker, *Geschichte der Schweiz*, II, 291.
49. Egli, *JSG*, XXI, 14–15.

A document once believed to be the product of Waldmann's negotiations with the papacy indicates the extent of the Zurich magistracy's power over the church in the first decade of the sixteenth century.[50] It is a petition presented to Pope Julius II in 1512 by the two burgomasters Marcus Röist and Jacob Meiss.[51] After the alliance with the Confederacy was concluded in 1510, Julius had renewed a number of old privileges for all the cantons. Zurich was not content with these and continued to negotiate independently, but without success: Julius rejected the city's petition. Though the representatives of the city probably only requested the confirmation of privileges that Zurich already exercised, had the petition been granted, it would have meant that the pope recognized the domination of the church by the civil power.[52] The papacy was not able to prevent territorial states from consolidating their authority by taking control of the external affairs of the church, but the formal recognition of the subordination of the church to the secular power posed a threat to the theory of papal monarchy. What had taken place could not be sanctioned in law by papal approval without undermining the constitution of the church.

The first two articles of the petition were concerned with the renewal of Sixtus IV's grant. The Roman curia had tried to profit from this grant by demanding higher taxes from the clergy appointed by the government during the "papal months." The city insisted that their appointees pay the same taxes as the other prebendaries.[53] Article three sought confirmation of an agreement over the probate of wills made with the Bishop of Constance in 1491. All members of the Chapter had the right to make wills for the benefit of the church, but bequests made by clerics for other purposes were to be subject to probate by the Council.[54] The magistrates naturally sought papal approval for an already established practice. However, it was one thing for a local bishop to give up the claim of the canon law that the church was heir to the property of deceased priests and quite another matter for the pope to do so.

The fourth article dealt with a grievance already mentioned in the ordinance of 1480.[55] The city asked that the income from the prebends

---

50. Rohrer, *JSG*, IV, 5.
51. Pestalozzi, 29–30; Egli, *JSG*, XXI, 27.
52. Pestalozzi maintains that the petition asked for more than the city actually practiced (Pestalozzi, 29–30). Rohrer calls the petition the *Magna Charta* of the Zurich state church (Rohrer, *JSG*, IV, 18). The petition itself stated that it merely sought the approval of customary rights.
53. Rohrer, *JSG*, IV, 10.
54. Steffen-Zehnder, 58.
55. Rohrer, *JSG*, IV, 10.

of clerics who were fugitives from justice be used to repair and support the church in the vacated prebend, rather than be divided among the rest of the clergy. The Council also asked the right to compel the clergy to keep its residences repaired. The government's requests reveal its interest in maintaining the church for the sake of the common good.

The following article sought the confirmation of the Council's jurisdiction over "mixed" legal cases. The offences for which the Council asked the right to try the clergy were termed "civil" and included acts committed with "drawn swords" and "blasphemous oaths." The magistrates stated that they did not seek jurisdiction over crimes which involved excommunication. This request indicates that the clergy taxed the patience and the police powers of the magistracy, and that it was an attempt to get higher approval for the arrangement worked out with the Bishop of Constance in 1506. Papal acquiescence would have set precedents for the destruction of clerical immunity. The next article, which demanded that the Council be recognized as the arbiter in disputes arising out of taxes and tithes due to the church, also sought to confirm the jurisdiction of the government over the clergy. The arbitration of tax and tithe questions had been carried out at Zurich by the *Zinsrichter* ("interest judges") since 1460.

The seventh article dealt with taxation of the clergy. The magistrates argued that the clergy enjoyed civil privileges and protection along with the rest of the citizenry. Therefore they asked permission to tax the ecclesiastical foundations and the clergy in time of war. In petitioning for this privilege, the Council asked for far less tax power than it already exercised over the spiritual estate. The request shows the incompatibility of the mediaeval church and its immunities with the development of central government in the territorial state.

Article eight sought the right to supervise the affairs of the church. It was followed by a request for formal approval of the Council's power to police the public assemblies and behaviour of the clergy. The tenth article tried to validate the Council's authority to hold a priest in prison while investigating a crime.

The three final sections asked for recognition of the Council's competence to judge marriage questions, its right to alter the terms laid down by the church for bequests, and the authority to prevent the canons of the Chapter from using Chapter funds to pay legal fees.[56]

Almost every request made in the petition referred to practices long accepted at Zurich. Had Pope Julius received the petition favourably he would have renounced his own right to control the temporal affairs of the church. Such a precedent would have threatened the foundations

56. *Ibid., JSG*, IV, 12, 15–16, 25–7.

of papal power. The fact that such a petition was seriously presented to the Roman curia indicates the magistracy's sense of power and the extent to which it had already taken *de facto* control over the external affairs of the local church. The petition of 1512 is the best summary of the progress made by the city in its attempt to dominate the church. It does not express a pious hope, but represents an effort to legalize existing practice.

In the course of two centuries the magistracy had so limited the church's immunities that the clergy had become in fact, if not in theory, a part of the citizenry, subject to the same laws and taxation.[57] The Bishop's jurisdiction had been virtually nullified by the city magistracy,[58] and the Council stood at the head of a unified corporate society, supervising the affairs of the church and society as the delegated representative of the city assembly.

The last line of demarcation between clergy and laity, ordination, which gave clerics control of the channels of grace, the sacraments, remained until the Zwinglian reform; but before that time the clergy was shorn of the secular symbols, the immunities in law and taxation which had proclaimed their sacramental office to the world. The first step toward the universal priesthood of all believers had been taken before Zwingli preached his first sermon.

This is the tradition Zwingli accepted and built upon. As Schultze has shown for the German cities, and Moeller, as well as von Muralt, for the Swiss cities, there was no idea in the towns before or during the sixteenth century of a separate legal entity known as the church congregation.[59] For Zwingli, as for most of his contemporaries, Zurich was a Christian city, striving to realize the rule of God under the direction of a Christian civil magistracy. Consequently, it is difficult to accept the assertion that Zwingli first championed the principle of congregational autonomy, as we understand it, and that he then retreated from it. The place of the magistracy in the religious life of the community was as natural to Zwingli as the separation of church and state is to the American Protestant.

57. Bluntschli, 386.
58. Steffen-Zehnder, 69.
59. cf. chap. I, n. 10.

2 The Influence of Mediaeval and Humanist Traditions upon Zwingli's View of Society

EVEN IF THE LOCAL TRADITIONS WHICH ZWINGLI ACCEPTED had not allowed the magistrate an important place in ecclesiastical affairs, the intellectual tradition which molded his thought would have led him to demand it. As it was, the ideas he brought to Zurich fitted the state of affairs in the city remarkably well. For example, his belief that the acquisition of secular authority and wealth had corrupted the clergy was a theme common both to the leading late scholastics and to the humanists of the northern Renaissance, especially Erasmus. Zwingli had come to this conclusion from his study of these sources and, above all, from his knowledge of scripture and from his personal experience. He was one with Erasmus in the desire to put the wealth and power of the church in the hands of the secular magistrate to free the clergy to preach the Gospel.[1] At Zurich the transfer was already well under way, and the earlier achievements of the magistracy doubtless inclined Zwingli to an even more willing acceptance of the government's role in the affairs of the church. Zwingli's ideas, pertinent and sympathetic to the actual situation in Zurich, won the support of a majority, at least in

1. Geldner argues that Erasmus sought to reduce the church to the position it had held during the first three centuries of its existence. Erasmus believed that it should have no rights in the temporal sphere and that its sole influence should be pedagogical. According to Geldner, Erasmus opposed forceful secularization of the church and hoped that it would divest itself of wealth and power which he said were a burden and the cause of ecclesiastical tyranny. Erasmus felt that the church's renunciation of secular concerns would free the state from the illegal power exercised by the church. Geldner also asserted that Erasmus defended the prince's right to restore order in the church when the hierarchy failed to do it (Geldner, *Die Staatsauffassung und Fürstenlehre des Erasmus von Rotterdam*, 98–100, 140). Maurer claims that Erasmus' view of the clergy's place in the *corpus christianum* represented a revival of the Franciscan ideal and that the logic of Erasmus' conception led to the absorption of the church by the state (Maurer, *Das Verhältnis des Staates zur Kirche nach humanistische Anschauung vornehmlich bei Erasmus*, 23–5). Moeller asserts that Erasmus placed a religious gloss on the state and incorporated the church in the state as an educational institution (Moeller, 49).

the Great Council, and aided the magistracy in bringing policies begun long before to their full fruition.

Except for the Baptists, no one in the sixteenth century seriously advocated the establishment of a "free church." Indeed, the idea of a magistracy which tolerated numerous sects and reserved for itself a sphere of activity divorced from religious life would have been an unspeakable heresy. The men of the sixteenth century still believed in the *corpus christianum*—the idea that society was a single Christian body.[2] The *corpus christianum* was divided into two realms, the spiritual and the secular, which were ruled by the priesthood and the magistrate. Together they governed the citizens of the Christian world. At the head of both was God, the creator and the sustainer of the Christian body, which existed to realize his purpose. As long as men believed in the *corpus christianum*, they lived in a society which was dominated by a theocratic aim, but not necessarily a society ruled by the clergy.[3]

In the course of the middle ages the relationship between the priesthood and temporal power within the Christian body had been radically altered. The early middle ages were dominated by the theory of Pope Gelasius, which asserted that emperor and priest were supreme in their respective kingdoms.

There are two things, most august Emperor, by which this world is chiefly ruled: the sacred authority of the priesthood and the royal power. Of these two, the priests carry the greater weight, because they will have to render account in the divine judgment even for the kings of men.[4]

Gelasianism tended to ignore the divine sanction of the emperor and to stress the superiority of the clergy. But neither Pope Gelasius nor his successors tried to claim a decisive role for the clergy in mundane affairs. They sought only to protect their supremacy in ecclesiastical affairs.

Until Gregory VII was raised to the papal throne in 1073 the church was dominated by the German emperors who developed the theory of "royal theocracy." They believed the divine sanction of their office empowered them to intervene in spiritual matters and to claim a position in the earthly hierarchy over the clergy. Gregory VII rejected all that. He denied the sacramental character of the imperial office and announced that clerical authority, due to its nature and function, was superior to secular, even in the affairs of the world. Earthly rulers did not receive

2. G. Locher, "Die Evangelische Stellung der Reformatoren zum öffentlichen Leben," *Kirchliche Zeitfrage*, Heft 26 (1950), 11–12; "Staat und Politik in der Lehre der Reformaoren," *Reformatio*, I (1952), 204.

3. cf. *supra* ix.

4. Quoted in Tellenbach, 33, 34.

their authority directly from God; the power they exercised was delegated to them by the pope. The Holy See had in theory, if never completely in practice, placed itself as a mediator between the earthly ruler and God.[5] Thus, the Gelasian theory was replaced by a doctrine which subjected the secular power to the spiritual.

In both the early period of "royal theocracy" and the era of papal supremacy, the tendency to fuse secular and religious authority was apparent. This was the result of the assumption that society had an ultimate and single divine purpose, and, however much the scales may have been tipped towards monarch or pope, the basic idea of the Christian society, oriented to God's will, remained throughout the middle ages.

Although by the sixteenth century the high water-mark of papal authority, as practised by Innocent III or proclaimed by Boniface VIII, was long past, the church remained a secular power. It controlled vast wealth and was deeply involved in political affairs. During the two centuries prior to the sixteenth, the extent to which wealth and power had corrupted the church was revealed in the fiscalism that accompanied the centralization of the church administration. The fourteenth and the fifteenth centuries were eras of rapid growth and centralization for secular government. European rulers sought to curb the financial drain imposed by the See of Peter's fiscalism and to limit the exercise of secular authority by the higher clergy. Developments in Zurich illustrate these efforts. The obvious solution to the problem was found in the establishment of national churches, which, though still loyal in dogma, cult, and adherence to the papacy, were effectively controlled by the local government.

Such far-reaching changes were not carried out without recrimination on both sides. Kings, princes, and magistrates found it necessary to seek authors to defend their policies. These were not hard to find among laymen and theologians. Two of the most important were the clerics, William of Occam, a founding father of the late scholastic *via moderna*, and Marsilio of Padua. They were active in the early decades of the fourteenth century and elaborated a view of the church which denied it wealth and secular power.

Though both men devoted their intellects to the cause of Lewis the Bavarian and attacked the basis of Pope John XXII's claim to secular power, the main lines of their thought were not similar. Marsilio's hostility to the independent authority of the church and his use of corporate theory to justify the control of the clergy by the secular government reveal his experience as a citizen of Padua and reflect, in part,

5. *Ibid.*, 35–6, 60, 156, 158.

his native city's solution to the problem of the church's disruptive influence in the affairs of the commune. By identifying the *universitas civium* with the *universitas fidelium*, i.e., the state with the church, Marsilio was able to rationalize the complete subordination of the clergy and all aspects of spiritual life to the authority of a government which represented the will of the people, or better, the "weightier part" (*pars valentior*) of the people. Marsilio rejected *in toto* the pope's claims to the *plentitudo potestatis* which he believed could rest only in the people, and asserted the authority of councils, representing clergy and laity, over the entire ecclesiastical hierarchy.[6] In order to preserve the peace of the state, he denied the clergy any secular function and limited them to their spiritual tasks: the proclamation of the Gospel and the administration of the sacraments.[7] His conclusions were a radical departure from past tradition.

Though Marsilio contributed to a climate of opinion which undoubtedly influenced the development of Zwingli's thought, it is doubtful that he had a direct effect upon Zwingli's intellectual development. Zwingli worked within a similar urban environment and used corporate theory to rationalize the control of the external affairs of the church by the magistracy and to identify the members of the church with the citizenry of Zurich. However, unlike Marsilio, he never gave the government authority over spiritual matters and did not seek to subordinate the clergy merely to preserve the state. Zwingli believed that good citizenship depended upon adherence to the Christian faith, while Marsilio made no such assumption.[8] The similarities between the two views are probably best explained by the fact that both men thought in terms of a communal environment which was dominated by a corporate theory of society and government.

Like Marsilio, Occam rejected the papal claim to unlimited power over all things temporal and spiritual. While recognizing the divine sanction of the pope's authority over the spiritual realm, he denied the pope and the clergy any rights in the secular sphere, except that of demanding the support necessary for them to perform their spiritual functions.[9] By asserting that kings and emperors received their authority from God through the people, not through the pope, and by limiting their power to temporal affairs, Occam sought to delineate the proper function of both the priesthood and the civil authority. He believed that the

6. Gewirth, I, 25–8, 182–3, 291–2, 258, 285–6.
7. Gewirth I, 207, 295; Seeberg III, 585.
8. Gewirth I, 293–4.
9. Boehner, 450–1; Seeberg, III, 587.

two were able to co-ordinate their jurisdiction because both served the same end, "the common good."[10] Occam's theory was far more moderate than Marsilio's and bears comparison with Gelasian dualism.[11]

Occam's view of religious authority and his definition of the church are of particular interest. Although he stressed the fallibility of the pope and asserted the authority of the scripture when he said, "Holy Scripture is not able to err . . . the Pope is able to err," he acknowledged the importance of an extra-scriptural tradition, passed along through the apostles and those who followed them, for the formulation of the truths of faith. He clearly was not the forerunner of Protestant biblicism but he helped to give the question of biblical authority a central place in late mediaeval theology. Occam defined the church as the *congregatio christianorum fidelium* assembly of faithful christians) and agreed that, when basic issues divided the church, a general council which represented it and derived its authority by delegation from the *congregatio* was superior to the pope.[12] Here again, however, Occam was far more moderate than Marsilio in his defence of councilliar supremacy; he viewed a council only as a portion of the whole church and put it on the same level with "provincial councils." In order for the council's decisions to have full validity, Occam maintained that it required the tacit agreement of all the faithful to its gathering and its actions; nor did he deny that in the normal course of events a pope should summon a council, or that a council which became heretical was subject to the supervision and correction of the pope.[13]

Many of Occam's ideas and much of his terminology were to appear frequently before and during the Reformation. Although it is possible to see certain parallels between Zwingli's definition of the church, his conception of the authority of councils and regional ecclesiastical gatherings, and his explication of the clergy's proper competence, it is difficult to establish a direct connection between Zwingli's thought and that of either Occam or Marsilio. If there was any one person who made a deep impression upon Zwingli, it was Erasmus. A number of Erasmus' ideas, especially those concerning the role of priest and prince in society, indicate that there was a certain amount of common ground between him and the major theorists who had opposed the secular activities of the clergy in the past.[14] In places his statements suggest a possible familiarity with Marsilio or Occam, and it is tempting to speculate that, via Erasmus, Zwingli was indirectly influenced by them.

10. Boehner, 445, 460, 463, 464.   11. Boehner, 468; Oberman, 422.
12. Oberman, 366, 399, 418; Seeburg III, 587, 588–9.
13. Gewirth, I, 289, 290.   14. cf. chap. II, n. 1.

However, Zwingli may well have had first-hand contact with the writings of Marsilio and Occam or with the work of their followers. When he studied at Vienna it was a centre of Occamist thought and, later at Basel there was opportunity for him to hear representatives of both Thomist and Occamist schools. Most scholars say that Zwingli was more closely associated with Thomism, but he himself refers to having studied both schools.[15] Zwingli no doubt had an interest in, and knowledge of, the Occamist tradition. The climate of opinion generated by the desire to limit the church to its rightful spiritual functions had existed long enough to become part of an accepted critical attitude. Zwingli could not have avoided absorbing some of it.

Various aspects of disaffection with the church were represented in German humanism, dominated by such figures as Erasmus and Hutten; consequently, it is necessary to examine with particular care Zwingli's connection with German humanism. After four centuries, this is not an easy task, but the work is made lighter by our knowledge of Zwingli's library. The three hundred and twenty books and twenty-eight manuscripts which are known to have been in it cover a wide range of topics and reveal Zwingli's contacts with the German humanists. The books included John Hus' *De ecclesia*, and William Bude's *Commentary on the Pandects of Justinian*, which was later influential in forming Calvin's view of the state.[16] There was, of course, Augustine's *City of God*, along with the works of Seneca, Eusebius, Lactantius, Jerome, Aristotle, and Cicero's *De Officiis*.[17] Although copies of Eberlein von Günzburg's pamphlets do not seem to have been in Zwingli's library, he did receive letters from Günzburg, and Günzburg's ideas may have interested him.[18] Günzburg hoped that the end of papal power in Germany would allow the Germanization and democratization of the church. He also sought social reforms for the benefit of the peasants.[19] Thanks to his friends in Basel, Zwingli had a copy of Hutten's edition of Lorenzo Valla's *De Donatione Constantini*, as well as some of Hutten's other pamphlets.[20] Shortly before his death Hutten sought and found refuge with Zwingli, but it is hard to say just what his influence upon Zwingli was; his "nationalist" interests may have strengthened Zwingli's Swiss patriotism. Conrad Celtis could have been another source for the development of

15. O. Farner I, 215, 218–19, 221–2.
16. Köhler "Huldrych Zwinglis Bibliothek," *NB*, LXXXIV, 6, 13, 21.
17. Usteri, "Initia Zwingliana," *TSK*, LVIII (1885), 617, 627; LIX (1886), 98, 103–4; Köhler, *NB*, LXXXIV, 17, 22.
18. Köhler, *NB*, LXXXIV, 14.
19. Fife, "Humanistic Currents in the Reformation Era," *GR*, XII, 83.
20. Köhler, *NB*, LXXXIV, 14, 21.

Zwingli's patriotism. Usteri believes that Zwingli's first two poems, the *Ox* and the *Labyrinth*, reflect the influence of the classical, political-patriotic themes stressed by Celtis[21]; but although he was at Vienna while Celtis was lecturing there, he never mentioned him as a teacher and could have derived these ideas from his own studies.

A more important contribution to Zwingli's thoughts on the relationship between the pastor and the magistrate may have come from Melanchthon. In the fall of 1522 the Ravensburg humanist Michael Hummelberg sent Zwingli a copy of Melanchthon's M.A. theses which dealt with the subject of the *"Double Magistracy."*[22] Melanchthon's theses reveal that he still thought within the framework of the *corpus christianum*. The government of the world was twofold, spiritual and corporal (*spirituale et corporale*); corporal government (*regimen*) was civil government and administered the external law, "the law of the flesh." The magistrates, princes, and judges who controlled civil government were, in Melanchthon's eyes, ordained by God to rule the external realm. He explained that the justice which they administered existed for coercion of those who lacked the spirit of God and that as long as the magistrates did not use the sword contrary to God's law, they did not sin.[23] Their justice, he concluded, was not of life but of death and the punishment of sin.

Melanchthon denied that the spiritual kingdom, which is ruled by God's Word and by those who serve it, had anything to do with secular power. He clarified his conception of the spiritual realm when he said: "They are miserably deceived who consider the [righteousness] of the spirit to be nothing else than the carnal righteousness of the world." This passage makes clear the foundation upon which the dual magistracy is based. It is based upon a twofold righteousness ordained by God, which

21. Usteri, *TSK*, LVIII, 617, 629.
22. In a letter to Zwingli, written on November 2, 1522, Michael Hummelberg informed him that Luther's answer to Henry VIII's attack had been published. If Zwingli did not have it, Hummelberg offered to get it for him. He advised Zwingli to read, in the meantime, Melanchthon's *Themata*: "In the meantime read these 'Theses Concerning the Double Magistracy' of the Melanchthon and you will see how they have confused the spiritual ministry of the Pope with temporal things" (*Z*, VII, 607, 8–10). Hummelberg's statement implies either that the *Themata* were already in Zwingli's hands or, as the use of *haec* makes more likely, they were being sent along with his letter. Since the work was known to have been in Zwingli's library, it is justifiable to assumed that it arrived sometime later in 1522 and was available to reinforce Zwingli's own views on the matter during the earlier stages of his career as a reformer. Köhler believes that the *Themata* may have influenced what he terms Zwingli's *staatstheoretische Anschauung* (Zwingli's theoretical view of the state); Köhler, *NB*, LXXXIV, 15, 21).
23. M, I, 595.

is necessary because many lack the spirit of God. If they had it, Melanchthon believed, the external law would become unnecessary.[24]

Melanchthon's conception of a dual regimen certainly appeared again in Zwingli. The sharp distinction which the former made between the worldly and the spiritual kingdom resembles Zwingli's division of authority between the magistrate and the pastor. Melanchthon, like Zwingli, justified the two powers in terms of a twofold righteousness established by God. The ideas found in Melanchthon's theses seem to have influenced Zwingli's sermon *On Divine and Human Righteousness* which appeared in 1523.[25]

It is to Erasmus, however, that one must look for a solid structure of ideas which enriched Zwingli's political thought. In addition to the Greek New Testament, Zwingli had twenty-three of Erasmus' works in his library and was familiar with ten others. Among these works were the *Complaint of Peace, Enchiridion, The Education of a Christian Prince*, and an edition of Erasmus' collected works published by Froben in 1519.[26]

Alfred Rich's admirable study of the beginnings of Zwingli's theology has shown the vital role which Erasmus played in Zwingli's early theological development. His careful analysis of the reasons for Zwingli's rejection of the Erasmian position in 1520–21 shows that there were certain points of continuity between the two even after the break. Both still saw scripture as the key to the revival of Christianity, though what each assumed the revival meant was radically different.[27] Rich does not consider the possibility that their attitude towards the place of the church in society remained the same. It is beyond the scope of this work to investigate the question thoroughly, but a few citations which indicate that they continued to agree should be mentioned.

Some have said Zwingli derived his principle of congregational participation in church affairs and his general attitude towards hierarchy from Erasmus.[28] The first assertion must be qualified in terms of the corporate tradition which dominated the political ideas of the city government and provided the frame of reference for Zwingli's consideration of the problem of church government which itself was a civil-religious issue. The most that can be said is that if Erasmus did aid Zwingli in formulating a conception of congregational participation in

24. M, I, 596.
25. Köhler, *NB*, LXXXIV, 15, 21.
26. *Ibid.*, 14–15. Egli, "Aus Zwinglis Bibliothek," *ZWI*, II (1907), 181.
27. Rich, 21–2, 26, 28, 82–3, 151.
28. Usteri was responsible for both suggestions (*TSK*, LVIII, 669–70). Köhler agrees with Usteri (*NB*, LXXXIV, 29).

church affairs, his influence was of secondary importance. The corporate tradition of government and the special place occupied by the Zurich Council in the affairs of all local assemblies were clearly far more important in determining Zwingli's solution to this question. The same applies to any general consideration of Erasmus' influence upon his political thought, for the two men worked in radically different contexts.

There is, on the other hand, considerable support for the claim that Erasmus helped to form Zwingli's attitude toward the hierarchy of the church. Erasmus' contempt for the clergy's lack of learning and for the greed and worldliness of the higher clergy was manifest. His bitter criticism of the clerical estate often concentrated upon these failings.

For one thing, they reckon it the highest degree of piety to have no contact with literature, and hence they see to it that they do not know how to read . . . some of them make a good profit from their dirtiness and mendicancy. . . . Our popes, cardinals and bishops for some time now have earnestly copied the state and practice of princes, and come near to beating them at their own game. . . . Nor do they keep in mind the name they bear, or what the word "bishop" means, labour, vigilance, solicitude. Yet in raking in moneys they truly play the bishop, overseeing everything and overlooking nothing.[29]

Erasmus objected to the confusion of the spiritual office with worldly authority which, he said, caused secularization and neglect of religion. Similar complaints appear more than once in Zwingli's writings. During the First Disputation he discussed the bishop's office:

And actually it concerns the little word bishop which, when one translates it into German properly, means nothing else than a guardian or supervisor, who should direct attention and care towards his people, being entrusted to instruct them in the divine faith and will, that is, in good German: a pastor.[30]

A comparison of the two definitions reveals that Zwingli and Erasmus share a similar conception of the bishop's task.

Speaking of the pope, Erasmus remarked:

As to the Supreme Pontiffs who take the place of Christ, if they tried to emulate His life, I mean His poverty, labors, teaching, cross and contempt for safety, if even they thought upon the title of Pope—that is, Father, or the addition "Most Holy," who on earth would be more afflicted . . . It would lose them all that wealth and honor, all those possessions, triumphal progresses, offices . . . In place of these it would bring . . . a thousand troublesome tasks. . . .[31]

---

29. Erasmus, *The Praise of Folly*, ed. Hudson, 85–6, 97 (hereafter cited as *PF*).
30. *Z*, I, 495, 22–496, 1.
31. *PF*, 98–9.

Zwingli, writing about the false prophet in *Der Hirt* (*The Shepherd*), passed a harsh judgment upon the hierarchy for living like the princes of this world.

Then it follows that they who have the staff, that is, worldly authority, along with the office of the shepherd are not shepherds but wolves; for Christ has forbidden the shepherd all ruling after the custom and manner of the princes of this world. . . . If they now have the staff which Christ has forbidden them, then they are false shepherds.[32]

The ultimate cause of Erasmus' disgust with the hierarchy was its propensity to cause war rather than to encourage peace, as the clergy should. Erasmus hoped for peace and religious revival in Christian Europe.[33] As he saw the situation, peace was possible if the clergy fulfilled its office and influenced the princes to follow wise policies. Needless to say, his hopes were never realized, but his ideals helped to crystallize Zwingli's opposition to mercenary service and his demand for Swiss neutrality.

Erasmus' pessimism about the clergy mirrored a general feeling which had long been present in European society. Despairing of the clergy's ability to reform itself he turned to the prince for help and assigned him the predominant role in the moral direction of the community. The introduction to the 1518 edition of the *Enchiridion*, written two years after the *Education of a Christian Prince*, gave a definition of the *corpus christianum* which summarized his opinion. He described the Christian body in terms of a series of concentric circles revolving around Christ as the centre. The ecclesiastical hierarchy constituted the inner circle. Much like Occam, Erasmus demanded the withdrawal of the hierarchy from worldly affairs and he based their superiority upon their spiritual function. Though he complained that the princes, the members of the second circle, often behaved like the common people, the members of the third, Erasmus gave them full control of society.[34] When he considered the prince's responsibilities in *The Education of a Christian Prince*, Erasmus said the moral example given by the prince to the people had greater effect than that of churchmen: "The studies and character of priests and bishops are a potent factor in this matter, I admit, but not nearly so much as those of the prince."[35] Erasmus had expressed the

---

32. *Z*, III, 57, 25–8, 31–58, 1.
33. Rudolf Liechtenhan, "Die Politische Hoffnung des Erasmus und Ihr Zusammenbruch," *Gedenkschrift zum 400 Todestage des Erasmus von Rotterdam*, 152–3, 158.
34. Geldner, 80–1, 140.
35. Erasmus, *The Education of a Christian Prince*, ed. Born, 157 (hereafter cited as *ECP*).

same idea in the *Complaint of Peace*. Using terminology reminiscent of Eusebius' description of Constantine as the upholder of God's image on earth, he exalted the authority of the prince: "I call unto you, O ye princes, at whose beck and commandment the matters and business of men most chiefly do depend, and that among men do bear the image of Christ."[36] However, he was careful to show the prince ruled for the common good, not for his own advancement: "[the prince] born for the common good . . . to whom no concern is of longer standing or more dear than the state. . . . The one idea which should concern a prince in ruling . . . the public need, free from all private interests."[37]

Erasmus' view of the service to the common good must have had a familiar ring to Zwingli in Switzerland, where the rising magistracies of the cities had long ago proclaimed in defence of their expanding power their devotion to the common good. The advice Erasmus gave to the princes concerning the conduct of justice indicates how great a moral task he gave to the ruler. Some of these ideas appeared later in Zwingli. Though the ruler to whom they referred was quite different, for Erasmus as for Zwingli, the governor's administration of justice had a didactic function: "Let the prince propose such laws as not only provide punishment in particular for the sources of crime but also have influence against sin itself. . . . The main purpose of law should be to restrain crime by reason rather than by punishment."[38] Speaking of the functions of judges and rulers, Zwingli wrote: "Therefore the judge and rulers are servants of God, they are the schoolmasters."[39]

One piece of advice given to the prince may have played a part in Zwingli's strategy of reform. Erasmus told the prince that the introduction of reforms required time and care.

However, if the people prove intractable and rebel against what is good for them, then you must bide your time and gradually lead them over to your end. . . . Yet he must not cease his efforts as long as he is able to renew his fight and what he has not accomplished by one method he should try to effect by another.[40]

Although as a diplomat Zwingli was no fool, this maxim might have been in the back of his mind.

There is no doubt that Erasmus was willing to expand the competence of the civil authority to achieve the purification of the church. The argument of a number of scholars, that Erasmus allowed the church to be absorbed into the state which then defined the church's task in

---

36. Erasmus, *Complaint of Peace*, ed. Hirten, 56.
37. *ECP*, 162–3, 140.   38. *Ibid.*, 222.
39. *Z*, II, 488, 4–5.   40. *ECP*, 213–14.

terms of its own conception of the common good, has already been noted.[41] Such a claim goes too far. Erasmus assumed that the prince, whose power he wished to enhance, was Christian. By definition, the power any Christian exercised was limited, and those who exercised absolute authority were pagans, not Christians. Erasmus made this point clear enough:

Never forget that "dominion," "imperial authority," "kingdom," "power," are all pagan terms, not Christian. The ruling power of a Christian state consists only of administration, kindness, and protection. . . . To subject his people through fear, to make them perform servile tasks, to drive them from their possessions, depose them of their goods, and finally even to martyr them—those are the rights of a pagan prince.[42]

Zwingli said much the same thing in the sermon *The Shepherd* which was delivered during the Second Disputation: "Seneca also considers royal power as a service; that is, the kingdom or the government is an office of doing good."[43] Erasmus and Zwingli both believed that a Christian prince or magistrate could not be a tyrant. They thought of society as a *corpus christianum* and were willing to trust secular authorities because they assumed that such men were Christian. The ideal bond for the prince and his people was Christian love, which Erasmus hoped the proper education would instill: "But where Christian love unites the people and their prince, then everything is yours that your position demands."[44] This is where Zwingli disagreed with Erasmus. For him, the ability to fulfil the love commandment was the gift of God's grace, not something which could be gained through education.

Erasmus envisaged "a government bound to the model of Christ."[45] By portraying the ruler as the bearer of Christ's image in the world, Erasmus made the exercise of absolute power in the pagan sense impossible. Any ruler who accepted the Erasmian standard had to conform to the principles of divine behaviour. Its essence was defined by Erasmus as the service of the good, an expression of love, and the service of the good excluded the possibility of tyranny. In a world ruled by a "limited" monarch, Erasmus could consider the restoration of a purified church, stripped of all earthly authority and devoted to its spiritual calling. Indeed he could even grant the prince the right to set in order the affairs of the church, when the clergy was unable to do so.[46]

The very fact that Zwingli did not remain an Erasmian, and that his thought developed under very different conditions than that of Erasmus,

41. Maurer, 23–4.
42. *ECP*, 175–9.
43. *Z*, III, 27.
44. *ECP*, 180.
45. Enthoven, *NJKA*, XXIV, 316.
46. Geldner, 84–5, 98–9.

makes it difficult to assess the importance of Erasmus' view of the state and its ruler upon Zwingli. In seeking a solution to this problem, Moeller's comments upon the subject are helpful. He notes the importance of Erasmus' conception of the state in the thinking of the northern humanists as a whole and states that Zwingli shared the general tendency to view the state as an organism, and that he also used this concept to justify linking directly the tasks of the church and state; but he claims that Zwingli's republicanism was a deviation from Erasmus' ideal state governed by a monarch. Without denying the significance of the humanists' political thought, in particular of Erasmus', Moeller asserts that for Zwingli as for Bucer the city environment in which they worked was a more decisive influence.[47]

Although Zwingli certainly did not derive either his faith in the Christian magistrate, or his belief in the *corpus christianum* from Erasmus, it is possible to conclude that Zwingli's belief in both was reinforced by his study of Erasmus and that Zwingli drew upon Erasmus' ideas and altered them to fit the local situation. Zwingli sought to remove the last vestiges of secular power and wealth from the hands of the clergy to free them for the preaching of the Gospel. He was in practice as willing as Erasmus was in theory to increase the authority of the magistrate. Though he spoke of the Christian magistrate in a different context, he employed terms similar to those used by Erasmus to describe the Christian prince. Zwingli believed that the magistrate could be trusted because he was a Christian magistrate, bound by Christian morality. He and Erasmus both viewed society as Christian and understood the offices of priest, prince, or magistrate as the organs of direction for it. This conception, though not so complete in Zwingli's case that it prevented him from propounding a right of rebellion against the government, explains much of his readiness to depend upon the magistracy for the success of his programme.

Thus, it probably would have shocked Zwingli to hear the product of his work described as a theocracy in the modern sense, i.e., as a society under ecclesiastical direction. All he sought was to restore the balance of authority within Christian society. To achieve this he called for an end to the wealth and power of the clergy. Only when the government was in full control of its rightful domain and the clergy devoted itself to the things of the spirit, could the rule of God be realized. This was Zwingli's "theocratic" ideal.

47. Moeller, 48–9, 51–3.

3   Zwingli's Thought and Work 1510-1520
and the Council's Mandate

IN THE YEARS BEFORE HIS ARRIVAL IN ZURICH, ZWINGLI'S primary concern was the defence of Swiss freedom, but his understanding of the nature of the problem and the solution which he proposed gradually changed. In the process his patriotism became entwined with a new theme, the Gospel faith. The resulting synthesis was the creation of a mind which functioned not only in the study but also in the world of political affairs: Zwingli's labours as a Christian humanist cannot be disassociated from his life as a good citizen.[1]

The threat to Swiss freedom which worried Zwingli was the result of the military reputation gained by the Swiss in the Burgundian and Swabian wars. The Swiss infantry was considered the best in Europe and, due to her military strength, Switzerland was recognized as a major European power. The Valois-Hapsburg struggle for Italy put good soldiers at a premium, and both sides, along with the papacy, vied with one another to gain Swiss infantry for their armies. They were willing to pay not only the soldiers but also those who aided in recruiting them. The payments, which were made in the form of pensions, affected virtually all office-holders at every level of government and were an invitation to corruption, since it was possible to receive pensions from several sources at the same time.[2] While the pension system corrupted the governments of the cantons, the habits which returning Swiss soldiers had learned abroad threatened to destroy public order in the Confederacy.

Not only did the Swiss lack a strong central government able to control such abuses, the Confederates were not eager to see them controlled. An attempt made by the Federal Diet in 1500 to abolish the pension system failed because the members of the Confederacy would not co-operate.[3] The Diet's effort, in co-operation with the cantonal governments, to limit recruiting and service by permitting the inhabitants of the cantons to serve only those powers with whom a recruitment treaty

1. Mueller, 52.   2. Guggenbühl, I, 317.
3. Gerig, 9.

had been made was never entirely successful.[4] Because Switzerland as a whole, and the original cantons, Uri, Schwyz, and Unterwalden, in particular, suffered from a surplus population which it could not feed, the chance to export men in return for money to pay for imports of grain and also luxuries made most of the cantons unwilling to consider putting an end to the system.[5] The French used the export of grain as well as the promise of favourable trade agreements to entice the Swiss to their side.[6]

As a result of their military supremacy, the Swiss were not content merely to serve foreign powers. The Burgundian and Swabian wars had brought territorial gains to the cantons of the Confederacy. For example, at the end of the Swabian war, Zurich won control over considerable territory along the Rhine which, together with the entry of Basel into the Confederacy, provided her with a defensive barrier against the empire. The existence of this buffer zone along the Rhine gave Zurich a security and freedom of action which helped to make possible the Zwinglian Reformation in the canton without danger of foreign intervention. Almost all the Confederates desired to expand their territories. The struggle for Italy provided them with a golden opportunity to use their military advantages; a surplus of first-class troops to embark upon a policy of territorial expansion in Italy.

Expansion required an efficient and authoritative central administration which the Swiss did not possess.[7] The cantons of the Confederacy had essentially different foreign interests. The western part of Switzerland, led by Bern, followed a policy of expansion at the expense of Savoy, while the original cantons were concerned with the absorption or domination of the Duchy of Milan and enjoyed the support of the other cantons as long as the policy was not too costly. Though, as Fueter says, Milan's importance as a grain centre played a significant role in motivating Swiss policy, its territories were the logical objectives for the ambitions of the original cantons. Allied with the Holy League against France, the Confederacy was dominated by the imperialist policies of Uri, Schwyz, and Unterwalden. For a few years the Swiss efforts were crowned with success; between 1512 and the disastrous battle of Marignano (1515) Milan was a Swiss protectorate.

Constant involvement in the Italian wars heightened regional tensions within the Confederacy. The events which preceded Marignano illustrate this. The Bernese and the other contingents from the western part of Switzerland withdrew before the battle. They favoured accepting the terms of peace offered by Francis I because they preferred a French to a

4. *Ibid.*; Guggenbühl, I, 393.
6. *Ibid.*; Guggenbühl, I, 426.

5. Fueter, 235–6.
7. Guggenbühl, I, 384, 316, 429–30.

papal alliance.[8] After the defeat, the Confederacy was deserted by its allies and was too divided to continue the war, or even to prevent the French from increasing their recruiting within its borders. Although Marignano did not put an end to the pension and mercenary system, it revealed the weakness of the federal government and thwarted Swiss ambitions to play the role of a great power in European affairs.[9] There was a growing feeling in the Confederacy that Swiss interests were not served by sending soldiers abroad for pay.

Zwingli's early writings reflect the shifting fortunes of the Swiss in Italy. His growing disenchantment with the system of mercenary service was based upon his own experience in Italy as well as upon the influence of Erasmus' Christian pacificism. Zwingli was not alone in fearing that foreign influence exercised through the pensioners might wreck the government of the Confederacy and lead to the absorption of Switzerland by one of the great powers. As his thoughts on the problem matured, he came to the conclusion that neutrality was the best solution to Switzerland's difficulty.

Zwingli's earliest work, the *Fable of the Ox*, composed in 1510, revealed a patriotic concern over the effect of mercenary service and the pension system upon the future of Swiss freedom. The poem refers to the complicated events of the year 1510. Julius II had turned his back upon the League of Cambrai and had formed a new alliance, the Holy League, to drive the French out of Italy. Through the clever diplomacy of Cardinal Schinner he managed to bring the Swiss into his system of Italian alliances.[10] The Swiss had understood their function as a purely defensive one and had agreed to protect the Pope from his nearest neighbours; but they soon discovered that they had been brought to Italy to aid Julius in his effort to expel the French. The Confederacy was in a difficult situation, for both Louis XII and his new ally, the Emperor Maximilian, threatened to attack it unless it withdrew from Italy. If it did retreat, it faced the danger of papal wrath and the loss of pay which would inevitably follow Julius' anger.[11] It was of this situation that Zwingli spoke in the poem.

Though Zwingli considered the greed and general collapse of public order which bribery and an unruly soldiery carried in their wake as serious threats, he was not yet ready to call for the abolition of military service abroad for pay. He advocated that the Swiss continue to support

8. Fueter, 236–7, 276, 279–80.
9. Guggenbühl, I, 424–5, 427.
10. O. Farner, II, 76; Guggenbühl, I, 397–8.
11. O. Farner, II, 77.

the Pope and he opposed the readiness of many to serve the French.[12]
This was a sensible argument because papal influence in the affairs of
the cantons did not menace Swiss freedom in the way an expansion of
French influence did. However, Zwingli's contention that the Confederacy would become so dependent it would lose its freedom by serving
the French can be seen as a general attack upon mercenary service.

The *De Gestis* of 1512, addressed to Vadian at Vienna, marked what
seemed to be a complete change of heart. There are no traces of worry
or concern about the effect of foreign influence upon Swiss freedom. The
account is full of pride at the deeds of the Swiss in papal service.
Although authorities disagree, it is quite likely that Zwingli took part in
the Pavia campaign as a chaplain and had personal reasons for satisfaction at the outcome.[13] He believed that Swiss interests were best served
by an alliance with the papacy and appeared to welcome the fact that,
as a result of the campaign, Milan had come under Swiss control, thus
enhancing the Confederacy's position as a European power.

Zwingli had become far more cautious by 1516. *The Labyrinth* contained the same patriotic emphasis as Zwingli's earlier works, but combined it with a new ethical and religious vein. The poem diagnosed the
country's ills and proposed a religious solution for them. Zwingli's years
of study had brought him to Erasmus and then to scripture.[14] Erasmus
had given him an understanding of, and enthusiasm for, Christian pacifism. Zwingli's fresh appreciation of the Gospel message was most important for the future. It was in the year he composed the *Labyrinth* that,
according to his later statements, he began to preach the Gospel of
Christ: "I began . . . to preach the Gospel of Christ in the year 1516."[15]

Erasmus and the study of scripture were not the only influences which
changed Zwingli's attitude towards Swiss military service in foreign
lands. In the *Labyrinth* enthusiasm for Switzerland's place as an ally of
the Pope is missing. Although this does not mean that Zwingli had
become anti-papal, his zeal for the "pastor" was a thing of the past.
As a chaplain serving with the troops in the campaign of 1515 which
ended in the disastrous battle of Marignano, he had a good chance to

12. Z, I, 12, 20–8, 18, 19–26.
13. Bullinger mentions only Novara (1513) and Marignano (1515), but Oskar
Farner suggests that Bullinger was not well informed about Zwingi's earlier life
and may have confused Pavia with Novara (O. Farner, II, 93–4).
14. Walther Köhler stresses the influence of Erasmus' pacifism upon Zwingli
(Köhler, 39). O. Farner agrees that Zwingli went a long way towards absolute
pacifism, but says that he never gave up his belief in military preparedness for
self-defence. The position which the poem reveals, Farner argues, is one of absolute
neutrality (O. Farner, II, 180, 184, 202).
15. Z, II, 144, 32–3; 145, 1–2.

see the seamier side of the "pastor's" role in Italian affairs. Even worse, he had witnessed the departure of the forces of Bern, Freibourg, and Solothurn, which were openly pro-French, before the battle. Prior to the battle he had preached to the soldiers and then had participated in the fight. Most authorities assert that his sermon was a plea for unity, but Oskar Farner maintains that it may have been more than that. He believes it is possible that Zwingli, speaking from a scriptural perspective, criticized the mercenary system.[16]

The sequel to the defeat was repugnant. The divided Confederacy, swamped with French gold and stunned by the disaster, made peace in the fall of 1516 and altered its foreign policy to favour the interests of France. The treaty and the Confederacy's subsequent change of policy laid the foundation for the alliance of 1521 with France.[17] This combination of events was surely difficult for a patriot to bear, and the impression they left is mirrored in the *Labyrinth*. Zwingli's public opposition to the developments after Marignano cost him his post at Glarus, where the pro-French party was in power. In November, 1516, he left Glarus to become pastor in the church at the Cloister of Einsiedeln.[18]

The *Labyrinth* reveals the new dimension in Zwingli's thought. The solution to national problems is no longer to be found by alliance with an earthly power, but is to be sought in the example of Christ which teaches peace and self-sacrifice. The troubled state of Swiss politics and the decline of public morality are not primary problems. They have become for Zwingli symptoms of man's failure to follow Christ's teachings.

> Look now on all human deeds, how
> they carry out everything without
> counsel. . . .
> There is no love of God in us which
> might remove so much evil. . . .
> Thus the world is now full of faithless
> cunning. . . .
> because we lack the likeness of
> Christ [we are] more like the heathen. . . .[19]

The new perspective became a central motif in his writings. The woes of the Confederacy are viewed as the result of its failure to realize the tenets of the Christian faith in the life of the community. Zwingli's aim is to rectify the situation. This is the key to understanding his conception

16. O. Farner, II, 174–5.
17. *Ibid.*, II, 184–5, 204–5; Guggenbühl, I, 427–8.
18. O. Farner, II, 202–3.
19. Z, I, 59, 13–14, 25–6, 30–2.

of the relationship between the Christian religion and the magistracy. The Christian faith must be the basis for the government of society.

The opportunity to proclaim Christ's teachings to a larger audience had come to Zwingli late in 1518 when he was called to Zurich as People's Priest at the Cathedral Church, where he preached his first sermon on January 1, 1519. At this time the full significance of the effects of Luther's Ninety-Five Theses had not been realized. No one could foresee the difficulties which Luther and his supporters were to cause the Emperor, Charles V. Still less would anyone have ventured to speculate that Zwingli's preaching was to reform the church at Zurich and win a substantial portion of the Confederacy, including Bern and Basel, for Christian renewal; nor could anyone have imagined that Zwingli's teaching would divide the Confederacy and cause its final withdrawal from active participation in the Valois-Hapsburg struggle for a European hegemony.[20]

Zwingli's conviction found further expression in the *Gebetslied in der Pest* (*Prayersong in the Plague*) of 1519. While he was visiting the baths at Pfäffers in August the plague broke out in the city. As the People's Priest at the Cathedral Church, he was obliged to be in the city during an epidemic, and so he immediately returned only to be stricken himself in mid-September.[21] The poem, written shortly after his recovery, shows a deepening of his spiritual life in the face of death and may also reflect his response to the tension created by the events which preceded his illness.

In February Zwingli had taken the lead in the expulsion of the indulgence-seller Samson not only from Zurich but also from the whole Confederacy. In this he had the support of the Bishop of Constance and the agreement of the Pope, whose political plans required military support from Zurich. Later that spring (April) a diet of the Confederacy sitting at Zurich declared itself in favour of Charles V's election as emperor. An opinion in favour of Charles' election was secured in spite of considerable French pressure for the Swiss to support Francis I. It was a difficult time for Zwingli, who favoured Charles and yet did not want to run the risk of being called a partisan of the Emperor, which he was not.[22] His preaching carried with it a challenge to France's use of Swiss mercenaries, and there was no point in angering the French further by openly supporting Charles. The French had considerable influence in the Confederacy and their hostility would certainly not help the cause of reform. Zwingli needed time to consolidate his position at Zurich.

20. Fueter, 50, 234, 238.   21. O. Farner, II, 352–3.
22. Köhler, 59, 55, 56.

Then came the plague. Oscar Farner believes that the news of the Leipzig debate must have reached Zwingli just before his illness and thinks that the knowledge of Luther's action, together with Zwingli's plague experience, helped to strengthen his decision to act more positively for the cause of reform.[23] In the poem Zwingli states his conception of his relationship with God:

> Do as you wish;
> Nothing is too much for me.
> I am your vessel,
> Make me whole or break me.[24]

This is the source of Zwingli's strength: he is God's instrument, and God's power works through him. The belief that man in the right relationship to God is called to serve as an instrument of his purpose can be applied both to individuals and to the community.

The evidence found in Zwingli's early works indicates he had already made the connection between the problems of politics and the solution offered by the Christian faith before he came to Zurich. Even if the corporate tradition of city government had not already given the magistracy a semi-religious character, it is not unreasonable to assume that Zwingli would quite naturally assign to a government in the right relationship with God a function as an instrument of the divine purpose.[25] Zwingli's intensive study of the Old Testament, where such a function is assigned to the whole community of the Israelites, the Lord's chosen nation, no doubt reinforced his willingness to accept the existing corporate theory of society and enabled him to identify the people and the government of Zurich with the children of the New Covenant. Thus the patriotism of Zwingli's earlier career could be identified with the purposive structuring of the community to fulfil the will of God for those who belonged to the people of the New Covenant. In this instance, political salvation must always appear as the by-product of the major aim: the religious salvation of the community. Zwingli's patriotic concerns and his discovery of the Gospel faith were a prelude to his work at Zurich. The connection which he had made between the two before his arrival helped him gain the support of the Zurich magistracy in a surprisingly short time.

According to Bullinger, the *Archeteles*, which appeared in August, 1522, summed up the main concerns of Zwingli's preaching from 1519–22.[26] Its contents will be considered later. The *Complaints* (*Klagschriften*) published in 1522, but written between 1519 and 1522,

---

23. O. Farner, II, 373–6.
24. Z, I, 67, 18–21.
25. Moeller, 15.
26. Bullinger, I, 30–1.

by Konrad Hofmann and another canon, probably Johannes Widmer, who had a reputation as a "bloody soldier," offer an excellent account of Zwingli's early preaching as seen through the eyes of those loyal to the old church.[27] The first portion of Hofmann's criticisms date from the period 1519–20. Zwingli, Hofmann complained, was too prone to criticize individuals and to weaken popular respect for monks and priests by his attacks on their conduct. According to Hofmann, Zwingli's preaching left the people so confused that they were no longer able to distinguish between major and minor sins, and he thought that they would cease to fear punishment for any sin, great or small.[28] It appears that Zwingli's sermons, which were drawn from texts in the Gospels, Acts, and the Pauline epistles, compared the behaviour of clergy and laity with the standard of conduct laid down by the Gospel.[29] The emphasis of Zwingli's preaching, which applied biblical norms to the problems of the community as a whole, reveals the close connection between him and Erasmus. Like Erasmus, he judged the conduct of society according to the *lex Christi sive evangelica* and sought to place it under the rule of God. The sermons about which Hofmann complained could scarcely have been delivered by an advocate of a separate, suffering church, made up of the sinless of the world.

Other aspects of Zwingli's preaching worried Hofmann even more. He was outraged at Zwingli's attacks upon the "customary laws and ordinances" and argued that even if these laws and ordinances, when subjected to the standard of the Word can be improved, Zwingli's method of criticism endangered not only the church, the fathers, the councils, the pope, and the hierarchy, but also threatened to stir up disobedience to the magistracy:

Thereby the holy church, the holy fathers, the councils, the Pope, cardinals, bishops, etc. are mocked, held in contempt and destroyed. And (thus) disobedience to the government (Romans 13), disunity, heresy, weakness and a lessening of the Christian faith arises, from which Christendom may receive the greatest damage and the Devil the greatest joy[30]

---

27. Egli's account of the two *Klagschriften* does not identify Widmer, but Pestalozzi definitely identifies him as the second author (Egli, 47; Pestalozzi, 79). According to Egli, the first section of Hofmann's work was put on paper between the end of 1518 and the early summer of 1520, before the bull against Luther was published, but after Cologne and Louvain had condemned Luther's teaching (Egli, 47; O. Farner, III, 180, 583). Widmer's contribution is sandwiched between the earlier and later portions of Hofmann's main work and was probably not written until 1522 (Egli, 47).

28. *E.A.*, 213.

29. O. Farner, III, 40.

30. *E.A.*, 213.

Hofmann's fear for the political stability of the canton and the Christian world demonstrates the general assumption of the period. Right religion is essential to society; heresy destroys public order. For both Hofmann and Zwingli the question of reform was as much a political as a religious issue. They disagreed not about the relationship between religion and society but about what was right religion.

Hofmann's *Complaint* points up the confusion of the conservative opposition. He himself saw the need for a limited reform of the church and for this reason had favoured the choice of Zwingli as People's Priest. However, once Zwingli began to preach, Hofmann became worried because he felt that what Zwingli said weakened the faith of the common man in the institutions and personnel of the church. He feared the results of a popular reform movement and became convinced that Zwingli was stirring up the citizens unnecessarily.[31] He and some of the other conservatives wanted reform and were anxious to have the Gospel proclaimed, but they had never dreamed that the result would lead away from established tradition, let alone stir up popular feeling against them.

Hofmann's dismay over the popular aspect of Zwingli's preaching probably had another cause. In general, the conservative element among the clergy was identified with the ancient families of the Zurich noble and merchant class, organized for political purposes in the *Constafel*.[32] In the Small Council, where the *Constafel* was strongly represented, the opposition to Zwingli was most marked. For example, during the visit of the bishop's commission to Zurich in April, 1522, the commissioners tried to have the Lenten fast violations, which were the cause of their visit, discussed before the Small Council because they knew that the Small Council was sympathetic to the old church.[33] Zwingli's attacks upon abuses in the church, and upon the morality of the clergy, were a threat to the *Constafel*. The monasteries and chapter house of the city served as a safe haven for the younger sons and daughters of the prominent families: within these foundations they found it easy to amass comfortable incomes by collecting prebends (pluralism).[34] Zwingli's demands for reform menaced their social position in the church and were a reminder to the ancient families that their power was in decline. This was bound to stir up a hostile reaction. His preaching also undermined their position in other ways, as the end of mercenary service would show. Hofmann could not avoid reflecting the concerns of this group over the social and political implications of Zwingli's sermons.

It was dangerous for Hofmann and his friends to go too far in

31. Pestalozzi, 41–3, 43–4, 48.   32. Steffen-Zehnder, 46.
33. Z, I, 138–9.   34. Steffen-Zehnder, 42–3, 46, 49.

attacking Zwingli or associating him with Luther's ideas, for the church's position on Luther was not clarified until the summer of 1520. Even in the late spring of that year, when Hofmann penned the second section of the first part of his complaint, it was unwise to accuse Zwingli of heresy. Zwingli had close connections with Cardinal Schinner, the pope's representative in Switzerland.[35] Schinner's defence of Zwingli was dictated in part by the desires of the pope himself, who wished to use Zurich as a counterweight against French influence in the Confederacy. All Hofmann could do was to advise Zwingli to refrain from discussing Luther's opinions so freely, until the Leipzig debate could be judged.[36]

Even though Zwingli was suspected of Lutheran heresy it was hard to prove it. Much of what he said had already been said by Erasmus and others. The line between a reformer ready to turn against the church and a Christian humanist, critical, yet loyal, was not clearly drawn, and Zwingli's caution gave his critics no help. His selection as People's Priest had been debated because some of the canons feared that he was an Erasmian and would demand a reform of the clergy; many still believed that he was merely another disciple of Erasmus.[37] Hofmann was not sure just where Zwingli stood, and the last part of the first section of the *Complaint* demonstrates his confusion. He warned against bringing questions best left to scholars before the people and cited Erasmus to give weight to his advice: "Erasmus himself writes that one should not reveal all his teaching to the people."[38] The remark indicates that Hofmann considered Zwingli an Erasmian and was both accusing him and warning him against going beyond his master. It also shows Hofmann's concern over popular sentiment in favour of the purification of the church.

The impact of Zwingli's activities was felt beyond Zurich. A letter written by Beatus Rhenanus at Basel in May of 1519 expressed admiration for his persistence and patience in the face of the hostile comment which his preaching had caused.[39] Zwingli replied and explained the reason for his patience. Matters at Zurich were going very well; the greater portion of his audience was drawn from the best people.[40] From the context of Zwingli's remark he seems to refer to the best, *optima*, in an ethical sense, but the reference could also imply that he had support from the more influential citizens of Zurich.[41]

35. Staehelin, I, 148.   36. *E.A.*, 213.
37. Pestalozzi, 61–2.   38. *E.A.*, 213.
39. Z, VII, 166, 3–10.   40. *Ibid.*, 171, 21.
41. The term *meliores*, the better people, was sometimes used to refer to the more influential segment of a city's population. However, its application was usually confined to the aristocratic element of the population, and Zwingli's remark surely did not refer to the Zurich *Constafel* (Moeller, 11).

Aside from theological considerations, Zwingli's preaching attracted and held his friends because of its patriotic vein, an element ignored by Hofmann. Many believed that Zwingli's sermons addressed themselves to the political problems of the entire Confederacy and in this they correctly understood his intention. Casper Hedio's letter, written on November 6 to express his relief at hearing that Zwingli was recovering from the plague, indicated that he believed that Zwingli's death would have affected the welfare of the fatherland: "For who would not bemoan the fact that the common salvation of the fatherland, the trumpet of the Gospel, the magnanimous trumpeter of truth is weak and perishes . . . ?"[42] Hedio obviously believed that he and Zwingli shared the same assumption: the well-being of the fatherland was intimately connected with the proclamation of the Gospel. He saw Zwingli as the agent of salvation for the nation. If he judged Zwingli's aim and the significance of his preaching correctly, his remarks provide further evidence that from the beginning of his career as a reformer Zwingli thought in terms of restructuring the public life of the community upon the foundation of the Gospel. This makes it more difficult to assert that at this time Zwingli believed that the true church was a suffering remnant. His preaching was directed to the community as a whole, and because it was, it must have accepted both the place which the civil authorities occupied in it and recognized their claim to be responsible for the common good of the community.

Hedio's letter also reveals that the desire for an alleviation of the political ills suffered by the Swiss through the application of biblical principles was shared by those schooled in the writings of Erasmus and dismayed by the results of Swiss participation in the Italian wars. However, reports of discontent over his preaching also came to Zwingli from as far away as Paris.[43] Myconius, writing from Lucerne in 1519, lamented that Zwingli was spoken ill of there; Zwingli answered with an encouraging word drawn from the apostle Paul: "For if till now I should please men, as Paul says, I would not be a servant of Christ."[44] In December Myconius wrote that at Lucerne Zwingli's doctrines were being called the work of the devil.[45] Zwingli's reply was calm and confident. Writing on December 31, 1519, he advised Myconius not to worry about the accusations of the crowd and assured him that they were not alone. He noted proudly the large following already won at Zurich: "For we are not alone: at Zurich more than 2000 children and adults, who are already sucking in spiritual milk, will soon make ready for solid food,

42. Z, VII, 214, 9–11.   43. Staehelin, I, 147.
44. Z, VII, 231, 2–3.   45. Ibid., 242, 6.

while the others starve."[46] The population of Zurich was between 5,000 and 7,000, and Zwingli's news indicated that a greater part of the populace had come over to the cause of the Gospel.[47]

The reply to Myconius is important for another reason: it gives us insight into Zwingli's attitude towards reform in his first year of public activity. Drawing upon the imagery of Hebrews 5:12, he discussed the progress he had made in terms of milk and solid food. The reference shows that he understood the need to prepare the people gradually, and, as his letters from the next year reveal, that he could never permit or sympathize with an incautious radicalism.

Despite the success which his preaching enjoyed at Zurich, Zwingli was not unrealistic about the difficulties which he and his friends faced. He pointed out to Myconius that the Gospel was bound to arouse opposition and that the struggle with the wicked, i.e., the opponents of Gospel, would be a continuing one.

There is nothing in common between this vain world and the Gospel; the demons are not able to be silent in the presence of Christ; and if, indeed, they are commanded to be silent, they rend asunder him whom they possess; the devil is torturous, between whom and the woman, that is the church, the pure bride of Christ, there exists mortal hatreds. . . . Further, for me the battle with evil is ongoing; it is not indeed that there is nothing in common between my morals and theirs, but their desire is to persecute Christ and the Gospel in me.[48]

Zwingli's identification of the opposition to the Gospel with the vain world, demons, and the mortal hatred which exists between the devil and the church sheds light upon his conception of the church. The charges that he and Myconius preached the doctrine of the devil, which Zwingli mentioned earlier in the letter, were made by members of the church itself.[49] Zwingli believed that this attack was the devil's, which would indicate that at this time he assumed that the church on earth was a mixed body containing believers and non-believers. In this case those who were truly of the world and the devil were making themselves known by their opposition.

The fact that he had won a sizable following was bound to affect the attitude of the magistracy towards him. If nothing else, the number of his supporters limited the ability of the magistrates to oppose him and influenced them in his favour. Their willingness to favour him was no doubt encouraged by his tact and careful preparation of his hearers for the full force of the Gospel.

46. *Ibid.*, 245, 13–17.
48. *Ibid.*, 245, 14–17, 21–4, 27–30.
47. *Ibid.*, 245.
49. *Z*, VIII, 245, 17.

Zwingli was able to maintain his position as People's Priest and gain the public support of the Council during 1520. Until 1520 it is difficult to isolate his ideas from the general programme of renewal outlined by Erasmus. Most scholars agree that Zwingli reached a full awareness of his reforming mission in 1520, and that the threatened ban on Luther, which was proclaimed in Switzerland during July, caused him to clarify his beliefs. Some time in 1520 he gave up his papal pension and began to move away from his earlier Erasmianism to a more theocentric conception of the Christian faith.[50] The attack upon Luther, and upon Zwingli's association with his doctrines, led the Zurich magistracy to take a firm stand on the question of church reform in the late fall of 1520. Its decision in favour of Zwingli established the Gospel at Zurich. As the second portion of Hofmann's *Klagschrift* reveals, all parties concerned accepted the ruler's right to make such a decision.

The development of Zwingli's intellectual independence was paralleled by a series of changes in the religious services of the Zurich church. The successful introduction of these practical reforms no doubt stimulated Zwingli to elaborate his own conception of the Christian life more freely. The changes reflected the impact of his preaching, but they were executed under the Council's supervision. The Chapter of the Grossmünster stopped singing the "Hail Mary" in March, and the Council assigned the endowments which paid for it to the city hospital. A little later the breviary was simplified with the approval of the Council.[51] The need to obtain the approval of the magistracy for such action was accepted as a matter of course.

Additional measures for the care of the poor were passed by the

---

50. Zwingli says he gave up his pension one year after he began to preach at Zurich, but he gives no exact date (Z, I, 396, 7). Erasmus believed that the corruption of the church was the result of an educational failure. He proposed the scriptures as an "absolute educational norm" which, when properly studied, would lead men to the correct understanding of Christ's law and thus achieve a renewal of Christianity. Erasmus' programme for the rebirth of Christianity was characterized by a "rational evolutionary . . . man centered quality." Though the scriptures remained central in the thought of both men, Zwingli, through the study of Paul and Augustine, as well as his own religious experience, came to understand the function of the scripture differently. To him, God's power and will spoke to men through the scriptures and compelled the believers to fulfil the law of Christ. The main difference between Zwingli and Erasmus was that Zwingli's view of the relationship between God, man, the Bible, and the rebirth of Christianity was God-centred rather than man-centred. This assumption was basic for the development of Zwingli's doctrines of sin, law, and justification, and conditioned the application of the Gospel to the problems of society and government. He believed that the proclamation of the Gospel would inevitably change the social order, because God's Word compelled men to act (Rich, 154–70 *passim*).

51. Köhler, 81–2; Staehelin, I, 183.

Council. They were instituted to benefit the *Hausarmen*, the poor who lived at home and were too proud to beg. Two *Pfleger* (overseers) were appointed to collect funds from contributors who were expected to give voluntarily.[52] In issuing the new ordinance, the magistrates included a long list of those to be excluded from public support. The list shows how far-reaching the control of the secular government was over the affairs of the city. Public beggars, pimps, drunkards, spendthrifts, and adulterers were cut off. Along with them, individuals guilty of failing to receive minimal religious instruction, to attend church, to confess once a year or to receive the sacrament at Easter, together with those under the ban and habitual blasphemers, were denied help.[53] No better example of the intertwining of secular and religious concerns can be found. A clear distinction between the various classes of offender is not made; all are excluded from government aid. Though such far-reaching supervision was an established tradition at Zurich, it is noteworthy Zwingli had no objection to punishing religious and moral offenders by depriving them of public support.

For the same reason Zwingli approved the execution of Uli Kennelbach, a farmer and a native of the Ducy of Togenburg, for mutilating a picture of Christ with a knife while in a tavern. When Kennelbach had ruined the picture, he said, echoing Zwingli's preaching, "the images are of no use there and cannot help us."[54] Yet Zwingli had no sympathy with him, for Kennelbach had acted on his own and by so doing had threatened public order.[55] Zwingli wanted a purification of religious practice on the basis of scripture, but he sought to implement it through the established government, not by the rash actions of individuals.

Throughout 1520 Zwingli continued his studies. He turned his attention, with the help of a new convert, Heinrich Engelhard, a canon of the Chapter of the Grossmünster and a doctor of Roman law, to the decisions of the councils and the canon law. The aim of the study was consistent with his biblical view of the faith; he sought to discover how great the discrepancy between the Bible and the canon law was.

No doubt the knowledge of canon law and its relation to scripture helped him in a clash with some of the canons. The issue raised appears to have concerned tithes. One of the canons delivered a lecture which maintained that tithes were founded upon divine law, and Zwingli demonstrated that they were not.[56] In view of the importance of this issue in his struggle with the radicals one point should be stressed.

52. Köhler, 82; *E.A.*, 132.
54. *Ibid.*, 126.
56. *Ibid.*, I, 154, 183.

53. *E.A.*, 132.
55. Staehelin, I, 130, 184.

Zwingli denied that the payment of tithes was sanctioned by divine law but he did not deny their necessity. The practical requirements of church life called for some way to support the clergy, reformed or Catholic, and Zwingli was well aware of these needs. This was a question which concerned the maintenance of religion for the sake of society, and it was consistent to deny the claims of conservative churchmen concerning the tenths and still, in principle, to support the system.

The clash with the canons raises another matter. Opposition from the adherents of the old church seem very slight during 1520. The ill-recorded debate with the canons stands out among the various unchallenged alterations effected by the Council at this time. Zwingli had so much support from the Council that he was free to go along almost unhindered.[57]

However, as the letters which passed between Zwingli and his friends reveal, hostility to him and to those who preached the Gospel elsewhere in Switzerland began to appear. In comparison with the difficulties faced by Luther in a comparable period, the opposition was not widespread but it was present. The forces at work were destined to affect not only Zwingli but also the government of the city. If this was a crucial year for Zwingli, it was a more decisive period for the members of the Council who supported him.

The universities of Cologne and Louvain declared several of Luther's opinions heretical in March, 1520. At about the same time a number of humanists who sympathized with Zwingli and were known to hold advanced views on the question of church reform felt the weight of popular disapproval. Capito was driven from Basel. Rhenanus was silenced by the authorities there, while Thomas Wyttenbach had to give up his post as People's Priest in Bern.[58] The papal bull which threatened Luther with the ban caused the line to be drawn between those loyal to the old church and those, who for the sake of conscience, took their stand upon scripture. It occasioned the correspondence cited earlier between Zwingli and Myconius, the latter of whom had been warned to keep quiet.

In one of his letters to Myconius, he lamented "the stubborn ignorance of certain men" which threatened the hope for Christian renewal and reminded him of the goal they both pursued—to achieve a "rebirth of Christ and the Gospel." He discussed the present situation in terms of the parable of the wheat and tares. The seeds have been planted, but the task has been complicated by the enemy who have sown tares among the wheat. The harvest must be brought to maturity and fruit; this

---

57. O. Farner, 192; Köhler, 83.   58. Staehelin, I, 170, 172.

requires care and a policy which will give the rebirth time to mature.[59] To gain a respite, he, Myconius, and others will have to suffer like the children of Israel at the hands of their foes. Persecution, Zwingli continued, is the "fire" promised by Christ, through which the work of the faithful is tested.[60] The difference between those struggling for God's glory and those fighting for earthly glory is all the difference between building on a rock which is never consumed and going up in smoke like straw: "Thus all who shall have built upon it, all who fight for His glory, and not their own, shall remain unharmed for all time.[61]

Zwingli then transferred the discussion of persecution from the individual to the church. The only way the church, which was born in blood, can be renewed is by blood. He then examined the role of the reformers in the church: as they see the filth filling it they are to arm many Herculeses to clean the stable. The only reward for their labour is the reward of those who serve Christ rather than men. Though they may be persecuted, Christ himself has promised retribution for their sufferings. It is possible to endure all for Christ's sake.[62]

Towards the end of the letter Zwingli spoke of Luther. Though Luther had been threatened with excommunication, Zwingli did not fear for his soul because he believed that when excommunication was unfairly inflicted it was more harmful to the body than to the soul.[63] He added that he had no fear for himself either; it did not matter if one perished for Christ's sake, regardless of the infamy attached to his name by men. He expected evil from clergy and laity alike. He was willing to testify for Christ and asked only: "that He may give me to bear all things with a brave heart, to break or confirm me, His vessel, as it pleases him."[64]

The letter demonstrates Zwingli did not believe his work would continue without opposition. He awaited a future harvest and realized that to reap the harvest, it was necessary to undergo a period of suffering. His appraisal of the situation is the key to his tactics during 1520. In keeping with Erasmus' admonition to the Christian prince, that he exercise patience when attempting a reform, Zwingli did not demand an immediate harvest. His concept of "rebirth" was expressed in terms of a gradual transformation within existing institutions and not in terms of a clean break with them. Zwingli, and those who followed him, were to arm Herculeses who would cleanse the church, not depart from it. His use of the wheat and tares image indicates that he considered the church to be a mixed body and that he expected conflict and persecution to

59. Z, VII, 341, 9–10, 13, 15–16.   60. Ibid., 342, 4–8, 30–1, 34–5.
61. Ibid., 343, 4–6.   62. Ibid., 343, 19–22, 28–9, 31.
63. Ibid., 343, 34–5; 344, 1.   64. Ibid., 344, 10–11, 14–17.

result from its transformation.[65] This is borne out by his assertion that
the church can only be reborn in blood. There is no way of interpreting
his words as expressing the ideal of a church made up of a suffering
remnant. Both those zealous for rebirth and those not in favour of it
are in the church. The reformers therefore face oppression because of
their labours within the structure not beyond it.

This is not the last letter of encouragement which Zwingli was to
write, nor were the dangers to be confronted less as the year went on.
By October, 1520, Luther had been officially condemned and the Papal
Legate, Pucci, appeared before a meeting of the Federal Diet at Baden
to demand that the Confederacy suppress the reading, publication, and
sale of his books.[66] According to Myconius, Pucci also demanded that
Luther's books be burnt. There was already a precedent for the request;
the emperor had begun to burn his books within his hereditary lands.[67]
No wonder Zwingli and Myconius, already identified with Luther's teaching by many, sensed danger. The demand that the printing and marketing
of Luther's books be stopped was a direct blow at Zurich where they
were being distributed from house to house.[68]

The Legate's demands and the Diet's compliance with them presented
fresh problems for Zwingli's friends. Myconius sought Zwingli's advice:
"First we wish to know your opinion concerning this matter . . . then
what your Zurichers may decide,"[69] and he was anxious for an answer:

It is voiced through the whole city, Luther and the school master [Myconius]
must be burned; although I never say anything concerning him [Luther] if
not among my [friends] and that most infrequently and I do not adduce a
single opinion from him, albeit I know why they always join me with
Luther: I say in school the things which are evangelical; . . . I speak also
whenever the thing demands it beyond this [I say] nothing. But because
these things agree with those [of Luther] . . . they think just what is actually
taken from the Gospel is copied from Luther.[70]

---

65. The parable of the wheat and tares has been applied to justify both the
persecution of dissidents within the church and their toleration (R. H. Bainton,
"Religious Liberty and the Parable of the Tares," *Early and Medieval Christianity*,
Series I of *The Collected Papers in Church History*, 95). Later in his career
Zwingli used the parable to advocate a moderate policy towards the *Täufer* in the
hope moderation might win them to his cause and avoid schism (Bainton, 107).
As it appears in this passage, the parable serves to encourage Myconius to be
tolerant of his opponents and to accept the difficulties which they have put in the
path of reform. In both cases the parable's use illustrates Zwingli's interest in
maintaining unity within the church.

66. *Z*, VII, 365–6.

67. *Z*, VII, 366, 1–2.   68. O. Farner, III, 212.

69. *Z*, VII, 366, 2–4.   70. *Ibid.*, 366, 10–17.

Myconius' problem was that of the Christian humanist who had arrived at a fresh understanding of the Gospel. Criticisms of the church resulting from the study of scripture were arrived at independently, but they sounded like Luther's ideas. Due to the official condemnation directed against Luther's views, the supporters of the old order were eager to claim that all their critics were followers of Luther and, on good legal grounds, to demand action against them. The tact and restraint which Myconius said he used were not enough to protect him.

Zwingli and Myconius faced the same dilemma and so did the Zurich magistracy. Zwingli was everywhere associated with Luther, but nevertheless, till now, the councillors had supported him. Now Luther was officially condemned and the Diet demanded the suppression of his books. The Council could not admit that Zwingli was a Lutheran and leave him free to continue his work with their blessing. If it did this Zurich faced the open hostility of the Confederacy, as well as of France and the newly chosen emperor. The safest thing to do was to expel Zwingli from the city.

However, Zwingli had been too successful in gaining a following, especially among the guilds, to be easily removed. The magistracy, with Zwingli's help, found an answer which protected him and allowed it to comply with the letter of the Diet's demand. It was based upon several considerations. Zwingli was not a Lutheran. He had arrived at his opinions via Erasmus and the Bible. Although Luther's ideas may have encouraged him, he could honestly deny being dependent upon them. For the moment the papacy wanted friendly relations with Zurich and tried to ignore Zwingli's activities; therefore the pope would be reluctant to sanction an attack upon Zurich in the name of the church. Finally, the loose construction of the Confederacy left the cantons considerable freedom of action. The magistrates exercised this freedom.

The solution took form in a mandate issued in the late fall of 1520.[71]

71. The mandate is not dated and does not appear in official records. The Council referred to it in 1524, when Zurich had been accused by the Diet of being a centre of the Lutheran heresy. It cited the mandate as part of their official refutation of the Diet's charge. Bullinger is the major sixteenth-century authority who places it in the fall of 1520. He claims it was the direct result of Zwingli's success as a preacher (Bullinger, I, 30-1). The absence of the mandate from the records of 1520 and the confused situation at Zurich during 1520 have led some to deny it was issued (Köhler, 82). Köhler claims similar mandates were issued in Germany after the Nürnberg Reichstag of 1523. They were framed in conjunction with the policy of the Reichstag which, to avoid either applying the Edict of Worms against the Lutherans or to allow them free preaching, called for the Gospel to be preached and supported by reference to reliable fathers of the church

The Council ordered the clergy of the canton to preach from the Bible and to keep silent concerning "innovations and man-made regulations."[72] The mandate was published to satisfy the Confederacy. The command to avoid mention of "innovations and man-made regulations" was not enforced in the canton, for attacks upon the abuses practised in the church continued to be voiced from the pulpit. The words "innovations and man-made regulations" were probably included in the mandate as a warning to the clergy not to mention Luther, and as an attempt to protect Zwingli and the city from identification with Lutheran heresy.[73] The mandate was a clever move; what it ordered conformed to the dictates of canon law, against which the Confederacy could not object.[74] Thus, for the moment, Zwingli was free to continue his work.

The distinction between Lutheranism and the preaching of the Gospel was not mere sophistry, as Myconius' letter shows. Both he and Zwingli derived their opinions from the Gospel. Zwingli made this clear when he wrote to the Reichstag in November of 1522: "I am not the defender of the cause of Luther here but of the Gospel."[75] A spirit of inquiry and respect for original sources was bound to produce independent thinkers. The significance of the Council's action cannot be stressed too much because it shows that the rulers' decision was made in keeping with their obligation to serve the common good. This included providing proper spiritual direction for the people as well as protecting Zurich from the interference of the other Confederates. No one questioned the Council's right to issue it.

(Köhler, 81–2). Köhler does not feel that the situation in 1520 could have led to the mandate (Köhler, 82).

In accepting 1520 as an accurate date, the suggestions made in Zwingli's *Sämtliche Werke* have been followed. Finsler, the editor of volume VII, believes that the mandate was the answer to Myconius' letter. The mandate sought to avoid the question of Lutheranism and to prevent any theological discussion. The best way to do this was to order the clergy to preach from scripture. Basel used the same tactics in 1523 (Z, VII, 367).

Oskar Farner accepts the same general solution and interprets the Council's order as the answer to the challenge posed by Pucci's activity and the Diet's decision (O. Farner, III, 215–17).

72. Bullinger, I, 32.

73. O. Farner, III, 217. As has been said, this was the tactic followed again in 1524 to refute charges of heresy made by the pope and the Federal Diet. The phraseology used at that time shows the pains the Council took to disassociate Zwingli from Luther. The Council claimed it had ordered the Word to be proclaimed: "before it had heard or known of Luther's teaching." The reference made in 1524 refers back to the mandate of 1520 and substantiates Bullinger's account (Z, VII, 366–7, 15–16).

74. O. Farner, III, 215.

75. Z, VII, 366, 38–9.

The mandate was a great victory for Zwingli. If it had not been issued Zwingli might have tended towards radicalism. It made the eventual break with his more extreme followers a foregone conclusion. The acceptance of the Bible as the sole authority governing the religious life of the community was essential for his reform programme. Once the Council recognized the place of the scripture there was no reason for him to deviate from his alliance with that body, because the ultimate victory of reform at Zurich was assured. Just as the government had acquiesced to the hierarchy's pronouncements on matters of doctrine and practice in the past, so in the future the magistracy accepted the interpretation of the Bible given by those competent to judge. Co-operation between the Zwingli and the political authority at Zurich made it possible to increase civil control over the external affairs of the church without the danger of outside interference. This filled the demands of the city government more perfectly than did the old ecclesiastical order. From 1520 on, the nature of Zwingli's task was altered; he had only to show the councillors what changes the Bible required. Then, in keeping with the pattern of government supervision over the affairs of the church, the Council could work out, with Zwingli's help, the timing and the method of change. Zwingli, as well as the secular magistrates, understood the need for caution. The Council often did demand time when Zwingli may have wished to press on, but he never had to worry about the outcome. The magistracy was Christian and accepted the Bible as the guide for religious life of the community. The reform could not fail unless a situation occurred in which those impatient for its completion attempted to force the Council's hand. This alone could ruin his plans.

So by the end of 1520 Zwingli had given up his papal pension, deepened his commitment to Christ's service, and secured the firm support of the magistracy for a Christian renewal in conformity with the norms of scripture. Despite all this, the final break with the old church had not yet taken place. In January, 1521, Zwingli's opinion regarding a suitable new priest was still requested by the magistrates of Baden, a city destined to become a stronghold of reaction.[76] Zwingli continued his attacks on the faults of the clergy and, some time after Easter, 1521, Hofmann took up his pen again to warn the Cathedral Chapter that it should silence him.[77] Though Hofmann objected to Zwingli, it proved impossible to prevent him from being elected a canon of the Chapter on April 29, 1521. The election made Zwingli a citizen of Zurich.[78]

76. *Ibid.*, 425, 12–14, 426, 1. 77. *E.A.*, 213.
78. Egli, 53.

4 The Rejection of the French Alliance and the Prohibition of Mercenary Service

THE COUNCIL'S NEXT STEP FORWARD, THE REJECTION OF THE French alliance, which the rest of the Confederacy had joined in 1521, and the prohibition of mercenary service, followed from the Mandate of 1520, and was the result of Zwingli's preaching. Zurich refused to join the alliance and forbade its citizens to serve for pay in foreign armies a few days before Charles V signed the edict against Luther at Worms.[1] The exact date is not given in Egli's *Actensammlung*. The reports from the country districts indicating the feelings of the people there, which were requested by the Zurich magistracy, were gathered between the sixteenth and twenty-second of May, 1521. Soon after the response of the local assemblies, which supported the Council's policy, had been received, the magistracy made its decision. It brought down the wrath of the Confederacy upon Zurich and prepared the way for the canton's final break with the Holy See. The hostile reaction to Zurich's decision reveals the risks involved in the Council's espousal of Zwingli's cause.

Typical of the threats which reached the ears of the Zurich magistrates is one brought to their attention some months after the final decision was made. The report ran: "The French would honour those within the territory of my lords with their cannon. . . . The French and the Confederates will make one region out of the Zürich See and give it as much money as to any other region."[2] Zwingli reported a conversation, said to have taken place in Zurich, which intimated that many people in the countryside favoured the French treaty. The participants in the discussion agreed that if the country districts of the canton were divided into four independent parts, it was likely that, once freed from the city, the four would enter the French alliance.[3] Both remarks imply that the country people did not agree with the city's policy and speculated upon what would happen if Canton Zurich were dismembered. The Council

1. *E. A.*, 167, 169, 170.
2. *Ibid.*, 187.
3. *Z*, I, 73, 1–6.

was bound to take such reports seriously but it felt strong enough to continue its new policy.

The abolition of mercenary service illuminates the patriotic element in Zwingli's reform programme. Believing that the Gospel provided the basis for political unity in the Confederacy, Zwingli hoped the example of Christian renewal at Zurich would win the rest of the cantons for the Word. A Switzerland united by the Gospel was to be the base for a missionary campaign to convert the rest of Europe.[4] Zwingli knew the Confederacy was becoming aware of the dangers of the mercenary system. He believed that in so far as the Confederacy looked upon the abolition of mercenary service and foreign pensions as a result of the Gospel's influence, they would be more willing to consider favourably the cause of reform.

It has been noted in the previous chapter that there were good political reasons for ending the practice of sending soldiers abroad for pay. The Swiss usually served the French and, as Zwingli and others saw, there was a real danger that Switzerland would succumb to French domination. Periodic dissatisfaction with mercenary service had been expressed long before Zwingli began preaching. Later, after the disasterous battle of Bicocca in May of 1522, even the original cantons considered abolishing the system.[5] The Council certainly recognized the wisdom of Zwingli's opposition to mercenary service.

The moral reasons for Zwingli's objections to the mercenary system were as cogent as the political. The steady influx of foreign gold had brought corruption in its wake. Magistrates in the cantons were willing to sell their influence in return for foreign pensions. Large bodies of men accustomed to the soldier's life did not adjust easily to civilian life. With the returned veterans came rowdyism and brutality which, even in those rough times, was alarming to the guardians of public order.

Regardless of the soundness of Zurich's policy it posed a problem for the rest of Switzerland. Swiss power in Europe depended upon the ability of the Confederacy to provide soldiers for the Italian wars. To profit from its surplus of soldiers the Confederacy had to agree upon a policy of mercenary service. The localism of the regions within the Confederacy and the lack of strong central authority made general agreement difficult enough, and Zurich's decision threatened to make even minimal co-operation between the cantons impossible.

Few realized in 1521 the extent to which Swiss fighting methods had been copied and improved by other powers (the disasters of Bicocca

4. Rother, 42.
5. Z, I, 156.

and Pavia were in the future). It would have seemed fantastic to say that the day of Swiss military ascendancy was over. Consequently, Zwingli's success at Zurich menaced Swiss power and prosperity. If the practice of selling soldiers were ended, the cantons, especially the original cantons, would be faced with a surplus of manpower. Without the money earned from the sale of fighting men to pay for grain, the supply necessary for survival would be cut off by France. When Zurich refused to enter the French alliance the Confederacy had reason to be angry. The effect of the Gospel did not please them.

The grounds for hostility were not merely political. The goal of Zwingli's preaching was not to end mercenary service; he demanded changes in the dogma and cult of the church. Even though the cantons had taken an independent attitude towards the local bishops and the pope, the ties of the Confederacy with Rome were close. The pope's guard was Swiss and was commanded by a Zuricher. Zwingli's programme attacked religious traditions closely identified with the beginnings of Swiss independence. This helped to complicate the already complex issue of mercenary service and added to it the fear, hostility, and violence which a religious question can arouse in an age of faith.

Opposition to Christian renewal at Zurich spread. Zwingli's foes in the other cantons kept close contact with disaffected groups in the city. These groups supplied the damaging rumours and false information which kept the Confederacy in a constant state of uproar over events in Zurich. The domestic forces opposed to Zwingli were led by the canons and chaplains of the Grossmünster, and several of them, including Canon Johannes Widmer, already mentioned in connection with the complaint of 1522, and the chaplain Johann Heinrich Göldli, had objected to Zwingli's appointment as the People's Priest. The fight against him was carried on in two ways. Some loyal to the old faith met Zwingli in public debate, while others plotted against him privately.[6]

The canons were closely linked to the *Constafel* families, who depended upon the revenues from mercenary service to compensate for the inadequate rents which their lands in the countryside yielded them.[7] At least some of the canons connected with the *Constafel* had the same interest in war and the pension system as their secular fellows. Evidence of this community of interest is revealed by the accusations, carefully investigated by the magistracy, that Johannes Heinrich Göldli was a pensioner of the French.[8] Both the canons and the *Constafel* were

6. Pestalozzi, 61–2, 199–200.
7. Birnbaum, *ASR*, IV, 18.
8. Pestalozzi, 64–5, 124.

supported by a small but influential element from the artisan strata of society, who had become mercenary leaders and profited from the system. The end of mercenary service stopped comfortable incomes and thwarted the hope of military careers for all of them. Since the old ruling class could not live from its land rents alone, the loss due to the prohibition of mercenary service represented a severe blow to their economic and social position in the city.

When the problems raised by the Council's action are considered, it is remarkable that the magistrates felt able to take such a step. If Birnbaum's contention that the new men who had joined the ruling class in the generation prior to the Zwinglian Reformation used the reform movement to replace the old elite is correct, then the reasons for the Council's action are easier to understand. The majority of the magistrates who favoured the abolition of mercenary service were not dependent upon pensions to maintain their status in society: most of them were still actively engaged in business. At this time the bulk of the artisan class supported Zwingli and were not alienated from, or indifferent to, Zwingli's programme, because it served the ambitions of those who wished to become the new ruling elite.[9] Even before the Reformation the majority of the artisans were concerned with local problems and did not share the interest of their betters in the wars of the period. They gained nothing from the system of recruiting soldiers and resented the profits which the aristocracy made from foreign pensions.[10] Zwingli's anti-mercenary stand appealed to them and the Council could be sure of their support. Although those who opposed Zwingli and his allies in the Council could be dangerous, at no time were they able to create a ground-swell of popular support for their interests in a return to the pension system and the old faith. They were a minority group often with common roots and common economic interests. Their subsequent inability to halt the attack upon the pro-mercenary party in their city during 1526 and to prevent the removal of members of the Council loyal to the old faith in 1528, which was the prelude to the reduction of the *Constafel* to the status of a guild in the next year, may indicate that the challenge of the Reformation simply revealed their political impotence.[11]

9. Birnbaum, *ASR*, IV, 18, 19–21, 28.
10. *Ibid.*, *ASR*, IV, 20.
11. Birnbaum asserts that the oligarchy tried to balance French and Hapsburg influence in the city by allying with the papacy (*ASR* IV, 20). He notes that the popular sentiment of the city was pro-Confederate and explains that Zwingli was brought to Zurich by the "notables" because he was an opponent of both the mercenary system and of the French. His claim that the pro-French party was

The Council had other reasons for confidence that its policy was well supported. Before the magistrates issued their mandate on mercenary service the question was presented for discussion and vote to the village assemblies, *Gemeinde,* in the outlying districts and to the guilds of the city.[12] Although the responses of the local assemblies were sometimes motivated by the desire to please the magistrates, the knowledge that its policies had been discussed and approved gave the Council reasonable security against unrest at home. Assured of domestic support, the Zurich government was able to pursue a policy deeply resented by the Confederacy.

---

finally "defeated" in 1521, as well as his statement that Zwingli appealed to the "common folk" and "crystallized a variety of social and religious discontents and demands," weakens his argument (*ASR*, 20–1). The pro-French party must have already lost ground before Zwingli could have been called to the city. Though it is possible that the governing classes may have assumed that Zwingli still retained his sympathy for a papal alliance, it is difficult to understand why, when they sought to pursue a policy of alliance with the papacy, the "notables" desired an outright opponent of mercenary service who was bound to appeal to an artisan class which was already discontent with the mercenary system. Gerig's suggestion that the Small Council was divided into two parties, an anti-French, pro-nationalist group, which included Mayor Röist among its number, and a pro-French faction, helps to substantiate Birnbaum's argument but does not clarify how Zwingli was chosen while the pro-French party still had influence (Gerig, 13). Zwingli's call to Zurich must have been a defeat for them and may indicate that the power struggle between the old elite which was generally pro-French and the new men had already begun. This would weaken Birnbaum's assertion that the Reformation ended a period of "relative political stability" in the city (*ASR*, IV, 17). If the Reformation did not cause a new period of political instability but became a factor in an already existing power struggle, then Birnbaum's assessment of its importance in enabling the new men to gain control of the government should be reconsidered.

12. The practice of addressing such enquiries to the local assemblies was well established by 1521. From about 1492 the Zurich government had issued statements to the local assemblies informing them of the government's plans (Dändliker, "Die Berichterstattungen und Anfragen der Züricher Regierung und die Landschaft in der Zeit vor der Reformation," *JSG*, XXI, 38–42). The first real *Volksanfrage* (people's enquiry) took place in 1503. At this time the Council requested the advice of the people concerning its policies on pensions, mercenary service, changes in the coinage and general security (Dändliker, *JSG*, XXI, 48; Gerig, 10). The rulers of the city wished to base their policy upon the firmest possible basis. Again in 1508, when the Confederacy was subject to strong pressures both from the Austrian and the French camps to provide troops, the Diet prepared to consider the whole question. Before sending ambassadors, Zurich's rulers instituted another *Anfrage* (Dändliker, *JSG*, XXI, 51–3). Dändliker is careful to add that the use of the enquiry was no indication of a belief in popular sovereignty. The magistrates were never bound to follow the wishes of the village assemblies. The rulers employed the *Anfrage* only for issues usually relating to foreign affairs to gain the maximum support for their policies and to secure obedience to them (Dändliker, *JSG*, XXI, 60–1).

The consultation of the village assemblies in matters of policy played a part in the Zwinglian reform. Zwingli often spoke of the right of the local *Gemeinde* to participate in the reorganization of its church. Many have said that he expressed a theory of congregational autonomy. This interpretation requires re-examination in the light of the relationship between the villages and the Zurich Council. The state's referral of the question of mercenary service to the villages offers a good beginning for such an examination.

The only local assemblies existing at the time were the *Gemeinde* to which the Zurich magistrates addressed their request for advice, *Anfrage*. In general, the membership of a local *Gemeinde* coincided with that of an individual parish, and it is reasonable to suppose Zwingli was speaking of the only parish gathering he knew, the *Gemeinde*, when he alluded to the congregation's role in the reform of the local church.[13] The *Gemeinde* met under the direction of representatives, either appointed or approved, if locally elected, by the central government at Zurich.[14] Those who presided over the meetings of the *Gemeinde* influenced debate so that the decisions reached there concurred with the policy laid down by the city. There was room for disagreement, but the function of the *Gemeinde* was to confirm and to facilitate the desires of the Zurich magistracy. They were not autonomous, and it is doubtful that when Zwingli discussed their functions with respect to the reform of the church he had any idea of congregational autonomy in religious matters. The deliberations of the *Gemeinde* gained wider acceptance for the decisions of the Council and guided the execution of reforms already introduced by the magistrates at Zurich.

Even though the replies of the *Gemeinde* may have been coloured to satisfy the wishes of the Zurich authorities, there is evidence that the average citizen was already dissatisfied with the system of mercenary service. After the battle of Marignano there was widespread dissatisfaction with mercenary service at Zurich, and popular agitation forced the government to arrest those suspected of pro-French feeling.[15] The Council's attempts to quash the investigation and its reluctance to prosecute

13. In making this assumption I am following the evidence presented by Schultze for the south German cities and Moeller, and von Muralt for the Swiss cities (cf. chap. I, n. 10). In both cases it has been proven that a separate assembly, called the church congregation, did not exist as a legal entity before the nineteenth century. If this was so for the cities, it seems logical that it was also true of the villages and local districts under the control of the cities. I can find no evidence to the contrary.

14. H. Steinemann's study confirms the fact that local officials were supervised by the Great Council at Zurich (Hans Steinemann, *Geschichte der Dorfverfassung im Kanton Zürich*, 122–24).

the suspects were due to the influence of the pro-mercenary party and its supporters in the Council of 50.

Though the anti-mercenary policy had popular support, the magistrates knew those hostile to it would not remain silent or inactive. The situation was not improved by the Edict of Worms, which demonstrated Charles V's intention to stamp out heresy. Events in Germany, as well as heightened tension within Switzerland, caused Zurich to abide by the treaty of 1515 and to send troops to the papacy in September of 1521.[16] This was a bitter pill for Zwingli to swallow but for at least a little longer he was protected by the magistracy from condemnation by the See of Peter. The more time Zwingli gained, the more secure his position in Zurich became.

The Council's reversal of policy in September, 1521, reveals both the strength of Zwingli's following and the efforts of his enemies to destroy him. The Roman curia was anxious to retain Zurich's support and sought a way to remove Zwingli. It was easy to find men who were willing to help discredit him. The letter to the papal legate in which Zwingli rejected his pension was given to them and made public at Zurich in August. It was used to prove Zwingli had been bribed to serve the papal cause, but fortunately for Zwingli the papal chaplain at Einsiedeln, Dr. Franz Zink, who had arranged for the pension, spoke out in his defence. In a letter to the magistracy he said Zwingli accepted the pension because he needed money, but he denied that he served papal interests: " . . . he never departed one finger's length from the Gospel on account of the pope, the emperor or any man, but he always supported the truth and educated the people with good faith." Zink also stated that Zwingli could have had double the pension, plus several prebends, if he had been willing to serve the papal cause.[17]

The effort to discredit Zwingli failed, but he was unable to prevent the dispatch of troops to Italy. It was probably too dangerous for the Zurichers to risk an open break with the pope so soon after their refusal to join the French alliance. Good relations with the pope made it simpler to deal with the domestic opposition and effectively prevented the rest of the Confederacy from attacking Zurich as a centre of heresy. The political reasons for over-riding Zwingli's objections were ample, and the Council's policy actually served Zwingli's interest by preventing, for the moment, an open break with the papacy.

15. Gerig, 12–13.
16. O. Farner III, 232.
17. Z, VII, 469, 15–19.

The new policy was only temporary. By January, 1522, the perfidy of the pope's policy caused Zurich to recall its troops and to issue a mandate which forbade all further service for pay abroad.[18] Rome's refusal to pay the troops heightened anti-papal feeling during the coming year and helped Zwingli gain support for his programme. The cause of the Gospel flourished under the protection of the magistracy, and Zwingli continued his attacks upon the corruption of the church without noticeable difficulty. The next crisis he faced was brought on by his own enthusiastic admirers.

18. O. Farner, 234.

5   The First Outbreaks of "Radicalism"

THOUGH ZWINGLI'S ENEMIES MULTIPLIED, AND THE RELATIONS between Zurich and the Confederacy became more strained, he was still able to expand his circle of admirers. One of the most important of those who were drawn to his teaching was Berchtold Haller. Haller took Thomas Wyttenbach's place at Bern and later guided the reform of the church in that city. Zwingli's letter to Haller on December 29, 1521, reveals his feelings a few months before the first confrontation with his more extreme followers.

Haller's theological opinions had not been well received at Bern, and he had appealed to Zwingli for advice. Zwingli, in reply, repeated the theme of suffering for Christ with which he had consoled Myconius. As far as practical policy was concerned, he advised Haller to be cautious:

I think the matter must be approached with the greatest mildness. For it is not fitting to act with yours as with ours, and, since the ears of yours are younger, they are not to be touched immediately with biting truth, as I believe Christ understood when he warned against scattering pearls before swine, who perhaps, having turned against you might tear you to pieces with great ferocity and hate forever the Gospel of Christ. Therefore these wild animals are to be handled more gently and, one must withdraw somewhat before their attack, until, conquered by our patience and intrepid constancy of heart, they are rendered tame.[1]

There was a good cause for Zwingli's advice. Bern, standing at the head of the western cantons, could, if won for the Gospel, provide a powerful ally for Zurich and a staging area for missionary efforts in the rest of the Confederacy, as well as in France. The prize was too precious to be lost by ill-timed zeal and, as Wyttenbach's experience had shown, the Bernese were still hostile to Christian renewal.

Zwingli's counsel summarized his policy. He might well have repeated the image of wheat and tares that he had used to encourage Myconius. The aim was the same: to reform the church from within and thereby to transform the life of the community, not to create a suffering remnant outside it. To achieve this Zwingli believed suffering and patience were necessary. He reminded Haller of the example of the apostles at Jeru-

---

1. *Z*, VII, 486, 29–39; 487, 1–4.

salem, who were beaten because they preached but did not cease from declaring their faith. Like Paul, Haller was to be all things to all people, and should above all avoid the suspicion of allegiance to the emperor or the French.[2]

Before the close of 1521 there was renewed friction with the Bishop of Constance over the refusal of the clergy in the canton to pay a special tax, the *subsidium*. A letter from the Bishop, dated November 21, 1521, demanded that the Council make the clergy pay, and the fact that he appealed to the magistrates demonstrates their control over the cantonal clergy.[3] But trouble with the Bishop was not the only problem which faced Zwingli. An undated hearing before the Council in January of 1522 mentioned a threat upon his life. When in his cups, Kärli Köchli, a dishwasher from the Dominican Cloister claimed he was at Zurich to kill the People's Priest.[4] Though Köchli was drunk and could not be taken at his word, the Council felt the matter important enough to investigate it. Perhaps the best indication of the situation in the city is the fact that at about this time Zwingli was given a guard for his protection.[5]

Threats made by men both drunk and sober were destined to be heard often in the next months as a result of the fast violations of March, 1522. Individuals and small groups publicly ate meat during Lent. This was a violation of both the established Christian practice and the city ordinances which forbade the consumption of meat during Lent. Those responsible were members of the reform party; their acts caused the first crisis within the ranks of those of Zwingli's disciples who were dissatisfied with the slow pace of the rebirth of Christ and the Gospel in the city.

The violations had many ramifications. They were a threat to public order and required the attention of the magistracy. As such, they affected Zwingli's alliance with the government and forced him to clarify his views on the ruler's place in the reform of the church. To the conservatives, breaches of established custom and public order were proof that Zwingli's doctrines threatened society. Zwingli's problem was to calm his followers and to retain the support of the magistracy in order to assure the progress of Christian renewal.

Two instances of misbehaviour are of particular importance. The best known concerned the violation of the Lenten regulations by a group of men, including Zwingli himself as a passive and surprised observer. It took place at the house of Christopher Froschauer, a printer. The second

2. *Ibid.*, 487, 7–8, 9, 13.   3. *E.A.*, 201.
4. *Ibid.*, 214.   5. Birnbaum, *ASR*, IV, 24.

involved a series of acts committed by a baker named Heini Aberli, who also took part in the meal at Froschauer's. On one occasion Aberli ate meat at the Augustinian cloister and, when criticized for doing so, attacked the clergy for not doing so and for not giving communion in both kinds. To make matters worse, Aberli, in the course of his condemnation, spoke favourably of the Hussite belief that the communion was valid only when taken by those who believed.[6] In view of Aberli's later activities as a Baptist, his comments on the communion deserve special notice, for it was the question of timing the abolition of the Mass which led to the open break between Zwingli and Grebel's followers.[7]

Both Aberli and many others present at Froschauer's home subsequently became Baptists. There has always been a question whether the radicalism of the fast violations was the work of an organized faction and whether this group became the nucleus for the Baptist Free Church organized under Conrad Grebel's leadership in 1524–25. H. S. Bender and John H. Yoder answer this question with a resounding "No!" J. F. Gerhard Göters, who re-examined the matter in his book on Ludwig Hätzer, said a connection definitely existed and that the first organized activity of the proto-Baptists took place in 1522.[8] If Göters is correct, the claim that the dissidents first gathered around Grebel in December, 1523, must be reconsidered. Göters' thesis also allows a re-interpretation of the circumstances which led Zwingli to deliver the sermon *On Divine and Human Righteousness*, and helps to clarify the reasons for the iconoclasm which occurred in the fall of 1523.

The best way to begin an analysis of the evidence is to refer to Bullinger, who, despite his prejudices, offers a number of valuable insights into the problem. Bullinger says that Anabaptism originated in the years 1521–22. At that time Thomas Müntzer conceived the idea of re-baptism and attracted Conrad Grebel, Felix Manz, and "other restless spirits" to his teaching.[9] But there is no evidence there was a connection between the Zürich Baptists and Müntzer, and the date Bullinger gives for the first contact between them has no foundation in fact. Müntzer was in Prague during 1521 and did not develop his views about baptism until later.[10]

6. *E.A.*, 233.   7. Staehelin, I, 203; *Q*, I, 159–63.

8. Göters, 31–2. Yoder says that it is impossible to be sure that a radical party did not exist at this time but he denies that Grebel had any connection with it (Yoder, 15). Krajewski takes the same position, while Bender is more emphatic in his denial both of the existence of a radical group and Grebel's connection with it (Krajewski, 39; Bender, 82–3).

9. Bullinger, I, 237.

10. Lohman, 6, 16, 30–2. Grebel's first letter to Müntzer was written on September 5, 1524, and it is not known if it ever reached him (*Q*, I, 13).

However, the date Bullinger gives, 1521–22, coincides with the violations of the fast ordinances during the early spring of 1522. Moreover, Oskar Farner's interpretation of the reasons for the Lenten violations lends credence to Bullinger's statement. He believes that the occurrences at Froschauer's house came as a surprise to Zwingli. Those responsible represented the radical wing of Zwingli's followers, and their actions, as his sermon reveals, caused him considerable anxiety. Zwingli was afraid that their premature radicalism would undermine the cause of Christian rebirth.[11] To prove his point Farner refers to a remark in Zwingli's sermon: "Thus eating meat is not forbidden at any time according to Divine Law. But where it wounds or angers the neighbour, one should not eat it without cause; one should before hand make those of little faith firm in faith."[12] But Farner's argument fails to explain Leo Jud's part in the violations.

Zwingli and Bullinger were close friends, and it is likely that Bullinger's chronology was derived from Zwingli. Zwingli's reason for identifying the Lenten violators of 1522 with the later Baptist movement can be found in the high correlation between those cited for their behaviour in Lent and the men later involved with Conrad Grebel and the re-baptizers of 1525. It is possible that Bullinger's reference to "restless spirits" concerned the very element to which Zwingli devoted his attention in the sermon *Concerning the Choice and Freedom of Foods*. If the violations of the fast were the result of an organized effort, it is possible that the zealots had come together and made their plans in the latter part of 1521 or early in 1522.

A significant number of the men present at Froschauer's home were subsequently identified with Conrad Grebel. Heini Aberli, Bartholomew Pur, and Hans Ockenfuss broke the fast and were mentioned by Grebel as his followers when he wrote to Thomas Müntzer in September, 1524.[13] Lorenz Keller reappeared in the report of hearings held in the district of Grüningen to investigate Baptist preaching.[14] Keller was charged with preaching against tithes, but the report sent to Zurich indicated that a number of clergymen had also been preaching about baptism and leading the people astray.[15] It would seem that the authorities in Grüningen identified the attack on tithes with the general programme of the Baptists. Hans Ockenfuss, Wolfgang Ininger, Lorenz Hochrütiner, and Hans, sometimes referred to as Claus, Hottinger attended Andreas Castelberger's "school" during 1523 and were involved

11. O. Farner, III, 244–5, 247.   12. *Z*, I, 112, 18–21.
13. *Q*, I, 19.   14. *E.A.*, 938; *Q*, I, 187.
15. *Q*, I, 187.

in the attacks upon the images in September, 1523.[16] Hochrütiner and
Hottinger were exiled for their part in them, and Hottinger's subsequent
radical activities led to his execution in the Duchy of Baden on March 9,
1524.[17] Hochrütiner later became a leading Baptist at St. Gall.[18] Among
the others present was Hans Uli. During 1525–26, the *Vogt* for the
district of Grüningen repeatedly mentioned the Baptist preaching of a
certain Uli.[19] Another "enthusiast" whose presence may have a certain
significance was Conrad Grebel's brother-in-law, Conrad Escher, a
member of the *Constafel*.[20]

Thus, among the men gathered at Froschauer's in 1522, four and
possibly a fifth, Uli, became known adherents of Grebel by 1524. One,
Keller, was suspected of Baptist preaching. Three were later connected
with Castelberger's school and the icoloclasm of 1523. One of these
three, Hottinger, was executed in 1524 for opinions which fitted the
Baptist pattern all too well. Still another, Escher, was related to Grebel.
On the other hand, Leo Jud, one of Zwingli's closest allies, was also
present and ate meat, but this was the only time he appeared among the
enthusiasts. None of the evidence is conclusive but it is enough to explain
the reason that Bullinger and Zwingli believed the Baptist movement
began in 1521–22.

Grebel was not involved in the fast violations, and it remains to be
seen if there was any reason for Zwingli and Bullinger to identify him
as the leader of the extremists in 1522. The records of the Zurich Council come to our aid. The first mention of the name Grebel in conjunction
with the enthusiasts appears in May of 1522, and Conrad Grebel himself
is cited and quoted in the Council's hearings of September, 1522, which
refer to Grebel's appearance before it on July 7, 1522.

Some time later in May, 1522, Heini Aberli, Claus Hottinger, and
his brother Jacob, a future Baptist also, planned a gathering in
Zwingli's honour at an inn called the Lindenhof. The plans for the meeting were made at Jacob Grebel's house.[21] But it seems unlikely that
Jacob Grebel, a respected member of the Council and the recipient of a
French pension, would help organize an assembly which the Council
considered dangerous enough to forbid.[22] The Council's investigation

---

16. *E.A.*, 415, 421, 623.
17. O. Farner, III, 245; *E.A.*, 415, 421; *Q*, I, 27.
18. O Farner III, 245–6.
19. *Q*, I, 170–1.
20. O. Farner, III, 244.
21. *E.A.*, 246.
22. Jacob Grebel was one of those executed during the purge of the pro-
mercenary party in 1526 for receiving foreign pensions. O. Farner asserts that contemporaries viewed this crime as evidence that the offender was a foe of the

of the men who arranged the gathering did not mention Jacob Grebel at all. It is more likely that his son, Conrad, who was still living at home, was the host at this planning session.[23] The gathering (Badenschenke), to which from three to five hundred people were invited, including guests from Zollikon and Höngg, was ostensibly being held to celebrate Zwingli's return from a cure at the baths of Baden.[24] Although the Council was suspicious of large public gatherings, ordinarily the matter would not have concerned them. However, as this was no ordinary assembly, the Council forbade it and ordered the organizers to explain their intentions.

The Council's hearing revealed that the meeting was planned to allow a discussion of the letters sent by the Bishop of Constance on May 24 to the Council and Cathedral Chapter. Many believed that the Bishop was trying to stop Zwingli's preaching at Zurich and to force the city to obey the church. The suspicion of the Bishop's intentions was justified, for his vicar, Faber, who had recently returned to Constance from Rome, had urged the Bishop to deal with the Zurichers more firmly.[25] Hottinger and Aberli, as Farner observes, planned the gathering as a demonstration of Zwingli's popular support, and they apparently hoped a fresh reminder of his popularity would strengthen the Council's determination to defend him.[26]

Oskar Farner believes that the two missives were dispatched to coincide with the meeting of the Federal Diet at Luzern. Pope Hadrian VI's letter to the Confederacy, sent on April 27, 1522, was to be discussed by the Diet. The letter reminded the cantons of their duty and called them to remain true to the church in this time of trouble.[27] Both the

---

Gospel, i.e., the Zwinglian reform (O. Farner, III, 124–5). Köhler notes that many believed that Grebel's execution was the price he had to pay for being Conrad Grebel's father. Though the charges brought against him were technically correct, his last proven offence had taken place in 1517 (Köhler, 155–6). There is little evidence to indicate that he was an outright opponent of Zwingli. Bender believes that Jacob Grebel may have been an early advocate of toleration (Bender, 250). But Jacob Grebel's social position and past participation in the mercenary system would certainly justify the assumption that he had the most in common with the conservative opposition to Zwingli.

23. Bender says the fact that the meeting was at Jacob's house may indicate that Conrad had a part in the affair (Bender, 250). Grebel was still living at home when he wrote to Vadian in September, 1523 (Q, I, 6).

24. E.A., 246; Egli, 65; O. Farner, III, 279. Egli first dated the affair in April but changed his mind when he wrote his History of the Swiss Reformation. The reason he moved the date to May was the connection between the gathering and the arrival of the Bishop of Constance's letters admonishing the Chapter and the Council to remain in the church (Egli, 65).

25. O. Farner, III, 277, 280.

26. Ibid., 279; E.A., 246.   27. O. Farner, III, 280; Egli, 66.

Pope's letter and the Bishop's words to Zurich indicate that a campaign against the spread of the reform was under way. It was a foregone conclusion that complaints about the effects of the reformed preaching would be heard, and that the Diet would advise the cantonal governments to suppress such preaching.[28] This was the first time the Confederacy as a whole recognized and discussed the impact of Zwingli's teachings.

This was no time to call undue attention to the progress of reform at Zurich.[29] A public meeting at which the Bishop's letters were criticized would be interpreted as a gesture of defiance by the Confederacy and would make it easier for Zwingli's enemies to claim that his teachings menaced public order and threatened the other cantons. If this could be done, then the Confederacy would have stronger grounds for intervening in Zurich's affairs. The Council was at pains to prevent this.

The hearing makes it obvious that some of Zwingli's disciples had taken matters into their own hands. Much as Zwingli was the innocent guest of those who planned to violate the fast, he is mentioned as the object of the celebration. There is no evidence that he supported the scheme or even knew of it. Some of the same men who ate meat during Lent planned the gathering at the Lindenhof, and this suggests the existence of a group with a conscious, though not necessarily fully articulated policy, whose chief characteristics was the desire to hasten the break with the old order. By May of 1522 members of this faction had met at Jacob Grebel's house and thus the possibility of a connection between them and Conrad Grebel appears.[30]

The official transactions of the Council refer to Conrad Grebel in September, but the events they record appear to have taken place in July, 1522, as an aftermath to the uproar over the fast question.[31] In the summer of 1522, the preaching orders, the Dominicans, Franciscans, and Augustinians, had become alarmed at the progress of Zwingli's teaching and had appealed to the government to restrain him. The Council agreed to consider the matter and turned its attention, not to Zwingli, but to a group of his followers who were most violent in their attacks upon the clergy and were causing great unrest among the people. The magistrates called Conrad Grebel, Heini Aberli, Bartholomew Pur, and Claus Hottinger before them on July 7.[32] Although Bullinger mentions the outcome, there is no complete record of the hearing. A fragment of it

28. O. Farner, III, 280.
29. Egli, 66.
30. *Supra* n. 23.
31. Most modern authorities assume that the hearing referred to in September took place on July 7, 5, 22 (Bender, 85; Egli, 68; O. Farner, III, 264).
32. O. Farner, III, 264; *E.A.*, 269.

is preserved in the minutes of a Council meeting which Egli says was held in September. Rumours of the verbal exchange which had taken place between Grebel and the guildmaster, M. Schliniger, during the July proceedings were still causing heated arguments, and the Council was anxious to stop the arguments.[33]

The cause of the trouble was Grebel's reply to Schliniger. After listening to Grebel and his friends, Schliniger remarked: "The devil sits in the Council chamber." To which Grebel retorted:

The Devil not only sits in the chambers, but he also sits among my Lords; for one sits among my Lords who has said, "the Gospel should be preached in a cow's ass." And in so far as my Lords do not allow the Gospel to progress further, they will be destroyed.[34]

Grebel's blunt remark did not alter the outcome. As a result of the hearing the magistrates decided by a slim majority to forbid further attacks upon the monks.[35]

The report shows that by July Conrad Grebel was openly associated with the same men previously involved in the fast controversy and the *Badenschenke*. He is not only numbered among them, but appeared before the Council as their spokesman. His position suggests an established relationship with the others. The report has further implications. It indicates that the men called before the Council had been working together. The monks had complained about Zwingli's preaching and yet the Council hailed Grebel and his friends before it. Apparently what Grebel and his associates were doing was sufficiently far from the norm expected by the Council, already committed to enforcing Gospel preaching, that the councillors found it necessary to silence them. The government's policy seems to have been to quiet Zwingli's most outspoken disciples and thus disassociate him from their activities.

It is worth noting that it was guildmaster Schliniger who spoke of the devil in connection with Grebel's activities. Zwingli's strongest support came from the guilds. Unless Schliniger was an exception, he probably shared the opinion of the majority of his guild, but he had no use for Grebel's programme. At this early date both Schliniger and the other

33. The context of the hearing which Egli dates in September makes it likely that he dated it too late. The concern the Council felt over the arguments caused by Grebel's comments to the magistrates would have been at their height soon after the July hearing.
34. *E.A.,* 269.
35. O. Farner, III, 264. Bender asserts that Grebel's part in the hearing reveals that he was one of Zwingli's most ardent supporters (Bender, 85). He leaves unanswered the question of whether or not Zwingli approved Grebel's tactics and whether Grebel's actions aided Zwingli's cause.

magistrates made a distinction between Zwingli and the men who followed Grebel. This fact gives further support to the argument that a radical faction appeared at Zurich early in 1522 which was directly connected with later Anabaptism.

Grebel's outburst also tells us a great deal about his own attitude. He believed the devil was represented among the city magistrates by those critical of the spread of the Gospel and he dared to threaten the Council. One wonders if Zwingli could have sanctioned these threats at a time when he was committed to an alliance with the civil authorities. Grebel's remark to the Council gives credence to the charge, made in 1525, that he had suggested it be replaced by a truly Christian magistracy. His hostile words show the drift of his thoughts, and this was a direction which made an eventual break with Zwingli inevitable. At the same time Grebel's words also reveal a great confidence in his own position. He appeared to feel free to insult and to threaten the Council. This behaviour was certainly based on a belief in the rightness of his cause and, possibly, reflects the confidence that his own education, ability, and social position gave him.

The evidence available supports Bullinger's assertion that Grebel was connected with the activities of the extremists at Zurich as early as 1522. There is nothing to substantiate Bullinger's claim that Manz was also a member of the group, but his remarks about the reasons the two embraced a radical programme provide an insight into the causes for Grebel's final repudiation of Zwingli's policy. Bullinger suggested that Grebel's and Manz's championing of the radical cause was motivated by non-theological considerations. He admitted that, as Grebel and Manz claimed, they were first taught by Zwingli but he maintained that they did not really want to learn from him. They followed Zwingli because they were ambitious. According to Bullinger, they proposed to set aside the canons of the Cathedral, drive them out of their prebends, and use their incomes to establish lectureships for teaching Hebrew and Greek. Manz wanted to be the Hebrew professor and Grebel wished to teach Greek. Bullinger attributed these ambitions to the social position which their families enjoyed in the city: "they believed also, that since they were citizens' children and of good families, they should be recommended (acceptable) to everyone." Zwingli promised to help them as much as he could, but, Bullinger added, what they wished was impractical: "One could not in this way pass by and cast out old, honourable people who have served well and were from old families and were most respected by the government. . . . "[36] If we assume that Bullinger was

36. Bullinger, I, 237.

repeating Zwingli's own opinion, then Zwingli's problem with them is clear. What the young men wanted was the immediate reorganization of the Cathedral Chapter. This was contrary to his policy and would arouse the ire of the old families, already threatened by the effects of the reform of the church. Such a move would also make an unfavourable impression on the rest of the Confederacy. Though he was sympathetic with their desire, Zwingli could not possibly have complied with it.

When Grebel's and Manz's ambitions were frustrated, Bullinger said they were "made wild by the Anabaptist spirit" and began to form a following to bring about the introduction of Anabaptism.[37] Among their supporters he listed H. Wilhelm Röubli, Brötli, Blaurock, and Hätzer, which indicates that he was referring to events that took place after Röubli's arrival at Zurich in 1522.[38] These activities caused "in a short time a wondrous, great confusion in Zurich." Bullinger's account tended to telescope events; he next described the Disputation of January 1525 and what he considered the Anabaptist's failure to maintain a consistent scriptural position. After this, despite the admonitions of the government, they caused trouble in Zollikon and began to set up their separate church.[39] Though his date for the beginnings of the separate church and his analysis of the motivations for such a move are of primary importance, the latter portion of Bullinger's narrative does not concern us here.

However prejudiced Bullinger's account may be, the stress he placed upon the impatience with which Grebel and Manz reacted to Zwingli's reluctance to comply with their wishes is worth consideration. It may

37. *Ibid.*, 237-8. Bender has raised serious objections to Bullinger's account. He notes that elsewhere in his history Bullinger says that Manz and Grebel would have been appointed when the Chapter was reorganized if they had not by then become Anabaptists. All that Zwingli achieved in 1522 was the appointment of Jacob Ceporin to a readership in Hebrew. Bender says that, at that time, Grebel and Manz were "warmest friends of Zwingli" and certainly would not have been offended by Ceporin's appointment. The reform of the Chapter was not begun by the Council until late 1523, the very time that Grebel began to break away from Zwingli, and the biblical lectureships were not established until June, 1525. Consequently, Bender concludes that frustrated ambitions played no part in the subsequent division between Zwingli, Grebel and Manz (Bender, 252).

Bender does agree that the two men were not willing to wait for a reform of the Chapter, and Krajewski also alludes to their unwillingness to wait (Bender, 251-2; Krajewski, 36). As Bender says, Bullinger was "probably fabricating a legend" when he attributed Grebel's and Manz's conversion to Anabaptism as the result of frustrated ambition (Bender, 252).

38. Bullinger, I, 238. Röubli had been expelled from Basel on account of his outspoken preaching, violations of the fast, and defamation of images (Göters, 31-2).

39. Bullinger, I, 238-9.

well reflect Zwingli's impression of their general attitude and reveal one
of the factors which he considered responsible for the split among his
followers. In fact, Grebel's career does reveal a pattern of impatient and
sometimes impetuous behaviour. While a student at Vienna he almost
lost a hand in a student brawl and later at Paris he was involved in a
fight which led to the death of two men.[40] Though Bender asserts that
Grebel had no part in starting the battle in Paris and felt no guilt about
his involvement in it, it would appear that Grebel had a rather fiery
temperament.

Despite the objections of his family, in February he married a girl
named Barbara, who must have been pregnant at the time, for their
first child was born in August, 1522.[41] When he had met her in the
previous year and his parents discouraged the match Grebel had sent
the girl off to Basel and joined her there for some months. Though they
had lived apart in Basel, Grebel's reaction to his family's advice certainly
reveals some signs of hastiness and impatience. The circumstances of
the marriage itself support this impression. Grebel's father was out of
town when the marriage took place, and Conrad's mother was very
angry about the union.[42]

Grebel had been associated with Zwingli's circle since the end of
1521, and Bender believes that he experienced a "rebirth" under
Zwingli's influence in the spring of 1522.[43] The next thing that happened
was his citation before the Council as the result of attacks upon the
city's monks. His remarks to the councillors do not indicate an excessive
moderation even when one allows for the sharp language customary at
that time. It does not seem totally wrong to see this affair as another
example of Grebel's tendency to impulsive, hasty action.

As far as Grebel is concerned, Bullinger's charge that he was impatient
can neither be dismissed out of hand nor ignored as a factor in the events
which led to the final break with Zwingli. It is quite possible that the
delay in the reorganization of the Chapter which was regarded with
impatience by Grebel and Manz did contribute to their ultimate rejection
of Zwingli's cautious method of achieving a reform of the church. Certainly in Grebel's case, slow, cautious reform does not seem to have
suited his temperament. An awareness of this personality factor should
not be allowed to obscure Grebel's genuine belief in, and devotion to,
the cause of Christian renewal but it deserves consideration in his break
with Zwingli and his methods. Taken as a whole, the scanty records that
we possess indicate that there were certain grounds for Bullinger's claim

40. Bender, 40–1.   41. Q, I, 5.
42. Bender, 60–2, 64.   43. Ibid., 80.

that Grebel was unwilling to learn from Zwingli and went ahead with his own schemes despite their impracticality.

Grebel's rash words to the Council in July of 1522 stand in sharp contrast to Zwingli's moderation, and his behaviour there explains Zwingli's frequent appeals that, for the sake of the Gospel, the extremists avoid giving offence. There may well have already been a gulf between Zwingli and Grebel which, because of their differing temperaments, was destined to widen. The question remains how much they ever really understood each other. If anything delayed the open break between them, it was probably the fact that Zwingli exercised the same caution with Grebel which he applied in his dealings with the supporters of the old faith. He no doubt did this because he respected his ability and hoped to conciliate him.

A radical element with a programme based upon the demand for a rapid realization of church reform began to pressure Zwingli in the spring of 1522. The appearance of this faction implies a prior organization which probably took place early in 1522. Though Grebel cannot be linked to the others before the summer of 1522, Bullinger was also right when he identified Grebel with them. Grebel's opinions, as well as his standing in the community, guaranteed him a place of leadership among the enthusiasts. From 1522 on, the activities of an organized radical party, which was the forerunner of the Baptist movement, were one of Zwingli's central problems. He was caught between the conservatives and the enthusiasts and the desires of both groups threatened his hope for a reform of the church at Zurich.

6   The Council's Policy, the Bishop's Commission and Zwingli's Sermon

THE VIOLATIONS OF THE FAST HAD CONSEQUENCES WHICH reached beyond Zurich. To prevent outside intervention Zwingli and the Council had to act quickly. Froschauer and others were imprisoned before the end of March, and some feared the Council would hand them over for trial to the Bishop's court.[1] Zwingli's problem was complex. He desired to protect his friends and to regain control over the movement which his disciples threatened to lead astray.[2] He preached the sermon *Concerning the Choice and Freedom of Foods* on March 23, 1522, as much to restrain his own followers as to defend them.[3] Nevertheless, his views caused consternation among the conservatives and they accused him of heresy.[4] The Zurichers loyal to the traditions of the church appealed to the Bishop of Constance, and Bishop Hugo, though reluctant to take action, was prevailed upon to send a commission to Zurich.[5] The Council reacted to the Bishop's decision and took measures to guarantee its authority over the church at Zurich. Froschauer was allowed to justify his behaviour. He defended eating meat by appealing to the Gospel: ". . . we must guide our life according to the rule of the Gospel, or we are not Christians," and he praised Zwingli. Froschauer stressed the fact that he did not intend to attack the laws of the community: "I have acted neither against you, nor against God with my meat eating. Indeed, I mean against your laws."[6] The main point of his argument was that he ate meat with a clear conscience, since the Gospel put no restrictions on such matters.

Then, to maintain a solid front in face of domestic opposition and the Bishop's commission, the magistrates referred the case to Felix Frei,

1. Staehelin, I, 204; *Z*, I, 75.
2. Egli, 59–60.
3. The sermon, when printed on April 16, was expanded to cover the events involved in the negotiations with the Bishop's Commission.
4. Staehelin, I, 205.
5. O. Farner, III, 252.
6. *E.A.*, 234.

the Provost of the Chapter, and to the three People's Priests.[7] The clergy suggested a compromise which fitted Zwingli's own previously stated policies and reflected the doubts and hesitation of the Provost.[8] They concluded that according to divine law no food is forbidden to Christians, but such freedom offends many, and Christ's wish is for peace. In so far as the faith was not damaged, they urged that the practice of eating meat in Lent be forbidden until a final decision on the matter would be reached. The response to the Council continued:

> that your honourable wisdom should act according to your consideration of the matter and in matters of the same type, as you may consider it good . . . for we are always desirous to remain in obedience until our rulers decide to set aside such things generally or to do something else.[9]

The terms of the clergy's reply confirm the findings of von Muralt, Schultze, and Moeller concerning the relationship between church and magistrate before and during the era of reform; they also foreshadow Zwingli's discussion of the secular and spiritual offices in the sermon *On Divine and Human Righteousness*. Like the sermon, the clergy's answer to the Council met the challenge posed by both the conservative reaction to reform and the demands for further changes made by Zwingli's zealous followers. To begin with, the clergy made a theological decision: eating meat in Lent is not opposed to divine law. However, in rendering it, the clerics did not claim the right to implement their opinion. They recognized an immediate alteration of past custom would offend many and, therefore, they cautioned restraint. They stated that the introduction of new customs was not their responsibility because matters affecting the public life of the city were the responsibility of the government. The reply presupposed that the secular arm respected the clergy's right to arrive at a theological decision and, when the time was right, that the Council would act upon the theologians' advice. Immediate changes were not expected. Each side respected the function of the other. The clergy assumed that the magistracy would implement necessary alterations as part of its larger commitment to the common good. Functioning togther, Council and clergy provided Zurich with a unified government.

Though Zwingli tried to prevent its dispatch, the Bishop's commission arrived on April 7, 1522. Zwingli's one consolation was the news that Dr. Johannes Wanner, preacher at the Constance Cathedral and member of the delegation, sympathized with his programme.[10] The Bishop of Constance and his advisers seemed to have believed that an open debate

7. O. Farner, III, 251.
9. *E.A.*, 235.
8. Staehelin, I, 205.
10. O. Farner, III, 253.

with Zwingli, who had wide support in the city, would strengthen his position. The commissioners were instructed by the Bishop of Constance not to mention Zwingli by name and to avoid any discussion with him. To achieve this, they attempted to negotiate with the Chapter, minus Zwingli, and with the Council of 50, where they knew they would find support.[11] In view of the predominance of the Great Council, the Council of 50 could not act alone, and so a joint meeting of the two Councils, which excluded Zwingli, was arranged for April 9.[12] However, the Great Council, which favoured Zwingli, demanded that he and the other People's Priests be given a chance to speak. Its request was granted. The very thing the Bishop's representatives had been instructed to avoid had occurred. Zwingli described what took place in a letter to Myconius: his opponents were cast down "as a high shore [does] a billowing waves of threats." In the same week, Zwingli told Myconius, Conrad Hofmann presented his *Complaint* to the Chapter. He added gleefully that the effect of the treatise over which Hofmann had laboured so long was nil.[13]

Hofmann's warnings have already been discussed, but one suggestion contained in the concluding section of his work is worthy of mention. Hofmann offered to debate with Zwingli before the Council. He suggested that, after the debate, the magistrates should refer the results to the Bishop and either limit preaching to the Bible or forbid attacks on "the old teachers" until the Bishop could consider the matter.[14] Hofmann's aim was to bring unity by forcing an open debate which he thought he could win. His demand for a debate was destined to bring his party disaster in January of 1523.

The role Hofmann assigned to the rulers of the city is noteworthy. They were to hear the debate and then to refer the matter to the curia of Constance. Hofmann never considered referring the issues directly to Bishop Hugo. Instead he asked for a debate before the Council which then would present the matter to the Bishop for comment. Hofmann's suggestion illustrates the extent of the Council's competence even in a religious controversy. It reveals that the Bishop's claim to authority in matters of doctrine was viewed by the traditionalists as ultimate, but that, in the eyes of all parties, the Council exercised supreme authority in the affairs of the city.

To be sure, Hofmann expected the government to leave a final decision to the Bishop, who was the proper authority for spiritual questions. The Council's action after Zwingli's debates with the commis-

11. *Ibid.*, 254.   12. *Ibid.*, 256–7.
13. *Z*, VII, 518, 6, 7–10.   14. *E.A.*, 213.

sioners shows that they respected properly constituted religious authority. However, the terms of the Council's statement to the Bishop after Zwingli's debate also show that, though spiritual authority was still respected, it was no longer viewed as being vested primarily in the hierarchy of the church. By this time the Council had begun to look to scripture as the final source of religious authority and to rely upon the advice of those competent and willing to interpret it. The stage was already set for the Council to call the First Disputation on its own initiative in January of 1523.

The magistrates incorporated the general solution to the problem of the fast suggested by Zwingli, Felix Frei, and the two other People's Priests. The councillors stated that eating meat in Lent did not violate God's law. They agreed to await the outcome of the Bishop's deliberations, as the commission had requested, and expressed a desire for a speedy solution to the question. In the interim they forbade eating meat during Lent.

The way in which the Council expressed its willingness to await the Bishop's reply demonstrates the impact of Zwingli's preaching:

[they] urge him with particular seriousness, that his grace may be concerned with it, without any delay, that he may wish to find help, be it with the Papal Holiness, with Cardinals, Bishops, Councils or with properly trained Christian people, so that finally a clarification and decision may be given, how and in what form one should act in such a case, and thereby that it may not be done against the precepts of Christ.[15]

At this stage in the development of the reform movement at Zurich, the Council was still willing to give heed to the Bishop and his followers. But the crux of their requirement was that the Bishop's response must not violate Christ's precepts, which Zwingli had taught them were to be found in scripture. In fact, if not yet in theory, the Council had broken with any conception which allowed the Holy See final authority in religious matters, or for that matter, the hierarchy alone. It is significant that once the magistrates had received the findings of the Provost of the Chapter and the three People's Priests, they themselves issued a religious pronouncement: God's law was not violated when meat was eaten during Lent. The corporate theory of city government had already permitted the magistracy's functions to take on a religious character.

The Council's pronouncement illustrates the exercise of this facet of its authority and is the logical outcome of the combination of the past precedents of city government with Zwingli's doctrine of biblical authority. Having accepted it, the Council was free from dependence

15. *E.A.*, 236.

upon the representatives of an outside spiritual authority and, from this time on, was able to control all aspects of public life, as the corporate nature of contemporary political theory demanded. For the moment, the magistrates were still willing to accept a compromise on the observance of the fast, but not upon what constituted God's law.[16] The Bishop never responded to the Council's request, and finally the Council called the First Disputation on its own authority. By so doing the members of the Council did not presume to decide by themselves what scripture said. They wished to act upon the findings of an assembly of Christian people, made up of theologians and laymen, which consulted the scripture, and, as Zwingli was to tell them repeatedly in the future, would be guided to the proper interpretation by the Holy Spirit. The result of the fast controversy was the First Disputation.

Rudolf Staehelin asserts that April of 1522 was the first time the government had acted to protect the Gospel.[17] This is not the case. The mandate of 1520 marked out the government's policy toward Zwingli. The occurrences of 1522 and the Council's behaviour were the result of its earlier acceptance of Zwingli's conception of religious authority. It always respected the authority of scripture and the conclusions derived from it by an assembly of Christian people which contained trained clergy as well as laymen. Though they remained the sole representatives of the Christian people of Zurich, the councillors recognized a division of labour in the society and a limitation of their own authority in spiritual matters. The magistrates sought the clergy's advice because as Christians they believed right religion was vital to the welfare of the body politic.

The political problems caused by the gradual reform of dogma and cult were manifested in the government's investigations of Zwingli's foes. On April 12 the Council considered the hostile activities of the conservatives at Zurich and elsewhere in the Confederacy. Certain persons threatened to remove Zwingli forceably from Zurich. Ulrich Schwab, a barber, repeatedly voiced such threats and, when questioned, excused himself on the grounds that he spoke while in his cups. He said that he had heard of a plot from a visitor newly arrived from St. Gall, to bring Zwingli to Constance. The Council also heard reports that Zurich would be destroyed if it continued to harbour Zwingli: "and

---

16. In arguing this point I am following Egli's interpretation (Egli, 61). A radical break with the past had already been made but the Council was not anxious to complete the formal break with outside spiritual authority, as long as this authority might still recognize that of Christ.

17. Staehelin, I, 205.

the entire city, Zurich, would be overrun and undergo great wrong and suffering if it kept him [Zwingli] any longer." Cornel Schulthess, a member of the *Constafel* and sometime diplomat in the service of the city, was alleged to have discussed the reasons for the Confederacy's anger at Zurich and to have expressed concern lest the Confederates might punish Zurich. He was accused of saying it would be better if Zwingli were elsewhere.[18] Later, another hearing recorded the warning given by Jakob Meyg of Bern who was apparently a mercenary soldier: "The Confederates would separate themselves from Zurich."[19] Still another investigation described how Claus Hottinger, by now a familiar name in the records, was awakened by a group of men pounding on his door, calling him and other followers of Zwingli heretics.[20] Zwingli certainly seemed to need the body-guard which had been assigned to him.

The Council wrote to the Bishop of Constance asking him what he knew about the plans to kidnap Zwingli. The Bishop admitted hearing the rumours, but denied he was involved. He expressed interest in the causes of the rumour and promised to pass on any information about the matter to the Zurich government.[21] The threats were directed against both Zwingli and the city. In the previous year, Zurich's decision to stay out of the French alliance had produced a similar reaction. Now menacing rumours were being heard in far greater volume, and there was every reason for the Council to proceed cautiously. In view of the situation, Zwingli's policy of slow reform met the diplomatic needs of the city. Even the compromise decision on the fast issue had stirred up trouble which was to come to a head all too soon. From this time on, considerations of foreign policy would increasingly circumscribe the activities of the Reformer and the government. Neither abandoned the course which had been taken, but both accepted the need to temporize.

The dangers that Zurich faced at this time because it supported Zwingli are well documented. The facts in hand refute Yoder who claims that the fear of war became the determining factor in Zurich's religious policy only after the Second Disputation.[22] The Council's records demonstrate that the danger of war was a live option even in April and May of 1522. Actually, from 1520 on, the Council's adherence to Zwingli's teachings had carried with it the danger that the other cantons, sensing a threat to their own religion, would act against Zurich. This danger did not suddenly emerge after the Second Disputation.

18. *E.A.*, 238.   19. *Ibid.*, 244.
20. *Ibid.*, 252.   21. *Ibid.*, 245.
22. *MQR*, XXXII, 134–5.

Zwingli's published account of the visit made by the Bishop's commission and his sermon *Concerning the Choice and Freedom of Foods* indicate his position at the time. The study of both places his political theory in clearer focus. As indicated above, although the sermon is generally assumed to be an apologia for his more restless followers, it is as much, if not more, a warning to them to avoid causing public disturbances. As a statement of strategy, it is remarkable for its understanding and restraint. In reading the sermon, one should remember that the support and sympathy of the Council were more than ever before vitally necessary. It is in connection with this need that Zwingli's remarks concerning the competence of the congregation to make decisions in religious matters are to be understood. They foreshadow the Council's decision to call the First Disputation and the theory of Christian government outlined by Zwingli in the summer of 1523.

Throughout the sermon Zwingli expressed apprehension over the rashness of those who had broken the fast. He likened them to the children of Israel who became impatient with the rigours of their journey in the wilderness and then later forgot them. Their haste, not their faith, was Zwingli's concern, and he was not convinced that all those who violated the fast acted from the love of God or for the sake of his commands. Some appeared to act only out of a desire to oppose what was generally practiced, and this Zwingli believed caused tumult and was wrong.[23] The reference to this element among the violators may indicate that Zwingli had doubts concerning the motivations of his more enthusiastic supporters. However, he agreed "it is fitting for a Christian man to eat all foods" because, as he noted a little further on, Christ had made men free.[24] Religious observances such as the Sabbath were established for men and these together with all the things of this world, were under his control.[25] The problem which men faced was how to use the freedom given to them. He stated that since God wished men to be free, man-made laws, i.e., religious observances, could not hasten the kingdom of God, and he warned that when men make regulations and assume that by following them they will become holy, they merely demonstrate their lack of faith in God.[26] Eating or fasting are unimportant; what matters is that the Christian man is free. "If you desire to fast, do it. If you do not want to eat flesh, don't eat it, but, in this, leave me, the Christian man free."[27] This is the gist of his concept of freedom. In

23. *Z*, I, 89, 7–9; 90, 7–11.   24. *Ibid.*, 98, 4; 101, 2–3.
25. *Ibid.*, 101, 4–8.
26. *Ibid.*, 102, 27; 104, 25–31; 105, 1–13.
27. *Ibid.*, 106, 15–17.

God's eyes fasting is an adiaphoron and thus men are free to make their own decisions. Of course when he said that men were free to decide for themselves Zwingli thought in terms of Christian freedom, which meant that as recipients of Christ's grace they would act within the limit of Christ's teachings.

The ensuing subsections of the sermon expounded Zwingli's basic theory. Man-made precepts were, he explained, the result of historical development and have been misused by the papacy to earn money.[28] Nevertheless, Zwingli did not advise ignoring these precepts, but rather he advocated compliance, when disobedience annoyed the majority: "But as the practice is neither bad nor dishonourable, one should peacefully follow it, as long and as much as the greater portion of men might be offended at its violation."[29] To clarify his position he stated that there were two causes of scandal. The first was the result of the preaching of the Gospel which caused those who were wicked to demand the preaching cease. He opposed yielding to such people. The second type of scandal was that which was caused by men themselves, often deliberately.[30] Zwingli used the fast question as an example of the second type of scandal. Since keeping the fast was not harmful to the faith and did not hurt anyone, it clearly did not fall into the category of necessary Gospel-preaching which was bound to offend some. Consequently, the violation of the fast fell into the second category of offence. Therefore Zwingli concluded that for the sake of one's neighbour one should not violate the fast. The crux of his argument was that the firm in faith should be patient with the weak and should seek to strengthen their faith rather than anger them.[31] Indeed, Zwingli warned that the violation carries with it a danger, for, if a man doubts and still eats meat, "what does not occur from faith, that is sin." The strong should have patience for the sake of the weak.[32]

To bolster his argument, Zwingli had reminded his readers of the aims of the kingdom of God. "For the kingdom of God is not food or drink but rather piety, peace and joy in the Holy Ghost." In conformity with the teachings of the kingdom, he advised: "Therefore let us strive for the things which lead to peace and let us instruct each other properly."[33] He alluded to Christ's willingness to pay taxes to the government in order to avoid conflict: "Listen to this, Christ gave the penny, so that he would move no one to anger."[34] Zwingli did not

28. *Ibid.*, 109, 1–15; 110, 10–13.
30. *Ibid.*, 111, 12–13, 14–16, 28–9.
32. *Ibid.*, 115, 26–29.
34. *Ibid.*, 119, 31–2.

29. *Ibid.*, 111, 7–9.
31. *Ibid.*, 112, 15–21.
33. *Ibid.*, 115, 13–14, 16–17.

call for mere passivity. He tempered his demand for patience with a call for the education of the weak. The references to the kingdom were aimed at quieting those who found patience so difficult. He was anxious to remind them of the distinction between the temporal world, the world of human affairs and justice, and the world of the spirit, the world of divine justice and the ultimate aim for those living in the external world.

Another example cited by Zwingli to support the policy of patience is important both because of its latter application to the struggle with the Baptists and because of its aptness as an illustration of his strategy. He spoke of Paul's attitude toward circumcision. Paul allowed Timothy to be circumcised in order not to annoy the Jews who wished to keep the ceremonies of the Old Testament after they had received the Gospel.[35] Then, as Zwingli went on to show in the next part of the sermon, when the Jewish Christians were better instructed, Paul was able to prevent Titus' circumcision.[36] The references demonstrate the tactics Zwingli felt it necessary to employ. Patience did not mean inaction, but continued quiet activity, so that, when the time was right, a more radical change could be made.

Zwingli also addressed his own disciples directly. The argument which he used paralleled the milk and solid food imagery which he had employed to describe the progress of his preaching to Myconius during 1520. He was anxious to remind his own followers that because Christ had made them free they were better able to be patient with their weaker fellows, until they were ready to receive solid food, which is what Christian love required. The issue of the fast was not central to the faith or its preaching and therefore could be treated as adiaphoron—the fast could be obeyed or ignored as the situation dictated. Zwingli's attitude towards change is clearly illustrated by the argument of the sermon: change must be carried out with patience and there must be time allowed to prepare those who were weaker in the faith for the solid food which was to come. His approach to the problem in 1522 is the same as it was in 1520 and would seem to indicate what his reaction would be to those who caused public dissension in 1523. The policy which the government followed after the Second Disputation of 1523 provided time to prepare the people for the abolition of the Mass and seems consistent with the position which Zwingli took in this sermon.

Zwingli wished to calm his followers and also to reassure the government of his own peaceful intentions. The Council was willing to aid him but could not be expected to permit any group to endanger the

35. *Ibid.*, 119, 3–6.   36. *Ibid.*, 123, 21, 25–30.

security of the city by an ill-considered offensive against established custom. Zwingli recognized that political survival depended upon slow change.

The sermon was not merely a plea for restraint; Zwingli also devoted his attention to a study of the way in which abuses were to be removed. To begin with, he asserted the need for change. His reason illuminates the connection he made between the welfare of the city and Christian religion. If malpractices were not removed, God would inflict his punishment upon the people:

Thus it is better, [that] we do it ourselves, so it will not be done by God and flagrantly punished as Paul teaches . . . (I. Cor. 11:31 ff). If we judge ourselves, we will not be judged by God; [if] we take the degradation ourselves, it must not be taken with the judgment of God.[37]

The idea Zwingli expressed was drawn from the prophets of the Old Testament. Just as the prophets called for reform to save the people of Israel from God's wrath, so Zwingli called for a reform to save the people of Zurich. The prophets presupported a covenant between God and his people, and Zwingli assumed that the same covenant existed between the Zurichers, the people of the new covenant, and God. Salvation was for the whole society, and not for individuals or a select group within the society.

Zwingli explained what the reform should encompass. In Matthew, Christ counselled the removal of various parts of the body, if they were offensive. In like manner Zwingli called for the removal of bishops, preachers, or rulers who placed unbearable burdens on the people. He defined the true nature of the bishop's office:

And the Greek word bishop [means] with us keeper. . . . Listen a little while, here is your office; to watch over the sheep, to feed them, not to oppress, to fleece, to load them with unbearable burdens. That is nothing else than to give offence. . . . Yes, even if they [the bishops] are as necessary for the support of life as a hand or foot, still one should remove them, if they misuse their predominance.[38]

He was careful to qualify his statement and to call for cautious change:

the offence [abuses in the church] should be done away with and one should not suffer it eternally, but all this with seasonable council and reason; nothing should take place according to ones own judgment and whim.[39]

These words were for his enthusiastic followers. He did agree with their aim but demanded reforms in keeping with the situation and reason.

37. *Ibid.*, 120, 25–9.   38. *Ibid.*, 121, 8, 13–16, 31–122, 1.
39. *Ibid.*, 122, 2–5.

These remarks were no doubt as pleasing to the secular power as they were discouraging to his impatient friends. He could not have been more explicit.

Once again he advised his disciples to make all due allowance for those who are duller and have less understanding of the Gospel:

Look, one should not let the stupid person remain stupid but rather proclaim the truth, not with hair splitting, through which one will become more doubtful, but rather with the clear, simple truth, so that all doubt may be removed from him.[40]

This passage leaves no doubt concerning Zwingli's method of carrying out reform: it must be done through patient and careful teaching.

Zwingli was at pains to prevent his supporters from diverting their attention from the essentials of the reform programme. This concern that the issue of the fast which was a non-essential would obscure the primary aim of his movement was manifest when he said: "Therefore consider the other things, like eating meat, working on feast days, which are means, after God's Word has been heard and the Communion celebrated."[41] If secondary issues were confused with primary ones there was a danger that the reform programme would never be realized. Zwingli obviously considered the preaching of the Word and the administration of the sacraments as primary questions, and it is fair to ask if he would have advocated the policy of patience and called for a period of instruction if the issue had concerned essential matters; for example, a reform of the Mass. As long as Zwingli was free to preach the Gospel, and the mandate of 1520 guaranteed this freedom, he had no reason to doubt that the reform would eventually be carried out. The policy which he advocated in dealing with the problem of the fast, which was a non-essential, was equally applicable to that of changing the Mass, an essential question. The opportunity to proclaim the Gospel which would transform men's hearts was the real prerequisite for his programme. The fact that the Council had given this opportunity to him enabled him to proceed with care and to take time to prepare the people for further changes. He sought to avoid tumult, especially over a secondary matter, during 1522, because public disturbances might cause the Council to change its mind and forbid him to preach. The discussion of the observance of the fast explains much of Zwingli's current and future policy.

The concluding segment of the sermon, which was added after the departure of the Bishop's commission in April, defined good works as

40. *Ibid.*, 122, 16–19.
41. *Ibid.*, 126, 4–6.

sprung from God alone and applied this definition to the fast question.[42] Zwingli maintained that he did not think the violation of the fast was in itself bad. When it occurred with divine inspiration, it was undoubtedly good, but he added that when it took place out of fear of human law and was valued as a divine command, the violation was damaging and did not please God.[43] What concerned Zwingli was the motivation of those who ate meat, not the fact that they broke the Lenten fast. Those who did not fast to please God could be as wrong as those who fasted. The problem was to find a way to regulate Christian conduct according to God's will. He then explained how this could be done. The explanation presupposed the authority of scripture and was expressed in terms of Zurich's political structure.

As in the political life of the city, so, for Zwingli, in the affairs of the church, an assembly of the whole could establish proper norms of conduct for Christians. The point which he stressed was that neither individuals nor particular bishops could do so:

Indeed only a generally assembled church can make laws which will also be binding in heaven . . . this work is not commanded of an individual member of Christendom [and] indeed never of particular bishops who for some time have ventured to impose laws according to their own will, the common people not having been consulted.[44]

Zwingli's comments about the authority of individual Christians and the bishop are important. When he denied individuals the right to make rules, he was no doubt referring to his following, who took the law into their own hands. He reasserted this position whenever the radicals pushed ahead on their own, and his attitude reveals that the gulf between them was clear enough in 1522 to refute the charge that he arrived at this conclusion later in his career. The rejection of the bishop's competence to make regulations was Zwingli's answer to the Bishop of Constance's attempt to interfere in the fast question. This was manifest when Zwingli went on to deny that the silence of the people or their failure to oppose a bishop's action implied consent. The people were silent, because, lacking the Gospel, they were fearful and ignorant. "The pious unity of Christians has remained silent about too many things, out of fear, and because no one has proclaimed their freedom to them from the Gospel." Now that the people have the Gospel, he continued, the clergy are afraid and wish to regain control over them. If the priests had not held that so many abuses were God's commandments, they would have been spared much difficulty.[45] Although the statement

42. *Ibid.*, 126, 22–4.
43. *Ibid.*, 127, 5–11.
44. *Ibid.*, 127, 13–17.
45. *Ibid.*, 127, 18–20, 29–30; 128, 1.

"indeed only a generally assembled church can make laws which will also be binding in heaven" could be interpreted to be a reference to a general council of the church, in this case, especially in view of the purpose of the sermon which spoke to a specific problem in the city, it is more likely that Zwingli used the term "generally assembled church" to refer to a Christian assembly which could be gathered at Zurich.[46] When he questioned the right of a bishop to make regulations governing religious practices without first referring to the common people, he definitely focussed his attention upon a problem which applied directly to Zurich's difficulties with the See of Constance. In questioning the Bishop of Constance's authority, Zwingli was able to refer to the Zurich constitution. The city assembly was a general gathering of Christians, and, according to Zwingli's definition, had the right to make laws governing the conduct of Christians. Of course at Zurich the assembly delegated its powers to the Council. In effect, because the Council was the delegated authority of a general gathering of Christians, Zwingli placed the authority to regulate external religious observances in the hands of the magistrates, and he denied such rights to the Bishop, because the Bishop did not, under the current circumstances, possess the requisite consensus to exercise such authority. The Council was seeking to control its own policy on the question of the fast and required justification not only for this but also for its support of Zwingli's reform. Zwingli's argument secured the Zurich Council from the traditional view of ecclesiastical authority and from the pressure of radicals who took matters into their own hands. His theory gave the government freedom to act without challenge.

Having defended the competence of the assembly to establish rules which were binding in heaven, Zwingli proceeded to distinguish between these ordinances and other rules which the assembly might issue. He employed the term *allgemein versamlung der Christen* (a general gather-

---

46. Many years later the English divine, John Jewel, returning from exile in Zurich to England, wrote Peter Martyr concerning the right of a "provincial church" to institute reforms. Jewel asserted: "that every provincial church, even without the bidding of a general council, has power either to establish, or change, or abrogate ceremonies and ecclesiastical rites, wherever it may seem to make for edification" (Robinson, ed., *The Zurich Letters*, I, 11; Booty, ed., *John Jewel, An Apology of the Church of England*, XXIV). Jewel was writing at a time when his Zurich experiences were fresh in his mind. It does not seem too much to suggest that he had derived his idea of the "provincial church's" right to carry out reforms from the model he had found at Zurich. Though Zwingli had been dead for almost thirty years and many changes had taken place there, the essential structure and rationale for the reformed church in the canton remained as Zwingli had evolved them.

ing of Christians) in place of *gemeinlich versamlete kilch* (a generally gathered church), but its use and the reference to Zurich remained the same. Such an assembly, Zwingli said, could make laws governing the fast but could not impose these laws as eternal law, i.e., divine law. The way to prevent confusion between laws made by an assembly of Christians which were not eternally binding and those which were was simple. To discover divine law one refers to the Bible; because it is impossible to add to or to change scripture, its use prevented error.[47] Regulations based upon it were binding in heaven and on earth. The passage touches upon a twofold conception of law which Zwingli fully clarified in the sermon *Concerning Divine and Human Righteousness* and reveals the crucial position which his doctrine of scripture held in his conception of the magistracy's competence to deal with religious problems.

This section of the epilogue was followed by an *excursus* on the manner in which the people are to be freed from man-made percepts which have been falsely imposed. Zwingli, like Luther, asserted that the Christian man, who was free, was bound only to the law of love. To eat flesh did not violate this law, if it was preceded by proper instruction which granted freedom from the old law:

And we are bound to no law, save the law of love; and free choice of foods does not damage the love of neighbour, for when it has been rightly taught and properly known, then we are not bound to the same command or law. . . . For what God has cleansed you should not call unclean.[48]

Zwingli's meaning was clear and served as an admonition to his restless friends. The people must be taught what the essence of divine law is and then they will not take offence at the eating of meat. Education must precede action.

In closing, Zwingli again considered the clergy's authority to command the observance of fasts and concluded that if a priest should command men to follow such a usage, he exceeded the limits of his office:

. . . the spiritual rulers not only do not have authority to command such things but rather, when they command it they clearly sin; for whoever rules and does more than is permitted him, he is punishable. . . . Therefore I leave each to his free judgment in this matter. . . .[49]

Zwingli's word indicate his view of the clergy's office; the right to command is not a part of it. The reduction of the clergy's authority to

47. *Z*, I, 134, 46, 9–10; 24–5.   48. *Ibid.*, 135, 12–15, 30.
49. *Ibid.*, 136, 1–5, 7–8.

its proper sphere was a central element in the programme for a rebirth
of Christ and the Gospel. However, at first glance, Zwingli's assertion
of freedom of conscience in matters like fasting appears to nullify any
policy a Christian assembly might lay down. This is not the case.
Zwingli's conception of Christian freedom called for those who have
faith to recognize the needs of their weaker fellows and to accept the
custom of fasting until the majority had been prepared for its abolition.
This position repudiated "individualism" and left it to the government
to supervise the practices associated with the observance of Lent. Zwingli
was willing to do this because he believed that a Christian assembly, or
its representatives, which recognized the teachings of scripture would
arrive at decisions compatible with the divine command.

The debate between Zwingli and the suffragan Bishop of Constance,
Melchior Fattlin, the leader of the commission which Bishop Hugo had
sent to Zurich, presents the issues involved in the fast question once again
and grants further insight into Zwingli's thought. As seen through the
eyes of a loyal churchman like Fattlin, the doctrines taught at Zurich
underminded respect for human teachings and ceremonies and consequently menaced the laws of society and the Christian faith. To threaten
or to undermine religion meant the destruction of the society. Although
Zwingli differed radically with the Bishop on most points, he, too,
believed there was an indissoluble link between right religion and the
stability of secular society.

Fattlin raised other issues when he described the ceremonials of the
old church as a *fons virtutum* (a fountain of virtues) and warned the
Zurich Council to remain within the church, because outside of it there
was no salvation.[50] Since it is not the purpose of this study to analyze
every argument in detail, Zwingli's response will be examined only in
connection with his comments concerning the nature of the church and
the relation between the church and the secular arm.

Zwingli answered the Suffragan's charges directly. First, he noted the
good results of the Gospel teaching: "There is greater peace and quiet
in Zurich than in any other region of Helvetia for which all good citizens
give credit to the Gospel."[51] In other words, the reformed doctrine,
rather than the traditional, results in greater social stability. This is quite
enough to refute Fattlin's claim that the new teachings threatened the
fabric of the community. Neither questioned the central role of the
Christian religion in society. This was not an issue at Zurich until the
rise of Anabaptism.

50. *Ibid.*, 145, 18–19, 22; 146, 8–9.
51. *Ibid.*, 145, 32–3.

To Fattlin's charge that he denied all human teachings or rules Zwingli responded:

Nevertheless I deny that I am of this opinion, that I consider no human precept is to be served or endured. For what is to be borne more readily [than] whatever the harmonious opinion of all Christians shall have decided?[52]

As in his sermon, Zwingli rejected priestly authority and called for decisions on church policy to be made by general agreement. Since the impossibility of gathering all Christians together is manifest, his argument left room for a theory of action by local gatherings of Christians or their representatives. His answer refuted Fattlin's insinuation that he denied all tradition. What he rejected was the misuse of traditional practices and their identification with divine law. This was the point of his reform programme: the existing institutions must be purified, not abolished.

Zwingli also responded to Fattlin's assertion that his opinions encouraged disobedience to the laws of the community. Disobedience to the laws of society was, as far as he was concerned, contrary to the spirit of Christ and the Apostles: ". . . I have denied that to be from the mind of Christ or of his Apostles. He said: 'Give to Caesar those things which are Caesar's, etc. . . . and contribute tribute or assessment. . . .'" He went on to say that Christianity had always maintained justice but added that a distinction between Christianity and ceremonies had to be made: ceremonies have never improved society:

Christianity has always served the public justice most powerfully, nor can the faith of Christ be abolished, when ceremonies have been everywhere abolished, but rather ceremonies have by no means achieved anything other than to defile the heart from Christ and his faithful, to destroy the doctrine of the spirit and to divert [men] from invisible things to the elements of the world.[53]

Ceremonies divert men from spiritual affairs and deny society the advantages which the Christian faith in pure form grants. The issue between Zwingli and Fattlin was drawn over the essentials of the faith. By offering a new definition of what the essentials were, Zwingli was able to represent the Christian renewal as a sounder vehicle for the preservation of the faith and the support of society.

Zwingli then devoted his attention to Fattlin's claim there is no

52. *Ibid.*, 149, 18–21.
53. *Ibid.*, 149, 25–8, 33–8.

salvation outside the church. He agreed with Fattlin and then explained
who the members of the church were and where they could be found:

Yea, in every nation and place, whoever confesses; with his mouth that
Christ is the Lord, and believes with his heart that God raised him from the
dead, he is saved, whether he may be among the Indians, or the Scythians
and certainly it is sure no one is saved outside of that [church]. . . .[54]

Zwingli's definition was in the tradition of Augustine. The true church
outside of which there is no salvation is a universal body of believers.
Zwingli included two requirements for membership: confession with
the mouth; belief in the heart. Confession with the mouth is external
and makes it possible to talk of a Christian society, while belief in the
heart is known only to God and is the acid test for membership in the
Church Universal.[55] The citizenry may not all belong to the Church
Universal but they can all confess Christ and hence belong to a Christian
community which must, by nature, always remain a mixed body.
Zwingli's agreement implies a twofold definition of the church: the true
church made up of all who believe in their hearts and the external church
consisting of those who confess with the mouth but do not necessarily
believe. Since the church in this world is a mixed body, it is governed
by the same laws that apply to secular society and its affairs are the
concern of the civil magistrate. Zwingli's theory leaves no place for a
believer's church.

The debate ranged to still other topics and then returned to a point
which had direct relevance to Zwingli's political theory. Fattlin had
stressed Bishop Hugo's concern to avoid scandal in the church. Zwingli
suggested that if this were the case, the clergy should give up their
immunities and bear the burden of the community as Christ had done:

Whether the Bishop should not at some time command his priests, according
to the custom of Christ, that . . . they should bear the public burden with
the remaining Christian brothers, that they should pay tribute and taxes?
For Christ was not scandalized to pay those who required a didrachma,
adding to it also a miracle (Matt. 17: 24–27); it can not be denied [that]
every people among all the nations have cause of complaint that the idle
priests, monks and nuns have been supported and nevertheless give nothing
either of substance or of labour for the public service.[56]

---

54. *Ibid.*, 152, 13–16.
55. Brockelmann claims this is the essential point for an understanding of
Zwingli's conception of society. The basis for membership in the congregation was
the external adherence to the Gospel and its regulations: "From the first, Zwingli
knows a Church, whose foundation is not faith but rather a compliance with the
external" (Brockelmann 37–8).
56. *Z*, I, 153, 17–24.

Zwingli repeated an old grievance. For centuries the immunities of the clergy had plagued the development of secular government. Though in the Confederacy, and canton Zurich in particular, these immunities had been sharply curtailed, the principle, stoutly defended by the church, still remained. In accordance with the biblical norm, Zwingli called for the renunciation of all special privileges. This was the crux of the new teaching. The priest is not set apart from secular society; he is a responsible member of it and, as such, must bear its burdens. This task is his Christian duty. Zwingli's demand attacked the external structure which the old church had built up to protect it from the control of the secular ruler. His comments reveal a tacit assumption, later made overt in the sermon *On Divine and Human Righteousness*: secular government fulfils a divine purpose and requires the support of Christians. Of course, Fattlin's response was that the matter lay beyond the competence of the assembly and the scope of the debate.

Zwingli fought for the essentials and compromised on the adiaphora, waiting for a propitious moment to introduce change. He provided the Council with a doctrine of the church based upon popular consent, which freed it from the last vestiges of control by the hierarchy. Zwingli believed the church on earth was a mixed body which found tangible expression in the structure of the society.

7   Further Opposition:
the Campaign of the Church
the Pro-Mercenary Party
the Radicals

IN CLOSE CO-OPERATION WITH THE FEDERAL DIET THE CHURCH
redoubled its efforts to thwart the reform movement. Bishop Hugo was
reluctant to take action against Zwingli, but Faber, his vicar, newly
returned from Rome, and the alarming spread of Zwinglian doctrine
within the Confederacy drove him to it. The campaign launched by the
See of Constance took many forms. The main thrust of its effort, which
was backed by the Federal Diet, fell upon the Zurich Council. There was
no direct attack on Zwingli but neither the Bishop nor the Diet did
anything to stop the flood of rumours which purported to reveal the
depravity of the reform party, or the clumsy attempts made in the late
fall to kill Zwingli. Although these did not have the official sanction of
the church they were the product of its open hostility to him. By
November, 1522, Zwingli and the Council were forced to take the
defensive measures which culminated in the First Disputation.

The preliminary moves in the church's offensive were made in May
of 1522. Bishop Hugo, at the behest of Faber, issued a mandate to the
Council on May 2. It called on the city to remain true to the faith and
practice of the old church. The mandate produced no effect and so two
other missives were dispatched to the Council and Chapter respectively
on May 24, which urged the councillors to end the "scandal" at Zurich
themselves.[1] The terms of the appeal suggest that Hugo contemplated
further action himself, and threatened intervention on a broader front.
Pope Hadrian's letter to the Confederacy, written on April 27, was due
for consideration at the May 27 meeting of the Federal Diet. When it
was discussed, the Diet sent a copy to each canton, accompanied by a
warning that the sermons of certain pastors were causing unrest and

1. The letter to the Chapter, written in Latin, was the work of Faber. *E.A.*,
251.

should be stopped. The Bishop's letter and the Diet's action were probably part of a general plan to frighten Zurich into submission.[2]

The Council's suppression of the demonstration in favour of Zwingli, which was planned as an answer to the Bishop's warning, indicates that the magistrates saw some connection between the letters and the meeting of the Diet. Demonstrations at Zurich in favour of reform could easily be interpreted by the Confederates as a provocative act. The Diet's response to the Pope's plea made it obvious to the Zurich government that its religious policy concerned the entire Confederacy.[3] Bishop Hugo's letter to the Council also demonstrated the church's difficulty in dealing with the challenge posed by Zwingli's preaching. The Bishop told the Council that he saw no need for Zurich's hostility to the church because "it was constant in its loyalty to the Gospel, the teachings of Paul and the holy Christian faith."[4] As yet, conservative theologians were unable to clarify their conception of the relationship between the authority of scripture and that of the church.[5]

At a meeting of the Diet held at Baden on July 4, the Bishop's representatives complained that the Diet had failed to stop inflamatory preaching. They called upon the Confederacy to aid the See of Constance in its struggle to defend the faith.[6] Just as the help of the government was basic to Zwingli's reform, so also, the defence of the old faith demanded the close co-operation of the secular arm. A formal alliance between the Confederates and the Bishop was a foregone conclusion.

The next phase of the Bishop's offensive began on August 10. Bishop Hugo had ignored the petition, framed on July 2 by Zwingli and his friends, which requested him to permit the Gospel to be preached and the clergy to marry. Finally, on August 10, he issued a mandate which answered the July petition. Hugo again asked the cantonal governments to help him suppress heresy. In making his appeal he complained that despite the ban on Luther and his teachings preaching hostile to the old order continued.[7] The mandate assumed that Zwingli was a Lutheran and dashed his hopes of winning the Bishop for reform of the church.

Zwingli was protected from the full force of the traditionalist reaction by the policy of the Holy See. Rome still had need of Zurich for its Italian wars. Even as late as October, 1522, Pope Hadrian sent a

---

2. O. Farner, III, 280.   3. Köhler, 86.
4. *E.A.*, 251.
5. Tavard, 49, 57, 66, 80, 113, 117; Oberman's conclusions call for a revision of Tavard but also indicate that there was no uniform interpretation of the relationship between scripture and tradition (Oberman, 6, 372–3).
6. Egli, 71.   7. O. Farner, III, 303–4.

friendly letter to the Zurich Council which contained no word of complaint about Zwingli's activity in the city. This was still true on the eve of the First Disputation, when the Papal Nuncio, Ennio Filonardi, passed along to Zwingli a letter from the Pope which called him a "beloved son" and urged him to consider the advantages of serving the cause of Rome.[8]

Though hindered by its conflict with Rome's desires, the alliance between the Confederacy and the local ecclesiastical authorities began to bear fruit. Myconius reported in late July that Zwingli's petition to the Bishop, which was read before the Federal Diet at Lucerne, received a cold reception. Myconius' letters, which reached Zwingli in the first weeks of August, revealed the effect of the co-operation between the Diet and the Bishop and indicated the nature of the Bishop's answer. He informed Zwingli that clergymen were being persecuted because they had married.[9] This marked the beginning of a repression at Lucerne which in a few months' time closed the city to the progress of Christian rebirth and set the pattern for the expulsion of the married clergy in Schwyz and Zug, which, by the late fall, were closed to Zwingli's followers. Soon, their only haven in the area was Cloister Einsiedeln, presided over by an abbot friendly to reform and protected, for the moment, from outside intervention by its special status.[10]

An agitated letter dated August 19 announced that Myconius had been expelled from Lucerne.[11] Two days later another letter explained the reason: Myconius was a Lutheran. The charge against him reflected the terms of the Bishop's appeal, issued on August 10, which classed the new movement in Switzerland with Lutheranism, an officially recognized heresy. Myconius' situation underlines the difficulty which confronted Zwingli's followers and his allies, the Zurich magistrates, and illustrates a major reason for Zurich's cautious policy. If the charge that Zwingli was a Lutheran could be substantiated, there was legal precedent to justify the forcible suppression of his teachings.

Pressure was brought to bear on Zwingli from another quarter. After reading Zwingli's *Archeteles*, Erasmus warned him of the seriousness of his actions: "Consult learned friends, before you publish something in general."[12] Erasmus, like Hofmann in his *Complaint*, and Bishop Hugo himself, saw the need for reform, but feared the effect of stirring up the mob with new ideas. This letter and Erasmus' letter of December 9 shows how far apart the two had drifted.[13] To the moral suasion of

8. Staehelin, I, 250–1.   9. *Z*, VII, 545, 1–5, 8–12.
10. Staehelin, I, 227.   11. *Z*, VII, 561, 11; 563, 11–12.
12. *Ibid.*, 582, 5–6.   13. *Ibid.*, 631.

Erasmus' warning were added damaging rumours, including one which asserted that Zwingli had preached in favour of adultery.[14] These rumours were conceived to alienate as many as possible from his cause and all of them revealed the malice and fear of the conservatives.

As the summer passed, Bishop Hugo was aroused by the failure of his efforts in the Confederacy, and by those of the monks at Zurich, to silence Zwingli. He began to work against the Zwinglians in closer co-operation with the Bishop of Lausanne. With the support of this prelate, he intervened in Canton Zurich itself and arrested Johann and Rudolph Ammann, two brothers who held parishes at Rifferswil and Knonau.[15]

The arrest of the brothers was a warning to Zwingli that his preaching would no longer be tolerated. It may also have been a test case to see what the Council would do when the Bishop moved his attack into their own domains. If so, the Bishop got an answer from the Council which showed the central role it played in protecting the reform movement. The magistrates informed the Bishop that the arrest of the Ammanns was a violation of the treaty which recognized their right to supervise the behaviour of the clergy within the canton. The city fathers also told the Bishop that his action violated the canon law, which required the publication of charges against priests who had been arrested. Denying the Council's interpretation of the matter, the Bishop punished both and placed Rudolph under the ban of the church; but he did send the Council a statement of the charges against them.[16] Neither Zwingli nor his

14. *Ibid.*, 613, 19–21; 643, 4–8, 12–13; O. Farner, II, 320–1.
15. Egli, 72.
16. *E.A.*, 270. According to the letter which Rudolf Ammann wrote to the Council in his own defence, the Bishop had accused him of informing his people that, until the beginning of the reform movement, they had followed a false faith and that he had preached against the cult of Mary and the saints. There were other charges also: Ammann did not hold with the sacrament of "final baptism," i.e., extreme unction, and had let a butcher die without it; he had committed adultery with two married women; he had worn red trousers and slippers while saying Mass. In his defence Ammann maintained that he had preached scripture, stressed salvation by grace, attacked the miracles of the saints, and the cult of the Virgin. He denied emphatically that he had ever neglected to perform any of the sacraments and asserted that he held all of them in high esteem. The charges of immorality were untrue, but he did admit that he had worn red slippers because of a physical illness, while he justified his red trousers on the grounds that he had received imperial authority to do so, because he was a notary (*E.A.*, 271). Ammann was known as an outspoken proponent of Zwingli's teaching in the Zurich countryside. His behaviour was not always circumspect and he was later removed from his parish and imprisoned by the Zurich authorities for committing adultery with his housekeeper during his wife's illness (*Z, IX,* 476). Ammann seems to have provided the Bishop with an excuse to embarrass Zwingli and his supporters in the Council.

followers were silenced by the Bishop's action. His behaviour only widened the breach between him and the Council. It was only a matter of time until his nominal jurisdiction in the canton would be ended.[17]

Again in November Hugo attempted to intervene, but this time his efforts did not succeed. Simon Stumpf, a pastor at Höngg, was cited before the curia at Constance for encouraging the peasantry not to pay tithes to their spiritual overlord, the Abbott of Wettingen. The Council claimed the right to judge the case, and the Bishop, after reminding the Council that he would defend his rights if nothing were done about Stumpf, turned him over to the Zurich magistrates. However, the Bishop was not easily satisfied with the Council's handling of the case, for as late as January 19, 1523, he wrote to the Council urging it to advise Stumpf and his friends not to repeat their disrespect of his authority. Finally, on the eve of the First Disputation, he expressed his satisfaction with the outcome of the case, and promised to do nothing more, as long as the Abbot of Wettingen made no further complaint.[18]

There was a reason for the Bishop's reasonableness in the affair. The Council's effort to defend Stumpf was a tactical victory for the church. No doubt with the Bishop's consent, the Abbot of Wettingen complained to the Diet in December that Zurich was protecting Simon Stumpf. By taking the responsibility for silencing Stumpf the Council should have been able to allay the charges of the traditionalists that it championed a movement opposed to public order. However, in the eyes of the Diet, the Council's behaviour confirmed the fact that Zurich supported a religious movement subversive to public order. This conviction inclined the Diet to act against Zurich, and its action was far more effective than anything the Bishop might do alone. Zwingli was supported by the political authority of the Zurich Council and only a stronger secular power could be expected to crush him. The delegates of the cantons may not have gone as far as the Bishop desired, but they did order Zurich to stop protecting Stumpf. At the same time, they renewed their admonition to the Confederates to suppress hertical preaching and remain loyal to the old faith.[19]

Another case made a deep impression upon the Zurichers and contributed to the decision to summon the First Disputation. Urban Wyss, a priest at Fislisbach in the Duchy of Baden, had preached the Gospel and won the support of his parishioners. He was arrested in November

---

17. The formal repudiation of the Bishop's jurisdiction took place in February, 1523 (*E.A.*, 332).
18. *E.A.*, 300, 323, 326.
19. Egli, 75.

and brought before the Federal Diet assembled in Baden. The Diet handed him over to the Bishop's court at Constance for trial and issued instructions to all local magistrates commanding them to report those who preached against the established faith.[20] These orders closed all the districts in the Confederacy which were under the joint administration of the cantons to Zwingli's followers.

If there was any doubt about the feelings of most of the Confederates towards the Zwinglians, a subsequent decision made by the Diet put an end to it. The Diet instructed Zurich and Basel to censor the publication of books favourable to the church reform. Zurich obeyed the letter of the demand and on January 3, 1523, set up a board of censors which included Zwingli among its members. The Council then reported it had complied with the Confederacy's wishes but did not say who was on the board.[21]

The Bishop's activity in the Confederacy emboldened the monks of the preaching orders within the canton to begin a campaign against the Zwingli.[22] Egli believes that the increased activities of Zwingli's opponents at this time were in part the result of a shift in the focus of his preaching.[23] Previously Zwingli had directed his attention to the doctrinal errors of the old church, but he was now apparently satisfied that his preaching had weakened the people's loyalty to the doctrines of the established church. Consequently, he began to place more emphasis upon the need to purify ecclesiastical institutions and liturgical practices to bring them into line with his interpretation of doctrine. The monks, in particular, were alarmed at this development and, led by the Dominicans, who had excellent connections with the Council and with Constance, they appealed to the Council for protection. By threatening to fight Zwingli from the pulpit, they persuaded the city fathers to forbid further criticism of the monastic orders.[24]

The councillors issued the order disallowing criticism of the monks on July 7, and it was on this occasion that they called Grebel and his friends before them and bade them be silent. The hearing, as has already been suggested, indicates that although the focus of Zwingli's preaching had shifted, a chief source of trouble for the monks came from the activist element within his following. The Council silenced Grebel and his friends and never mentioned Zwingli.

It seems logical to suggest that the monks were aware of the difference of opinion concerning tactics among the reformers. By attributing the

20. O. Farner, III, 327.
21. Egli, 75, 78.
22. Staehelin, I, 228.
23. Egli, 67.
24. Staehelin, I, 229–30.

excess of the radicals to Zwingli himself and appealing to the government, they hoped to undermine Zwingli's influence with the authorities. There was also the chance their stratagem might force him to repudiate Grebel and thus split the reform party, which would make it easier to destroy the whole movement. The way in which the Council responded makes this probable. Grebel and his associates were reprimanded by the civil authority and not by Zwingli. Zwingli was spared the necessity of publically reprimanding Grebel. He was given time to restore unity within the ranks of his followers. Although Zwingli did shift the emphasis of his preachings, it remains an open question how much the grievances of the monks were exaggerated in the attempt to embarrass him with the indiscretions of his disciples. In view of his cautious approach to the practical problems of institutional reform during the next eighteen months, it is possible he spoke more harshly against the religious establishment in order to retain control over his party and to head off the demands of the extremists.

The monks were not long in following up their initial success with the Council. The itinerant Franciscan, Franz Lambert, a future Protestant, but at that time a defender of the cult of Mary and the Saints, arrived in Zurich. The monks, hoping Lambert would be able to defeat Zwingli in debate, arranged a disputation. It took place on July 17, and Zwingli, arguing from the scriptures, forced Lambert to concede defeat. However, as soon as he arrived in Basel, Lambert gave a different version of the outcome.[25]

Lambert's failure only spurred the monks on to greater exertion and, at their behest, the Council appointed a commission to re-examine their complaints. Zwingli refused to accept the compromise, that the monks preach only from the scripture and that both sides avoid criticizing one another, which the commission tried to impose. He said that when he became People's Priest, he took responsibility as a spiritual guardian and had sworn an oath that he would fulfil the obligations of his office. Consequently, if the monks persisted in false teaching, he was obliged to attack them. When forced to choose between the two parties, the magistrates placed no restrictions upon the scope of Zwingli's preaching and once again ordered all the clergy, under threat of punishment, to confine their preaching to scripture.[26] If the previous policy of the Council had left any question about the government's commitment to Zwingli's programme, it was set aside. The outcome of the monks' activities demonstrates how futile any attack against him was as long as he retained the support of the Zurich government.

25. O. Farner, III, 265–6.   26. *Ibid.*, 267–9.

Zwingli pressed his advantage and delivered a heavy counter thrust. Early in August he obtained from the magistrates the right to preach to the nuns at Oetenbach. This broke the control of the Dominicans over the spiritual life of the nuns, and Zwingli's preaching there was so successful that by November they began to petition for the right to re-enter secular society. The Council, wishing to avoid a decision for the moment, delayed its reply to their request until June of the next year. In the interim it allowed the nuns to choose either Dominican or secular confessors, but ordered both to preach from the scripture.[27]

The monks made a further unsuccessful attempt to hinder the process of Zwingli's work. The circumstances reflect the interaction between their effort and the Bishop's campaign. Heartened by the strong line taken against Zwingli by the Federal Diet in December, 1522, they caused a scene while Leo Jud was preaching in the chapel of the Augustinian Order. Jud's sermon was repeatedly interrupted by one of the monks and a fight was barely avoided.[28] The uproar was followed by several attempts on Zwingli's life during December. Though neither the Bishop nor the Zurich monks were directly implicated in these attempts, a warning sent from Lucerne by Iodocus Kilchmeyer, a signer of the July petition, stated that two monks at Lucerne had hatched the plot to kill Zwingli.[29] These incidents led to considerable outcry in the city and were the immediate, though not the major cause, for the calling of the First Disputation[30].

Another group was present in the city which played its part, with outside support, in fomenting domestic discontent. It was made up of those who were opposed to Zurich's decision to put an end to service in foreign armies. This faction offered to the other cantons the perfect vehicle for undermining Zwingli's alliance with the government without involving them in an open clash with the Zurich magistrates.

During the summer and in increasing numbers during the fall of 1522 and the spring of 1523, Zurichers, encouraged by French recruiting agents operating in the canton and by those at Zurich who still received French pensions, violated the laws forbidding mercenary service.[31] It is not always possible to establish a direct connection between the policy pursued by the cantons in co-operation with the Bishop and the fact that a growing number of illegal recruits for the French army were

27. *E.A.*, 298, 300, 301.
28. Staehelin, I, 259.
29. *Z*, VII, 627, 10–14.
30. Staehelin, I, 260.
31. *E.A.*, 258. This report discusses the activity of French agents and the citizens receiving French pensions.

induced to leave Zurich. Nevertheless, it is obvious that the French agents could not have passed in and out of Zurich's domains without the help of the other Confederates. Nor, for that matter, could the Zurichers willing to join the French have done so. The evidence indicates that the growing unrest among the citizens anxious to serve for pay abroad was stimulated as part of a general attempt to force the Zurich Council to alter its religious policy.

The difficulties caused by the pro-mercenary party at Zurich must be reckoned as another factor which helped to convince the magistracy that the matters at issue should be clarified by a disputation. The problems caused by those favouring mercenary service did not cease with the First Disputation. Again, in the spring of 1523, the number of defections to the French increased and forced the Council to investigate the cause. The magistrates discovered that the pro-mercenary party in the city was in contact with the other cantons.

In a vain effort to stop the violation the Council had re-issued the mandate against mercenary service in June, 1522. This had no effect, and, in October, the Council received a fresh list of citizens who had recently entered French service. Once again the mandate was re-published and orders were given to apprehend and imprison violators. A decree was issued on November 15 which forbade, under the penalty of a heavy fine, any citizen to receive a pension from a foreign power. At the same time, all Zurichers in foreign service were ordered home to swear an oath of obedience to the new ordinances.[32]

None of these measures was successful and the reasons for their failure are varied. In the first place, there were economic factors involved. The pope had not yet paid the Zurichers who had served him in Italy, and there were reports that citizens who had not received their wages were attracted to the French because they needed the money. In order to remove this economic inducement, the June mandate had promised that current negotiations with the Holy See would bring about a speedy payment of the funds. The failure of the Council to obtain the money led some to join the French, but the pope's refusal to pay helped to discredit pro-papal elements in the city. The Council saw the pope's delay as an effort to undermine the government's control over the citizens and did not hesitate to accuse him of attempting to foment discontent.

The negotiations with the pope continued on into 1525. Pope Hadrian VI and his successor, Clement VII, made various promises and excuses,

---

32. *E.A.*, 259, 282, 283, 293, 296, 352. Staehelin lists the November decree as a part of the Councils' attempt to stiffen its resistance to those who were attacking Zurich from various quarters (Staehelin, I, 252).

and, in response to the delay, Zurich tried to force a general discussion with Rome of matters of mutual concern, i.e., the reform, contingent upon the payment of the money due the city. A partial payment was finally made in January, 1523, but it was not enough to satisfy the Zurich councillors, and the tone of their correspondence became more harsh. A letter sent to Rome in April of 1523 suggested that the pope was delighted with the difficulties his failure to pay was causing the Zurich magistrates with their own people.[33]

If the contention of the Council was correct, then it appears that despite the official attitude of the See of Peter, the papacy, much like the other cantons, desired to discredit the Zurich government and was willing to see Zurich's citizens recruited for service even for the French, its enemy in Italy, in order to achieve this end.

In the face of the illegal departures from the city, the town fathers were driven to take even harsher measures. These measures should have stirred up further unrest which would have played into the hands of those anxious to unseat the government, but this did not happen either before or after the First Disputation. During both periods the Council issued decrees and attached stern penalties for those guilty of entering foreign armies; but considerations of domestic and foreign policy induced the magistrates to a lax enforcement of its laws. There are no cases reported in which the prescribed penalties were actually imposed. By constantly asserting its position and yet either ignoring or dealing leniently with those guilty of breaking the law, the Council prevented the wave of unrest in the canton from reaching a crest. Thus, the combination between the forces favouring the mercenary system and elements hostile to Zurich in the other cantons did not result in the collapse of the magistracy's authority. The Council was able to ride out the storm and to continue protecting Zwingli, and, for a time, to divert interest away from the mercenary problem towards the greater issues of the First Disputation.

Zwingli's most serious troubles came from the activity of the enthusiasts, still counted among his friends. The clarification of the city's attitude toward Zwingli's reforming principles, and of Zwingli's own position, which was achieved through the First Disputation, was as much an answer to the extremists of the reform party as it was to the conservatives. The Council's dealings with the radical faction among Zwingli's following, led by Conrad Grebel, have already been alluded to. Although the government's admonition to Grebel, delivered in July, may have restrained him and his friends for a time, the brief reference to those

33. *E.A.*, 259, 357.

earlier events contained in the September hearing of the Council indicate that Grebel's friends were for from satisfied with the slow course which the reform was taking.

Even during the late summer there is some reason to believe that the behaviour of individuals in sympathy with Grebel caused Zwingli to take counter-measures. Andreas Castelberger, a travelling book-seller from Graubünden who arrived at Zurich in the summer, encouraged the dissidents. Although Castelberger's association with Grebel can be proven only during the next year, the nature of his labours in the summer of 1522 makes it likely that he was in contact with the enthusiasts almost as soon as he arrived in the city. Although he was no trained theologian, he began to give public instruction concerning the scriptures. This work was certainly in keeping with the wishes of the extremists to spread the new faith and to hasten the completion of church reform. It was also just the sort of activity to which the conservatives pointed to substantiate their charge that Zwingli was a radical, bent on stirring up the masses and undermining public order. Egli suggests that Castelberger's unlicensed teaching and the danger of similar developments caused Zwingli to redouble his efforts to instruct the people through trained clergymen. When an opening came at St. Peter's Church, Zwingli lost no time in filling it with Leo Jud, a long-time friend and supporter.[34]

The potential danger from Castelberger and men like him was nothing compared to the situation which developed in the fall of 1522. A series of attacks on the established customs of the church were carried out against Zwingli's wishes by individuals who can be identified with the aims of the radical faction. Not all the incidents fit into a pattern, but several of the more important ones were directed against the payment of the "spiritual" tithes to the church. They represent the beginnings of a rising tide of anti-tithe feeling which culminated in the summer of 1523. They key to understanding these outbreaks lies in the interpretation of the tithe question. Grebel's friends were deeply involved in the tithe agitation, which they sincerely hoped to utilize to achieve a more complete purification of the church's cultic practices. Although Yoder and Bender deny it, Göters says that the radicals felt that the "spiritual" tithes which were paid for the support of the parish clergy were the economic basis for the cultic practices of the established church.[35] If

---

34. Egli, 66.
35. Göters, 33–4. Yoder claims that the Baptists accepted Zwingli's position that although a Christian should not receive tenths he should fulfil the obligation to pay them if it were imposed upon him, or if he inherited it. Speaking of the

they were abolished, the performance of the mass, along with the other cultic practices the enthusiasts considered abusive, would cease. The extremists were not concerned with social protest and raised the question of the tenths to achieve a thorough reform of the church.[36] The attacks on the tithes which took place in the fall of 1522 and early summer of 1523 also reflect a social protest and need not be identified with the aims of the radical party alone; but, as the evidence considered in this section shows, the purpose of the radicals' participation in them cannot be denied.

Konrad Frei of Watt refused to pay tithes to the church and was cited to appear before the Council on September 10, 1522. He informed the Council he was acting in accordance with the advice given by the Pastor from Höngg, Simon Stumpf, whose relations with the Bishop of Constance and the Zurich Council have already been mentioned. While preaching at Affoltern, Stumpf had informed his hearers that no one was obliged to pay tithes. Under pressure from the Council, Frei paid the tithes due to the Cathedral Chapter but refused to pay tithes to the Abbot of Wettingen because he objected to the way in which they were used. Frei was imprisoned and later set free after the Council had issued, on September 22, 1522, a policy statement directed towards all those who had failed to pay the tenths. It is clear from the Council's decree that Frei was not alone in his action and that the Council was forced to formulate an opinion which would apply to a general category of offenders. The nature of the policy evolved by the Council provides

---

unrest of the peasants during the summer of 1525 in Grüningen, Yoder maintains that Grebel and the other Baptists did not seek to ally their movement with that of the peasants (Yoder, 170). Yoder notes that Zwingli distinguished between the Baptists and the opponents of tithes when he wrote *Who Causes Tumult* in 1525 (*ibid.*, 17, 37). Yoder is correct. Zwingli did distinguish between the two groups, and they were essentially different but it does seem fair to conclude that the *Täufer* were willing to fish in troubled waters and sought to use the unrest of the peasants to win them to their interpretation of the Gospel. The fact that they pursued this policy after the break with Zwingli sheds light upon the relationship between the enthusiasts and the tithe agitation in Canton Zurich during 1522–23. Bender, who denies that there was an organized group of proto-Baptists among Zwingli's followers in 1523, asserts that Grebel took no part in the tithe agitation of 1523 (Bender, 86, 95–6). He believes that the compromise which later led Zwingli to embrace the principles of a state church began with his reaction to the tithe question in June, 1523. Zwingli's co-operation with the government caused a change to take place in the attitude of the "more aggressive part of the evangelical population toward him." From this time on this faction became increasingly restless and dissatisfied with Zwingli's policy (*ibid.*, 94–5). Bender's account fails to put Zwingli's attitude towards the magistracy in the context of the corporate theory of society and government which dominated affairs of the city.

36. Göters, 33–4.

further evidence that the unrest was general. The councillors commanded all those who had not paid the tenths to do so or be punished, but they allowed anyone who believed he had a legitimate grievance one year's grace to present the matter to them.[37] The fact the Council left room for negotiations indicates that the magistracy hesitated to cause further dissatisfaction by merely issuing a blanket order that the tithes be paid.

Because Frei based his refusal to pay upon Stumpf's sermon the case presents the first clear link between the enthusiasts and the tithe agitation. In the next year Stumpf played a leading role in the opposition to the tenths and then joined with Grebel to propose that a believers' church, independent of support by tithes, be set up.[38] He later clashed with Zwingli in the Second Disputation and, because of his preaching and other activities, was expelled from Zurich on December 23, 1523. Although there is no information available to attach Stumpf to Grebel before the summer of 1523, it might be added that representatives of his parish were among those invited to the gathering in Zwingli's honour in May of 1522 which the Council prevented.[39]

This much can be said. Both he and Grebel were involved in the tithes question during the summer of 1523. In view of their intimacy at that time, it does not seem too much to suggest they had been closely associated before 1523. If Göters' assumption concerning the aim of the tithes agitation, which Frei's evidence bears out, is correct, then it is plausible to suggest that Stumpf was carrying out a campaign in keeping with the aims of the radical faction. The campaign leads logically to the proposals of the summer of 1523, and, when the indirect approach to a reform of the cultus completely failed, to the struggle over the Mass and the images in the fall of 1523.

Several hearings which Egli does not date exactly, but which appear to have taken place at some time late in 1522, give further evidence of unrest over the tithes as well as opposition to Zwingli. The first is most significant because the connection between the tithes and the Mass was directly referred to by the participants. The Council heard a report of a clash between the Pastor at Bülach, Ulrich Rollenbutz, and members of his flock. Rollenbutz was told by his parishioners that both the tithes and the "sacrifice," i.e., the Mass, could go on no longer. The Pastor's reply summarized the traditionalist view of the reform movement: he

37. *E.A.*, 267, 273, 274.
38. *Q*, I, 120–1. The interpretation found in the text assumes that Grebel can be connected with a radical element which formed the nucleus of the future Baptist Church as early as 1522–23. For full discussion of the problem see *infra* chap. X.
39. *E.A.*, 246, 441, 446, 463.

asserted that Zwingli and all those who heeded his teachings were heretics.[40] The members of the congregation referred to the Mass and the tithes as abuses which should be ended.

A second investigation held about the same time reported a fist-fight between some of Zwingli's critics and a group of his supporters. The fight began when Konrad Felk and Hans Wyss, both clearly defenders of traditional religious practices, used obscene language in speaking of Zwingli's preaching and said that the "evangelicals," Zwingli's adherents, took each other's money. The second reference made by Felk was apparently directed at some of those who used Zwingli's preaching as an excuse not to pay tithes. The two culprits apologized for their language. Another incident reported to the Council seems to foreshadow the attacks upon the images which took place in September of 1523. Melchior Küefer, a supporter of the reform movement, was imprisoned for six days and given a warning by the Council for saying that "he wished to love God and excreted on the old and painted idols, which stand there in the church."

The last report to be considered here was heard by the Council on November 1, 1522. Though it is not directly pertinent to the tithes question, the hearing concerned Wilhelm Röubli, who later while pastor at Wytikon in 1523, was a leading opponent of tithe payments and finally became a Baptist.[41] Shortly before he was summoned by the Council, Röubli had been expelled from Basel on account of his radical preaching, violation of the fast, and attacks upon the worship of relics.[42] The Council cited him for violating the fast regulations, and Röubli excused himself for reasons of health. He was pardoned by the magistrates and advised that if his health required it, he could eat meat but he should do it in secret and not annoy others.[43] The incident appears harmless enough and, at this juncture, it is difficult to attach Röubli to the radical faction at Zurich. However, it should be noted that his action paralleled the behaviour of the extremists in the spring of 1522.

The incidents cited above do not offer conclusive proof of the link between Grebel, a pre-existing radical element, and the tithes issue, but they do make the assumption that such a union was present far more plausible. Stumpf was involved in the initial refusal to pay the tithes and

40. *E.A.*, 314. The fact that at Bülach opposition to the tithes and the Mass were linked together weakens Yoder's argument that the opponents of tithes were farmers and that the later *Täufer* had no connection with them or the opposition to tithes (Yoder, 17, 37).

41. *E.A.*, 315, 317, 378; *Q*, I, 10, 11, 36, 112, 391–2.

42. Göters, 31.

43. *E.A.*, 285.

later became a close adherent of Grebel. The tithes were mentioned on
one occasion in connection with the Mass, and the evidence seems to
bear out Göters' interpretation that the tithes issue was raised in order
to demand a reform of the cult. The name of one other person, Röubli,
later known to be among Grebel's following, also appears. On one occasion the images, which were later the object of so much extremist
attention, were abused.

A letter written by Zwingli to Vadian, Grebel's brother-in-law, on
December 22, indicates that Vadian felt that the progress of reform at
Zurich was too slow. Vadian's opinion may have been influenced by
Grebel, who was in close contact with him and whose "diligence," along
with that of his father, Zwingli praised in the letter. Zwingli's response
revealed that he did not consider further delay a serious problem.

Otherwise the work goes along nicely however somewhat more slowly than
you wish . . . and you are not ignorant of how difficult the first dangers may
be. However the delay won't matter very much for what we have seen of it
[the work] is, by Hercules, very satisfactory.[44]

Though what Vadian thought about the pace of reform cannot be
directly attributed to Grebel's influence, Zwingli's brief reference to the
diligence "of the Grebels" which came immediately before this passage
might reveal that Zwingli had Conrad Grebel in mind when he discussed
his feelings about further delay. Zwingli's answer does show that he was
pleased with the way things were going, and, in view of the dangers
inherent in the situation, that he was willing to accept the need to wait
in order to realize his goal. His attitude stands in sharp contrast to the
one expressed by Grebel when he appeared before the Council in July.

The Council tried to restrain the dissidents and maintain order and
the magistrates were not unsympathetic toward the protest. In dealing
with the problem the councillors permitted appeals, but made it clear
payment would be enforced. The Council fought to protect Stumpf from
the Bishop of Constance and from the Federal Diet by merely warning
him to cease advising the farmers not to pay tithes, and Röubli was also
treated with moderation. The Council's aim was to avoid further internal
disorder, so that neither the Bishop nor the Diet would have a reason
for complaint or for attempting a direct intervention in the affairs of
Canton Zurich.

44. Z, VII, 630, 5–9. The passage is difficult to interpret because, as the editor
notes, it is not clear to what the word "work" refers. The author assumes that
work is used to describe that reform movement at Zurich.

8   Zwingli's Position:
Late Spring and Summer, 1522

ALL OF THE PROBLEMS THE COUNCIL FACED DURING THE LAST half of 1522 can be attributed to the impact of Zwingli's attempt to renew the faith of the *respublica christiana*. The efforts of the Bishop of Constance, the Federal Diet, the pro-mercenary party, and those zealous for immediate reform failed either to alter the course of Zwingli's programme or to break up the alliance between him and the Zurich councillors because the initial agreement between the two parties remained unshaken. The Council was committed to the Bible as the ultimate religious authority and Zwingli continued to believe that the magistrates had the right to supervise the purification of the church. Without the help of the Council, Zwingli and his party could not have met the challenges presented to them.

It is with this in mind that his behaviour and writings during the summer and fall of 1522 must be interpreted. Despite continuing threats upon his life, Zwingli maintained his campaign against abuses in the church. In a letter from Ravensburg written on May 1, Michael Hummelberg warned him of a plot on his life and entreated him to be careful.[1] Zwingli centred his criticism upon the Mass practice, the sacrament of confession, and the abuse of the tithe system. He told the people that divine law did not require the payment of tithes.[2] However, he never denied the Council the right to enforce their payment. His position was in keeping with the argument he had used in the sermon *On the Freedom of Foods*, which stated that the Council could make laws governing the fast but could not impose these laws as eternal law.[3] When the Council ordered Frei and other violators to pay the tithes, it did not seek to justify the command on the basis of divine law. The magistrates gave an order which they had a right to do, and Zwingli made on objection to it. He merely attacked the false basis upon which the payments had been collected. In addition he also condemned the clergy's abuse of

1. Z, VII, 512, 22–3, 25–8.
2. Egli, 67.
3. Z, I, 134, 9–10, 24–5.

the tenths. This was the position later taken by the villages. They refused to pay church tithes because the gifts were misused and not because they did not want to pay tithes at all. Zwingli's attitude was consistent with the plan for Christian renewal which envisaged the transfer of wealth from the control of the clergy to that of the magistracy. This was the only way the clergy could be free to preach the Gospel.

Zwingli's condemnation of the established church should not blind us to the fact that he attempted to pursue a conciliatory policy towards the Bishop of Constance. Zwingli and the Council awaited the Bishop's response to their appeal for a statement of policy concerning the observance of fasts. He still hoped to win the Bishop, as well as the other Confederates, for his programme and was careful to distinguish between Hugo and the influential anti-Zwingli faction gathered around Faber.[4] The hope that the Bishop might be won, as well as the heightened tension produced by the Diet's debates at the end of May, led Zwingli to delay answering the Bishop's letters to the Council and Chapter.

Another event occupied Zwingli's attention in May and for a while aroused his hopes that Canton Schwyz might be won for the Gospel. The news of the French defeat at the battle of Bicocca had reached Switzerland. The disaster confirmed Zwingli's opposition to mercenary service and Zurich's decision to remain outside the French alliance of 1521. Schwyz had lost many soldiers in the battle and public opinion throughout the canton was stirred up against the mercenary system. Aware of this, Zwingli hurriedly wrote his *Godly Admonition to the Oldest Confederates at Schwyz*, which arrived in time for the cantonal assembly on May 16, 1522. Even had Bicocca not taken place, Zwingli and his successor at Cloister Einsiedeln, Leo Jud, had left a following behind them in the canton.[5] The Cloister was, for the moment, a centre from which Zwingli's teachings were being spread. Zwingli also had many friends among the political leaders of the canton and there was every reason to believe his appeal would find a hearing.

The *Admonition* reflects the religious dimension which had first entered Zwingli's patriotic writing in 1516.[6] He was not primarily concerned with winning Schwyz for a policy of neutrality; the patriotic element of his opposition to mercenary service was subordinated to his religious concern. He believed that knowledge of the Gospel was essential to the political well-being of the Swiss people, and he hoped to convert the people of Schwyz to the programme of church reform now

---

4. O. Farner, III, 282.   5. Z, I, 156.
6. Cf., pp. 33–4.

under way at Zurich.[7] No wonder the Bishop and the Diet were alarmed at the spread of Zwingli's influence in the Confederacy.[8]

The *Admonition* is an excellent early specimen of Zwingli's political theory, which was based upon a biblical theology. Throughout the tract he drew a parallel between the Schwyzer and the children of Israel; both are in a special covenant relationship with God, and both won their freedom with God's help.[9] Schwyz faces serious difficulties because the Schwyzer have lost sight of the image of God, a harmonious image of unity, in which they were created.[10] They have been defeated because they ceased to worship God and took pride in their own achievements thus inviting God's wrath.[11] Greed for money and the selfishness of those who put their own interests above the common good have brought them to this ruin.[12] Like all nations which rise to power by war, they have set out on a path leading to destruction by war.

Zwingli was careful to add that he did not advocate complete pacifism. In certain circumstances war was justified, as the example of Israel itself proved. The Israelites fought both those who sought to bar them from the promised land and those who later attempted to drive them out from that land. As far as Zwingli was concerned, the grounds for war were either the repulse of an invasion or the rectification of a wrong.[13] The people of Schwyz were not hopelessly doomed, Zwingli maintained. The misfortunes which beset them were a warning by a gracious God to change their hearts and to bring them back to him. Here again the parallel which Zwingli saw between the Schwyzer and Israel is manifest. As God acted in the past for Israel, so he now acts to save Schwyz.

Having discussed the basic cause of Schwyz's misery, its failure to worship and obey God, Zwingli analyzed the secondary consequences of the people's apostasy. Quoting Cicero, he reminded his readers that constant foreign wars undermine law and order.[14] Men are blinded by bribes which corrupt even the law courts, and they forget the responsibilities of government. Ultimately, there is a real danger that amidst the corruption engendered by the mercenary system the mercenaries themselves will take over the government. In the face of this danger

7. *Z*, I, 157.

8. A letter from Berchtold Haller at Bern, written to Zwingli in July, revealed that the Bernese were annoyed that Zwingli had singled out the Schwyzer for such special attention. It did, however, give an optimistic report concerning the progress of reform at Bern (*Z*, VII, 533, 13–19).

9. *Z*, I, 170, 26–171, 3.   10. *Ibid.*, 168, 1–5, 169, 8–25.

11. *Ibid.*, 172, 4–7, 11–24, 173, 10–20.

12. *Ibid.*, 173, 21–4; 174, 16–175, 4.   13. *Ibid.*, 177, 15–16, 21–4.

14. *Ibid.*, 178, 6–10; 179, 3–9.

and on the basis of canon law, Zwingli justified disobedience to governments subverted by bribes from the mercenary interest.[15]

A further danger which the people of Schwyz face is that wealth gained through the sale of soldiers abroad will sap the people's virility and lead to a general collapse of morality. To this yet another misfortune must be added: the wealth acquired from the mercenary system has stirred up hatred and mistrust among all the Swiss: " . . . pensions have brought forth great hate and mistrust among us."[16] Finally, because of their involvement in foreign wars, not only the people of Schwyz but the entire Confederacy faces the danger that a foreign power will take control of their country. Zwingli ended his appeal to Schwyz by returning to the opening theme of the *Admonition*: the only sure defence the Swiss have is God's protection. Once again stressing the similarity between the position of the Confederates and the children of Israel, he cited God's promise of help to those who obeyed him: "If you [the children of Israel] walk in my commandments and keep my command . . . I shall give you peace. You will pursue your foes; they will fall down before you."[17] His last words were a warning against the influence of foreign powers: "Guard yourself from foreign lords, Oh, Schwyz; they have brought you to dishonour."[18]

This tract, written on the eve of the church's counter-attack against Zwingli, makes his conception of the role of religion in society clear. The cantons of the Confederacy stand in a *covenant* relationship with God; they are the Israel of the present. Political stability and national freedom depend upon the proper obedience to the Lord. Zwingli's purpose is to restore the right relationship between the Swiss and their God, and, in this context, his role becomes prophetic; he is carrying on the tradition of the prophet of old who called Israel back to God. The return to God which Zwingli demanded had a direct bearing on all of society. Hence, it is difficult to believe, as some scholars assert, that during his earlier career, he thought of the church as a separate body in which the chosen remnant, the elect, could find refuge. The pamphlet also shows the scope of Zwingli's plans. In concentrating upon the situation at Zurich, it is easy to forget that the city was for him the first target in his reform programme. It was to be the model through which the rest of Switzerland and then Christian Europe were to be called back to God.

The *Admonition* had the desired effect upon the Schwyzer, and the

15. *Ibid.*, 180, 4–7, 21–181, 5; 181, 9–17.
16. *Ibid.*, 183, 5–11, 16–18; 184, 10–11.
17. *Ibid.*, 185, 6–9.   18. *Ibid.*, 187, 15–18; 188, 12–13.

cantonal assembly decided to remain outside any foreign alliance for the next 25 years. However, what appeared to be a victory for Zwingli and a favourable omen for the prospects of reform in the canton proved to be an illusion. The pro-mercenary party regrouped and, aided by their supporters in the other cantons, was able to reverse the May decision in August.[19] The part which Zwingli's appeal played in the original decision of the Schwyzer no doubt frightened those loyal to the old church and stimulated their opposition to his programme.

June passed quietly enough. Zwingli still had hopes that he could win the Bishop and reports such as Haller's letter from Bern which announced that "The Christian affair gathers strength rapidly" kept coming in.[20] As July began the quiet ended. Two days before Bishop Hugo approached the Diet and gained its support for his programme of opposition to the Christian renewal, Zwingli and a number of his followers, including Leo Jud and Simon Stumpf, gathered at Einsiedeln. Under Zwingli's direction they framed a Latin petition to Bishop Hugo (*Supplicatio ad Hugonem episcopum Constantiensem*) which requested that he permit the Gospel to be preached freely and the clergy to marry. Simon Stumpf, Zwingli, and ten other men, all of whom were already married, signed the document, but for reasons of policy many others did not.[21] The signers came from the cantons of Zurich, Zug, Schwyz, and Lucerne, which indicates how far Zwingli's teaching had spread.[22] On July 13 a second petition, enlarged and written in German, appeared. The publication of the plea in German under the title *Eine Freundliche Bitte und Ermahnung an die Eidgenossen* made sure that Bishop Hugo, who had difficulty with Latin, knew what the *Supplicatio* requested.[23] The second petition was addressed to the Confederacy and bore no signatures.

The reasons for the publication of two petitions are difficult to assess. As far as the first is concerned, Zwingli probably still believed the Bishop might be favourably inclined to it. By the time the second appeared the results of the Bishop's appeal to the Diet at Baden were known and Zwingli's hopes were dashed. August Baur says that Zwingli and his friends realized that the petition had little chance of success but they issued it to show their determination to continue preaching. The fact that the second petition bore no signatures may have been due to this realization. The propaganda value of both petitions, especially the second, was enhanced by the appeal to the secular authorities for

19. *Ibid.*, 157, 158.
20. Z, VII, 533, 16–17.
21. O. Farner, III, 285.
22. Köhler, 86.
23. O. Farner, III, 295.

aid. The petitions left no doubt that the reformers desired religious change to be carried out in an orderly fashion and reflected Zwingli's positive attitude towards the magistrates. Baur suggests that Zwingli's appeal to the governments of the cantons for help and protection, though genuine enough itself, was also motivated by other factors. The conservatives asserted that Zwingli's movement was revolutionary and they sought to substantiate their claims by citing the disorders at Zurich. Zwingli stressed the legitimacy of his movement by affirming his desire to gain the co-operation of established governments. The petitions imply that the government has the right to institute reforms when the church fails to do so.[24] This assumption reveals that the already established traditions of city government had a direct bearing upon the principles which guided the Zurich magistrates. After the failure of their appeal to the Bishop the magistrates called the First Disputation on their own authority.

The petitions appeared at the same time that the Council censured Grebel and his sympathizers for their provocative behaviour. The stress upon co-operation with legitimate authority so apparent in these appeals may have been directed towards the extremists at Zurich. The petitions made Zwingli's position clear to them, for he left no place for individuals to introduce changes without the approval of the government.

The request for the freedom to preach the Gospel was more important than the demand for permission to marry. The right to preach from the Bible laid the groundwork for a reform of dogma and cult, and made possible a gradual transition from a traditional to a reformed order of worship. A method was laid down whereby this transition might be achieved. First, via instruction from the pulpit, a following was won and an atmosphere favourable to change created. As the understanding of the congregation was deepened, modifications in the cult could be introduced. This procedure commended itself to secular governments like the Zurich magistracy which could not afford to support an immediate change in the religious observance of the community.

In seeking approval for the marriage of the clergy, the petitioners sought to regularize the existing practice of clerical concubinage which the Bishop of Constance sanctioned in return for the payment of fees which netted him a considerable sum.[25] However, the request for

24. Baur, I, 109, 115–16.
25. McNeill, 14. Priests paid the Bishop 4 *gulden* a year for the right to keep a concubine. Each child born out of this union required the payment of 4 (later 5) *gulden*. It is estimated that about 1,500 children were born each year in such unions (Z, I, 225).

clerical marriage, though justified by the status of the signers, weakened the force of the petition. It was at best a secondary question in comparison with the basic demand for greater freedom to preach the Gospel and only provided another reason to assert that Zwingli's attack upon the customs of the church was revolutionary. Zwingli doubtlessly wished to seek sanction for his own marriage and the marriages of his followers but, if this were the only reason, it is surprising that he did not announce his own status.[26] Most scholars agree that the legal difficulties over his wife's inheritance and his desire to avoid public offence at this time led him to keep his marriage secret until April of 1524.[27] These reasons are valid but they make it more difficult to understand why he permitted the request to be included in the petition.

It is possible that the plea was included in the supplication as a concession to the enthusiasts. Zwingli's rejection of their individualistic activity which is manifest in the *Supplicatio*, as well as in the rebuke which the Council had delivered to them, called for just such a concession to prevent a split in the reform party. At the same time the context of the request, emphasizing as it did the need for official sanction of clerical marriage, made Zwingli's desire for orderly reform clear to the extremists of his own party. Simon Stumpf's presence among the signers could indicate the conciliatory purpose. It may also have eased Zwingli's conscience concerning his own marriage which was an example of the very individual action that he claimed to deplore among his followers. His marriage must have been known to Grebel and have given him good reason to believe that, despite his public utterances, Zwingli really favoured the type of action in which Grebel and his friends engaged.

In the Latin version of the *Supplicatio* Zwingli reminded the Bishop that the Gospel was shamefully neglected. Rather than persecute those who preached it, the Bishop should forward the cause of Christian unity by supporting them. Zwingli then defined in biblical terms the nature of the Bishop's office. The Bishop's duty was to preach God's Word and, to illustrate his point, Zwingli reminded the Prelate of the parallel between his task and the function of the prophets. The prophets reminded the Israelites of God's covenant with them and the Bishop should do the same for the Swiss.[28]

The passage re-affirms Zwingli's conception of the clergy's task, to

---

26. The exact date of Zwingli's marriage is unknown. At some time in the spring of 1522, he married the widow of Meyer von Knonau, the former Anna Reinhard.

27. O. Farner, III, 289–91.

28. Z, I, 198, 24–35; 199, 28–200, 8.

preach the Gospel, and re-emphasizes the fact that for him the Gospel applied to the whole nation. The terms in which the clergy's office was defined carried with them a total rejection of the hierarchical church, and the constitutive element in gathering the people together to form the body of Christ, the church, was the preaching of the Word and not the offices and external structure of the church. The description of the clergy's task foreshadows the creation of the preaching post at Zurich the following November, the logical outcome of Zwingli's interpretation of the clergy's function. The second portion of the Latin petition was concerned with the attempt to obtain official sanction to put an end to clerical celibacy. The crux of Zwingli's argument was historical; neither Christ nor the Fathers imposed total chastity. Christ left the matter free, "lest they should smear the sweet yoke of the Lord with wormwood."[29]

The German edition of the *Supplicatio* repeated the same arguments but with a different emphasis. From the greeting, in which the petitioners offered their "obedient, willing service and submission in the Lord Jesus Christ" to the political leaders of the Confederacy, to the end of the petition, Zwingli's desire was to assure his critics that there was nothing socially revolutionary in his efforts.[30] He defined exactly what he believed the New Testament message was. Baur notes that Zwingli's foes did not understand what he meant by the Gospel and tended to misunderstand his purpose.[31] The definition which Zwingli gave sought to allay their doubts. However, regardless of what he said, at a time when religious and political affairs were so completely intertwined, it was quite natural for his foes to remain unconvinced. They assumed that an attack upon the established practices of the church was necessarily a call for political revolution. Zwingli reiterated his belief that the Gospel held the key to the solution of the Confederacy's problems, and his words reflect the climate of opinion in the Confederacy. He was speaking to a society which still sought to be a *res publica christiana* and he could assume that no Confederate wished to oppose God's Word.

In the process of pleading for the freedom to preach the Gospel, Zwingli touched upon the false preaching so common at the time. He complained that preaching of this kind was concerned with payments of interest and tenths and opened the clergy to the suspicion of greed. He was careful to qualify this statement: "Not that an honourable, needy priesthood should not be supported with alms, tenths and other

29. *Ibid.*, 202, 25–8.   30. *Ibid.*, 214, 8–9.
31. Baur, I, 109.

things."[32] These words reveal his attitude towards the tithe question and demonstrate the difference between Zwingli, Grebel, and Stumpf, both of whom, in 1523, called for the establishment of a church unsupported by tithes. His remarks also anticipate the nature of the tithe opposition at Zurich, which centred upon the abuse of the tithes by the clerical estate, and also point towards the re-organization of the Cathedral Chapter in the fall of 1523. As a result of the re-organization, the funds derived from the tithes were retained to support teaching and charitable functions which Zwingli thought were the rightful objects of such payments.

Lest there be any further misunderstanding of the purpose behind the appeal for permission to preach the Gospel, Zwingli repeated that it was made for the good of the whole Confederacy. His statement refuted the charge that his programme was revolutionary and illustrated once again the connection between his patriotism and his scheme for Christian renewal. He warned his opponents that the labour which he had undertaken would continue, despite all opposition. The reason was simple; God was to be obeyed before men: "for we may speak, as the apostles spoke, when at Jerusalem they were forbidden to preach about Jesus . . . ; one must be more obedient to God than to men."[33] These words are the basis for his justification of resistance to a tyrannical government. Some of his readers may well have regarded him as a revolutionary.

Continuing in the same vein, Zwingli treated the opposition's attempts to silence with the charges of Lutheranism those who preached God's Word. Zwingli said he was not a Lutheran, but admitted that if he and Luther derived their doctrine from the same source, then they shared the same teaching: "If he has drunk there, where we have drunk, then he has the Gospel teaching in common with us."[34] Zwingli's consistent denial of the charge of Lutheranism was both a matter of truth and a matter of necessity for the defence of the reform movement at Zurich. Though his argument did not convince those loyal to the old church, it continued to be useful in making a full scale attack upon Zurich more difficult.

Zwingli's insistence that he merely preached the Gospel, which the canon law itself required, offered further assurance to the Confederates he was no firebrand who ignored public order. This is the theme to which he next turned his attention. He had already had difficulties with his own followers, whose lawless behaviour had focussed unfavourable

32. *Z*, I, 221, 6–12, 12–14.   33. *Ibid.*, 223, 28–30, 34–224, 3.
34. *Ibid.*, 224, 11–12.

attention on Zurich. There is no mistaking his hostile attitude towards the incautious preaching of rash individuals:

But where someone is importune in proclaiming the Gospel, it is well to remember, that it is not wrong when the same is commanded to be silent. But this we do not wish to do at all, if God wills; rather, we wish to proclaim the Gospel with all faithfulness and diligence for the good of the faithful.[35]

Zwingli distinguished between the right and the wrong way to proclaim God's Word, and the distinction was made as much for the benefit of the extremists as it was to re-assure the Confederates. It reminded radical and conservative alike that the only purpose in preaching the Bible was to serve the well-being of all Christians.

The second part of the German version of the petition repeated the arguments against clerical celibacy. Zwingli castigated severely the greed which sanctioned the violation of celibacy in exchange for a money payment. In order to condemn the practice of clerical celibacy he cited Christ, Paul's words, the practice of the early church, and the canons of the Council of Gangra (c. A.D. 340), which called for the marriage of the clergy.[36]

His argument for the validity of the Council of Gangra's canons summarizes his idea of the relationship between the authority of scripture and that of the church. He accepted the Council's decisions because they were made in accordance with the Gospel and the teachings of the Apostles, a fact which he regarded as proof that the Holy Spirit had been present to guide the assembly: "If the Council of Gangra was gathered in the Holy Spirit, as it was, since it has acted in accordance with the Gospel and apostolic teaching, why have those who came after, who have annulled the law without Scriptural cause, not let the same remain?"[37] For Zwingli, the authority of the church gathered in council was valid when the assembly obeyed scripture. The Council's subordination to the Bible guaranteed it the inspiration of the Holy Spirit. Thus the authority of the church depended upon its proper use of the scriptures and, according to Zwingli's words, apostolic teaching. This conception was the basis upon which the Zurich Council felt justified in accepting the decisions of the First Disputation. The Disputation complied with the requirements for a valid council; scripture and the teachings of the Apostles were referred to, so presum-

35. *Ibid.*, 224, 28–225, 2.
36. *Ibid.*, 228, 30–229, 5, 15–22; 230, 7–11; 231, 4–11, 19–27, 232; 8–11; 234, 5–8.
37. *Ibid.*, 234, 14–18.

ably the Holy Spirit was present. The magistracy no longer had to refer to the representative of the old church before reforming the institutions of the local ecclesiastical establishment.

Zwingli's theory not only offered a conception of religious authority which fitted the tradition of local autonomy so dear to the hearts of the individual cantons, but it also demonstrated that he had a strong sense of history. Unlike the Baptists a few years later, he did not call for a return to the norms of the early church; he called only for a return to the traditions of the church which were derived from the proper sources: scripture and apostolic teaching illuminated by the Holy Spirit. He demanded that all the present institutions of the church be scrutinized by this standard and, where they failed to live up to it, that they be altered according to its requirements.

To explain his attitude towards the traditions of the church more fully, Zwingli examined the right of other councils to set aside the canons of the Council of Gangra. He concluded they could not set them aside because the Council of Gangra had acted in keeping with the norms of scripture: "When one examines the Council of Gangra, it can suffer the probe, for it has conformed to the divine sanction, therefore it has to remain, and that which does not conform to the divine will, should without doubt not remain."[38] In the summation of his argument Zwingli discussed what the results of the failure of the petition would be. In the event the Bishop rejected it, Zwingli asserted that he and his party would exercise the right of self-help. He suggested, first, that even if the Bishop did not heed the appeal, he might still wish to defend Zwingli and his friends from the reprisals of the pope or the clergy. Then if the Bishop refused to do this, the reformers would defend themselves "with the solace and refuge of the Scripture." He added that if the scripture did not support their cause, they would expect to take the consequences.[39] He revealed his faith in the justice of his cause and his willingness to stand correction if he misused the Bible.

Zwingli's belief that scripture offered him a secure refuge must be seen in connection with the Zurich Council's acceptance of its authority. As long as Zwingli could defend his policy with the Word, he could depend upon the Council. Since he and the magistrates had access to the ultimate source of religious authority, they were free to direct the affairs of the church in the canton. The First Disputation spelled out what Zwingli meant when he referred to the right of self-help via an appeal to the authority of the scripture. The section devoted

38. *Ibid.*, 235, 20–3.   39. *Ibid.*, 246, 21–6.

to the problem, in the summary of the petition, provided the theoretical ground-work for the Council's action in January, 1523.

In order to press his demand for the Bishop's protection, Zwingli reminded him that Swiss tradition called for the defence of those threatened with wrong. In this case, he argued, the Bishop's protection of the petitioners who desired an end to clerical celibacy was more than justified, because many of the cantons already obliged a priest to take a mistress so that he would leave the other women of his parish alone.[40] This was also a reminder to the Confederates that the demand for the marriage of the clergy was not far removed from the actual practice. It re-affirmed the fact Zwingli was no radical.

Zwingli closed the petition with the promise that married clergymen would not try to pass their prebends on to their sons. He also vowed, if the request were granted, that the clergy would subject their marriage plans to the supervision of the government.[41] The latter stipulation illustrated once again the importance which Zwingli placed upon the position of the government in the affairs of the church. He was, above all, anxious to show that married priests would be good citizens, an approach which may not have appealed to the Bishop.

On August 10, 1522, Bishop Hugo issued the mandate calling for the Confederacy to repress the reform movement. There was no longer any question about winning Hugo to the cause of reform, and it remained for Zwingli to strengthen his defences. The Zwinglians were not slow to answer the Bishop. The clergy of the Zurich countryside gathered at Rapperswil on August 19 and agreed to preach nothing but the scriptures. The agreement was evidence of the support Zwingli enjoyed in the canton. This move was followed by the publication of the *Apologeticus Archeteles* (August 23), which was a delayed answer to the Bishop's letters of May 24, and appeared with the official sanction of the Council. Though there was little hope of gaining the Bishop's support, Zwingli still maintained a friendly attitude towards him in the *Apologeticus*.

Before considering the *Apologeticus*, it is important to know what Zwingli's attitude was at the time. The best source for such information comes from Zwingli's replies to Myconius' anxious letters announcing his expulsion from Lucerne. He advised Myconius to gain the support of the Lucerne Council by refuting the charge that he was a Lutheran:

". . . that you [Myconius] should go to the senate and there make a speech, worthy of Christ and of you; that is of such a kind, which is able to prick

---

40. *Ibid.*, 247, 3–8, 10–13.
41. *Ibid.*, 248, 4–10.

them, not excite [them], and one which blames none, not alone not by name but not even by way of suggestion, [one which] denies you are a Lutheran, but asserts you are a Christian. . . ."[42]

The policy of a firm but moderate stand in the face of opposition was the means by which Zwingli had succeeded in maintaining his alliance with the Zurich Council. What requires stress is the importance that he placed upon winning the good will of the magistrates. A second reason for Zwingli's counsel was his desire to hold Lucerne for the reformed cause. He was determined to expand the movement and believed that it was still possible to do so. He told Myconius: "Lucerne must not be deserted, unless you are forced [to] by extreme danger."[43]

His next letter, written on August 26, repeated the same theme. To give heart to Myconius, Zwingli defined the whole purpose of the Christian renewal: those engaged in the struggle to introduce it do not seek an earthy home, but rather seek to prepare for citizenship in the Heavenly City: "for we do not have a city here, in which it is given to remain perpetually, but we seek a future [city]. . . ."[44] No passage could demonstrate more clearly the theocentric conception of human life and society. All human goals were subordinated to the purpose or reaching the Heavenly City. In this sense the society of the sixteenth century was dominated by a theocratic ideal.

The *Apologeticus* was an officially sanctioned statement of the reformed faith. The fact that it was issued with the approval of the government bears out the assertion that Zwingli's views on the relationship between the church and the magistracy remained consistent during his first years at Zurich. He began by asserting the primacy of divine things over human and cited the failure of most bishops to fulfil the requirements of their office. He refuted Hugo's charge that he was destroying the unity of the church by claiming that he was attempting to renew it through simple preaching, comprehensible to the Swiss.[45] The stress on simple preaching easily understood, repeated the suggestion found in the second July petition and earlier, that the old church had failed to meet the needs of the Swiss people.

As he had done in the *Ermahnung* of July 13, Zwingli summed up the message of the Gospel and then used the summary to question the sacramental function of bishop and priest: "I do not consider that, if the occasion so demands, I have any need for a Bishop, or a priest, who

42. *Z*, VII, 566, 7–11.
43. *Ibid.*, 566, 26–7.
44. *Ibid.*, 569, 5–6.
45. *Ibid.*, 278, 28–33; 279, 14–17; 280, 4–6, 14–24; 285, 29–286, 1.

may give satisfaction for me, for Christ has already made it."[46] In other words, Zwingli is saying that if the services of the clergy are denied him, probably as a result of an interdict, he does not believe that he has need of them. The statement implies a denial of the sacramental function of the clergy. When he answered the Bishop's warning against false prophets a few paragraphs later, he denied anyone the right to claim that they controlled Christ's presence. Those who said that Christ was here or there and showed his presence by false signs and miracles were the false prophets. He cited Matthew 18:20 which contains Christ's promise that wherever two or three are gathered together in his name, he is with them.[47] The two passages point up a central motif in Zwingli's thought: they stress God's power to act and man's inability to control the activities of the Godhead. Implicit in Zwingli's statements, especially against those who claim to be able to reveal Christ's presence by signs or miracles, is a denial that the priesthood depenses Christ's body and grace via the sacrament. This line of thought threatened one of the constitutive elements in the traditional doctrine of the church.

These views had practical application. The priesthood's claim that it alone could preside over the re-enactment of Christ's sacrifice and bring an infusion of grace to sinful man was the basis for the clergy's hold upon the laity and for its demand for special status in society. Ultimately, Zwingli freed laymen from dependence upon the clergy for the benefits of God's grace and prepared the way for the redefinition of the clergy's function later expressed in the establishment of the preaching office. Zwingli's reasoning deprived the priesthood of the opportunity to amass wealth and secular power, and consequently denied them the means to pose a threat or hindrance to the authority of the secular government. Though, in practice, the Council had stripped away most of the clergy's power and wealth before Zwingli began his work, the theoretical basis for them had remained. Now Zwingli sought to remove even this, so that the clergy would perform the only task which the scripture allowed it: the proclamation of the Gospel. There are parallels between Zwingli's conception of the clergy's role and that of Marsilio and Occam. Zwingli, like Marsilio, thought in terms of a city republic but his conclusions concerning the clergy's role were less radically secular. His use of scripture, his conception of the relationship between scripture and tradition, and his view of the hierarchy differed from Occam's, but he and Occam were agreed upon what the primary task of the clergy was.

46. *Ibid.*, 286, 17–19.
47. *Ibid.*, 288, 14–20.

In the *Apologeticus* Zwingli elaborated his conception of the clergy's office and clarified two other problems relevant to the place of the church and magistrate in society. Bishop Hugo had warned those who led the people away from the church that they would be left to perish outside of the church without their Bishops. Zwingli agreed, but made his agreement contingent upon the proper definition of the Church of Christ and who true bishops were. As he saw the matter, they were those who were installed according to the rule which Paul had laid down for Timothy and Titus.[48]

A little later the Bishop gave Zwingli the opportunity to explain the connection between the church and the Gospel. Hugo said he was willing to permit the Gospel to be preached, as long as the message did not remove anyone from the unity of the church, for if the unity of the church were broken the Gospel could not exist. Referring to the period of the Arian heresy, Zwingli demolished the Bishop's argument. At that time, he noted that both the Orthodox and the Arians quoted the Gospel, which proved that it did exist while there was division in the Church. Zwingli then drew the logic of this assertion to its natural conclusion: "Therefore the church which rightly believes and has the Gospel is able to exist, even if it does not have the Roman pontiff. . . ."[49] Continuing to attack those who wished to exalt human traditions above the Gospel, he criticized the position taken by Augustine when he had said "I should not believe the Gospel, if the church had not approved the Gospel."[50] According to Zwingli, it was an open question whether Augustine spoke more audaciously or more imprudently. The crux of Zwingli's counter-argument appeared in his definition of what the Gospel was: ". . . thus far, however, the Gospel was the good messenger of God's grace, 'til now it was the agreement [*commercium*] which God entered upon by his grace with the lost race of men. . . ."[51] He then denied that the Gospel depended upon any man or Council and castigated such a view as the greatest impiety; divine matters do not receive authority from men, but rather "are born from the mouth of God."[52]

The use of the convenant idea marks the difference between his understanding and the Bishop's of the Gospel's place in the church. For Zwingli, the Gospel is the account of God's promise to men; it provides the constitutive element for the church of Christ. The church is subordinate to its norms and hence directly dependent upon God's authority.

---

48. *Ibid.*, 267, 10–13; 290, 32–4.
49. *Ibid.*, 267, 21–2; 292, 17–23; 293, 1–2.
50. *Ibid.*, 293, 6–7. Zwingli's version of Augustine's statement was not accurate but rendered the sense correctly.
51. *Ibid.*, 293, 8–12.   52. *Ibid.*, 293, 27; 294, 11–14.

The Bishop's assertion that the Gospel can not exist without the unity of the church, which finds tangible expression in obedience to the pope and hierarchy, was unacceptable to Zwingli. In Zwingli's opinion the Bishop placed the Gospel under the authority of an institution founded upon the precepts of men rather than the commands of God.

The elucidation of Zwingli's conception of the Gospel's authority which followed reveals that he was not a literalist. Quoting the passages of canon law which condemned Marcion and Basilides, he said ". . . the Gospel is not in the words of the scriptures, but in the sense; not in the surface, but in the marrow, not in the pages of words, but in the root of the meaning." The reference to the canon law was followed by a citation from Paul's Epistle to the Romans (Romans 1:18): "The Gospel of Christ is the strength of God for the salvation for all who believe."[53] His position on this question is consistent with the tradition found among the church fathers, especially Origen, whom Zwingli had studied, and follows the one which Erasmus had taken.[54] As Zwingli's distinction between word and "sense" reveals, it is not a view of scripture which inevitably leads to literalism.

After explaining that the rock upon which the church was built was not Peter but Christ, Zwingli denounced the pope's usurpation of Christ's place in the church, and then turned to examine how the pope's and the bishop's office had been abused. According to the canon law, the bishops were to administer "the bread of the heavenly Word" to the churches in their care, but they had failed to do this. Instead, in violation of the law of the church and Christ's precepts, they seek wealth, wage wars, mix in secular affairs, and presume to act as judges in worldly cases that do not concern their office.[55]

Bishop Hugo had complained that the attack upon the church's traditions was not in accord with piety. Zwingli responded that past traditions could be reverenced only when they were in harmony with the tenets of the Gospel and the Apostles. As an example he compared the biblical grounds for excommunication with the contemporary use of it as a means of forcing repayment of loans, and warned that once the people became aware of the abuse, they would no longer tolerate it. In the same vein he attacked the use of ceremonials and the penitential system for financial gain.[56]

He answered in detail Hugo's claim, contained in propositions 41 and

---

53. *Ibid.*, 294, 22–4, 33–4.
54. Spitz, 218, 217–18, 220, 234; cf. Yoder, 24.
55. Z, I, 295, 19–25, 33–296, 6; 296, 24–8, 32–9; 297, 4–6, 10–16.
56. *Ibid.*, 267, 29–32; 300, 13–15; 19–21, 23–35; 302, 16–24.

42, that ceremonies and practices could be devised from the traditions of the Apostles and general councils. Repeating the argument concerning the authority of the councils employed in the petition of July 13, Zwingli suggested that their canons be re-examined according to the standards of the Bible. Those in harmony with the divine law contained in the Word should be retained and the others set aside. To emphasize the danger in relying upon usages sanctioned by men, he reminded the Bishop of Christ's warning that what is revered by men is an abomination before God. He used such terms as *testimonium dei* (testimony of God) and *divina lex* (divine law) interchangeably with *scriptura sancta* (Holy Scripture) which demonstrated the reformed doctrine of biblical authority. The Bible is the standard by which the councils and canons of the church are to be judged, not because of the written word found upon its pages, but because the power of God stands behind it. He reaffirmed this when he explained that when he spoke of scripture, he did not mean the letter which killed but the spirit which gave life.[57]

The articles considered thus far have been concerned with theological questions, but these issues had direct bearing upon the political situation in the entire Confederacy. In articles 44 to 49, Hugo of Hohenlandenberg, Bishop of Constance, noted this fact. He said that the attack upon the traditions and ceremonies of the church by rash individuals menaced "all political order."[58] Zwingli also saw the connection but interpreted the situation differently. He spoke of the Gospel's relation to national life in terms of a covenant ideal and insisted that God chose nations for specific purposes. Doom awaits those nations who fail to fulfil their appointed task:

And you, Oh, Germany, whose vigorous and bold heart I have drawn away from the tumults of wars to true piety, and made rich with all kinds of teachings . . . that you may wisely, fitly, purely proclaim . . . the religion defiled with filth by some. Whether on account of this thing which you have indeed begun, your praise will be exalted to the heavens, [if] you in truth will not have carried it through to the end? Not in the least! You shall be thrust down to hell, because you have neglected the light coming into the world . . . in truth, a more mild judgment shall befall the unbelieving citizens of Sodom than to you. . . .[59]

The passage reflects very clearly the setting in which Zwingli lived and thought. The cause of reform is a national issue and not merely a matter of individual salvation. A national policy based upon the Gospel guaranteed security to the people, which, in turn, guaranteed salvation

57. *Ibid.*, 303, 4–10; 305, 8, 19–21, 25, 27, 28–31; 306, 4–9.
58. *Ibid.*, 268, 2–10.
59. *Ibid.*, 307, 24–30; 308, 1–2.

to individuals who were subordinate to the community. It was not the individual's task to save the nation, but rather the nation's task to save the individual by choosing the right religion. Zwingli's perspective has much more in common with the prophetic themes of the Old Testament and the view of society found in the classical tradition of Greece and Rome than it does with the modern mind, which is influenced by the individualism of classical liberal political theory, as well as by the emphasis upon personal salvation engendered by a Protestant pietism.

Although in the immediate context Zwingli's use of *Germania* applies to the Confederacy, *Germania* can be employed with reference to the German nation, and its appearance here indicates the wide scope of Zwingli's reform plan. The hostility to foreign wars mirrored in Zwingli's words reveals the influence of Erasmian humanism upon his thinking. However, the major significance of the statement lies in the intimate connection which he made between reform and the welfare of the nation.

He pressed his case for the abolition of ceremonies which were not in keeping with the scripture. He argued that if eventually the ceremonies must be abrogated, there was no reason for not doing so immediately, and he lamented that this was impeded only by the greed and corruption of the bishops.[60] His anger at the greed of the hierarchy was nothing new, and his impatience with the delay in the reform of the ceremonies was significant, for undoubtedly Grebel's circle was encouraged to assume that Zwingli would stand with them in the next phase of their effort to push for the rapid completion of reform at Zurich. The concept of biblical authority which Zwingli elaborated and used to destroy the foundations of the hierarchy's power provided both a summary of his previous teaching and a blueprint for further reform. Grebel and many others must have seen this clearly and have waited eagerly for him to act.

As Zwingli continued his reply, the way in which he wanted the changes in the ceremonies to be made was explained. He was one with Bishop Hugo in assuming that the proper observance of the faith was necessary to the welfare of the society, but he argued that his programme of biblical preaching served the interests of the commonwealth better than the Bishop's, which was based upon the shaky foundations of human reason:

But indeed this our city is the most Christian of all [and] is adapted to it [the Christian faith]. It appears in the laws and the magistrates of the people; it [the influence of the Christian faith causes men to pay] pays tribute to whom it is due; it pays tax to whom [it is due] and no man calls

---

60. *Ibid.*, 308, 5–6, 12–15.

anything his own, but all things are considered in common; each desires to anticipate the other with kindness, to oblige with gentleness, to share the labour of the other, to lighten his burden, for each cares for all as brothers; blasphemy is abominated, piety is esteemed and is increased among all.

Wherein, that I may draw together all things briefly, you have received into the canon, that writing inspired of God that is the Scripture . . . divinely inspired, which remains forever unshaken; but the writing of bishops can be rejected . . . not alone by councils, but also by anyone who is more learned, if indeed they should differ from those [the scriptures].[61]

The two passages quoted show Zwingli's purpose. The first passage reveals that he desired to put religion on a theocentric basis and describes how the influence of the Gospel served the interests of the community. The section foreshadows the main themes of the sermon *On Divine and Human Righteousness* and indicates the optimism of his political thought. Not only does the Evangel encourage men to filfil the obligations of citizenship by paying taxes but it also produces a moral attitude which transforms the relationship of men to their property and to their fellow citizens. Those who possess property view it as a responsibility which they administer for the good of all.[62] If Zwingli had not explained what he meant when he said that all things were thought of in common, his words might be interpreted as a description of Christian communism. They are not. The passage illustrates his faith in the power of the Gospel to transform the attitude of men towards their property, their neighbour, and existing institutions. It helps to explain why he later said that where the Gospel was preached the city was nothing else but the Christian church.[63] When Zwingli's statement is considered within the context of his twofold doctrine of righteousness, it demonstrates how well his conception of the impact which the Gospel would have upon the city fitted the requirements of the corporate view of society which dominated Zurich. The message of Christ led men to exceed the mere dictates of human law and to improve the standard of life in the whole community, thereby serving the common good, as well as the will of God.

Zwingli's boast that a Bible-centred faith upheld the laws and the magistrates also reveals the factors which automatically limited his impatience to remove abusive ceremonies. Changes which were made had to conform to the laws of the city and could not threaten the

61. *Ibid.*, 308, 38–309, 5; 213, 2–6.
62. Locher, 35–6. Locher's general interpretation of Zwingli's attitude towards private property and the effect of the Gospel in transforming the traditional attitude towards it is presupposed in this analysis.
63. *Ibid.*, 32.

welfare of the community. None of the advantages resulting from the proclamation of the Gospel were available from man-made religious decisions. He took great pains to illustrate the unreliability of such decisions, which in turn proved that they could not serve the needs of the city.

Zwingli also reminded the Bishop in his answer to article 53 of the Bishop's letter that the Gospel leads men "to a sure harbour of salvation."[64] If one examines his logic, it becomes apparent that he replaced the traditional conception of sure salvation within the external structure of the church by sure salvation in the harbour of a spiritual church whose only tangible focal-point was the Gospel. If there is a weakness in his idea of the church it is his tendency to neglect the external vehicle, which must guarantee the preaching of the Gospel. After all, the institutional development of the old church was, to a great extent, the product of a defensive reaction to the encroachments of a hostile, secular world. But Zwingli believed that society and the magistrates were potentially Christian.

His definition of the clergy's office and his doctrine of salvation must be seen in connection with his earlier discussion of the Gospel's effect upon civic affairs. The city state is the frame of reference within which Zwingli evolved his theories concerning the relationship between Gospel, clergy, and salvation. He assumed that the society of the city state provided the object and the framework which made possible the proclamation of the Gospel. His assumption represented the confluence of both a historical process which had taken place at Zurich before he arrived and a tradition of critical thought which demanded that the activity of the clergy be confined to the concerns of the spirit. He spoke from the practical circumstances of the situation at Zurich, where the worldly affairs of the church were in fact controlled by the Council. He merely carried the logic of an historical process to its obvious conclusion.

In keeping with his "spiritualization" of religious affairs, Zwingli pointed out to Bishop Hugo the fallacy of using force to win converts: "[Christ] denies that his kingdom was of this world."[65] This assertion was central to Zwingli's ecclesiology and explains why he identified the visible church at Zurich with the political assembly. In answer to the sixtieth proposition, which reminded Bishop Hugo's readers that Leo X had condemned the new doctrines of Luther as contrary to the church, Zwingli elaborated upon the nature of the church. He asserted that Leo's condemnation was false because these doctrines were tested by valid

64. *Z*, I, 315, 11–13.
65. *Ibid.*, 316, 27.

authority, the Gospel.[66] In the ensuing articles Bishop Hugo had reminded those who governed the church, i.e., the clergy, that they had been appointed to rule by the Holy Spirit, and he exhorted them to keep the church free from abomination and schism by setting aside the new teachings and maintaining the church's religious customs. Zwingli countered with Paul's statement of the clergy's responsibility: "that you may feed the church of God." This was the task for which the Holy Spirit had appointed them: "shepherds feed, they do not rule." The church was born in Christ's blood and Christ purchased men with his blood, therefore neither individual Christians nor Christ's church can be ruled by men.[67] Everyone who believes that Christ won the church with his blood is a member; faith, not membership in the institutional church, is the ground for salvation: "Therefore, whosoever shall have believed it firmly is of this church of Christ, which He prepared by His blood; for faith alone is the cause of salvation."[68] Using this argument Zwingli drew a sharp distinction between the true Church of Christ, sprinkled with his blood and the church of the wicked, *ecclesiam malignantium*, whose crime is that it rests not on Christ but upon flesh and blood, i.e., the traditions of men.[69]

In these passages Zwingli opposed the church whose authority rested upon scripture, and whose membership was based upon faith in Christ, to the church defended by Bishop Hugo. It is an opposition between a spiritual church and an institutional church whose constitutive principles are centred upon a non-scriptural amalgam of law and ceremonial. Zwingli refused to the true church, the servant of God's kingdom, the secular power that carried with it the means to compel obedience. His doctrine of the church was far more likely to fit the structure of the Zurich city state, whose government desired no competition from a church which had the means and organization to exercise independent authority. Zwingli's ecclesiology left, by default, the exercise of all secular authority to the guardians of the kingdom of this world.

However, Zwingli set sharp limits to the power of the magistrate. Though the magistrate might use force to regulate the external practices of the church, he had no power over the true church, the Church Universal, because God alone granted men the faith which admitted them to it. The ruler could not force one to believe, for the realm of faith, Christ's kingdom, had nothing to do with the world. The true

66. *Ibid.*, 269, 4–10; 319, 7.
67. *Ibid.*, 269, 10–16; 319, 15, 17, 21, 22–3, 25–9.
68. *Ibid.*, 320, 3–5.
69. *Ibid.*, 320, 6–8.

church obviously did not depend upon the Zurich government, nor was it confined to the limits of the canton; it was universal. Nevertheless, Zwingli said Zurich was a Christian city.

The very nature of the Church Universal allowed him to say this. When arguing with Melchior Fattlin in April, he had said that membership in the church rested upon two requirements; the confession of faith with the mouth and belief in the heart. As was suggested earlier, it followed from this that those who did believe were known only to God, who gave them faith. Men might confess faith with their mouths, but no one who heard them could ever be sure of their hearts. Thus the church at Zurich was a mixed body, and Zwingli could identify it with the political assembly of the city. Its external affairs were the magistrate's concern. However, indirectly, even the spiritual church depended upon whether or not the Gospel, which quickened the hearts of the believers, was preached or choked out by the false ceremonials of the established church.

This is why the alliance with the magistracy was essential. By enforcing external standards in the spirit of the Word of God and protecting, as well as supporting, the proclamation of the Gospel, the magistrates made possible the gathering of the believers. It also explains, as Brockelmann has noted, how Zwingli could define the Church Universal as a spiritual body and yet talk about a Christian society. Society was Christian only in so far as it fulfilled God's will for men in the world by enforcing a modicum of peaceful external behaviour and allowing the proclamation of the Word of God.[70] Society was rewarded for its effort by the quickening of the souls of the believers whose spiritual power lent the community strength. Although the basic relationships between the church and the government were present in practice and presupposed in much that Zwingli wrote, he had not yet fully elaborated his position. One reason for this was that, for the moment, his task was to win the people away from their loyalty to the old church. As dissension mounted at Zurich among the reformers themselves, he was forced to explain himself.

The Bishop had expressed the hope that the negotiations at Zurich would be concluded with patience and mercy and that the spirit of unity conferred by Christ would prevail. Zwingli responded that it would, if the scripture was consulted.

do you [his opponents] not see that the Spirit of God is everywhere like itself and always the same? . . . and as it is a spirit of unity, concord, peace

---

70. Brockelmann, 34–5, 37–8, 39, 40–1, 49.

and not of contention and dissension, so it provides that those who are not learned, provided they are pious, perceive the Scripture most naturally according to the mind of God.[71]

In the light of later developments at Zurich, Zwingli's faith in the Spirit appears naive, but it was to remain the basic assumption of his belief in the authority of scripture.

Bishop Hugo had closed the letter to the Chapter by expressing the hope that God might deign to preserve his church in peace and its members unharmed. Zwingli answered him with a description of the internal peace which the Gospel had brought to Zurich.[72]

The *Archeteles* summarized and clarified the major themes which Zwingli's preaching had developed since January 1, 1519. The church and all its officers were subordinate to the Word of God. The institutions of the old church were rejected, in so far as they depended upon human, rather than divine, authority. He defined the true church as a mystical body, gathered and quickened wherever the Word was preached. Membership in the body depended upon the belief God gave through his Spirit. Zwingli's ecclesiology left the Church Universal free of domination by any human power and also made it possible for a part of it to be housed with the physical body of the city state. As Zwingli conceived of it, the quickening of the mystical body guaranteed health to the physical body: Christ's church was the soul of the community. When the body and soul functioned in harmony they prepared men for life in the Heavenly City.

The *Apologeticus* also offered a coherent justification for the reform movement at Zurich, carried out under the leadership of the Council. In the sermon *Concerning the Choice and Freedom of Foods*, Zwingli had insisted that the consensus of the universally gathered church was necessary for the promulgation of valid rules to govern the conduct of the Christian life. The *Apologeticus* defined the authority of the scripture and gave assurance that those who read it and were illumined by God's Spirit would find unity and know God's purpose. Zurich possessed scripture, the consensus of a Christian people, and presumably the guidance of the Holy Spirit. The *Apologeticus* demonstrated that there was no reason for the city to depend upon any other authority in proceeding with the purification of the ecclesiastical establishment. The tract was not only a refutation of the Bishop's charges, it provided a blueprint for the Council to carry on Zwingli's programme.

One point remains to be discussed. Zwingli allowed a laudatory poem

71. *Z, I*, 321, 35–6; 322, 1–3.
72. *Ibid.*, 270, 3–6; 325, 18–22.

written by Conrad Grebel to be affixed to the published version of *Apologeticus*. In the poem Grebel rejoiced that the truth was once again being proclaimed, and he prophesied that the dominion and oppression of the Bishops, whom he described as rapacious wolves, was at an end.[73] Many assume that the presence of Grebel's poem indicates a close relationship existed between him and Zwingli.[74] They are no doubt correct, and certainly the presence of the poem proves their case; but Grebel's relation to the radical movement at Zurich and his behaviour before the Council in July makes it possible to suggest another reason for the inclusion of the poem. Zwingli, who recognized Grebel's promise and yet was concerned at his lack of patience, may have allowed the poem to be printed as a conciliatory gesture to the young man and some of his friends. Like the request for the marriage of the clergy, included in the appeals to the Bishop and the Confederacy, his willingness to add Grebel's poem to the *Apologeticus* was an act of good will which might have been expected to temper Grebel's impatience. Yoder has noted the difference in tone between the *Archeteles*, whose very title, he argues, indicated that Zwingli wished to end the fight with the Bishop, and that of Grebel's poem. According to Yoder, Grebel delighted in the struggle with the Bishop and, indeed, there is a sharp, relentless note in the work which reflects a temperament that could easily misunderstand the nature of Zwingli's policy.[75]

73. *Ibid.*, 327, 17–18, 19–20, 23–30.
74. Bender, 81; Yoder, 14.
75. Yoder, 14.

9   Zwingli's Position:
       Fall, 1522

TWO SERMONS PUBLISHED IN SEPTEMBER, 1522, CONTINUED to educate the populace for the next stage of Zwingli's programme and were the prelude to the changes introduced in November. Neither adds a great deal to the understanding of Zwingli's developing political theory. The first, *Concerning the Clarity and Assurance of the Word of God*, enlarged upon Zwingli's doctrine of scripture. The second, *A Sermon Concerning the Eternal, Pure, Maid Mary*, demonstrated the essential conservatism of Zwingli's attitude towards tradition when it conformed to scripture.

The sermon on the *Clarity and Assurance of the Word of God*, delivered to the nuns at Oetenbach, was prompted by the opposition of the monks who did not accept the loss over the nuns without a struggle. It was re-published for propaganda purposes in 1524. Zwingli's advice to the nuns is illustrative of his general method of reform. Rather than call for an immediate end to celibate life, he merely discussed the authority of scripture. The nuns were left to draw their own conclusions and to take action themselves. Once the rationale for the monastic life was considered in the light of the scripture, monasticism should begin to decline of its own weight. The contrast between Zwingli, who saw the need for education through preaching, and the enthusiasts, anxious for an immediate attack upon the institutions of the old church, is manifest. By proclaiming the authority of scripture, Zwingli destroyed the basis upon which the cult was built. The success of his sermons made it possible for the magistrates to initiate a reform of the cult, as the practical situation allowed. He proclaimed the Gospel, which he believed was the only task assigned to the clergy, and left the councillors free to implement the demands for a purification of the church which he hoped would result from his preaching.

In the foreword to the first published version of the sermon Zwingli informed his readers that he had preached the sermon at the behest of the Council, which recognized "that there is no more pernicious hunger than the hunger for God's words whereby . . . the soul perishes."[1] The reference explains the Council's position. As the guardian of public welfare, it was concerned with the spiritual, as well as the physical, needs of the people. Zwingli raised no question about the Council's right to sanction his preaching. He accepted it as a matter of course.

Assuming the dual nature of man, Zwingli proved that the preaching of the Gospel was essential to life. The soul which was created in God's image, and links man to God, seeks Him because of its nature and therefore preaching is essential because men long for God's Word.[2] Zwingli's interpretation of man's nature was central to his conception of society. In the sermon *On Divine and Human Righteousness*, delivered during June of 1523, he relied heavily upon his notion of man's nature to explain the relationship between the church and the magistracy. The church preached to the souls of men, while the magistrate ministered to their bodies. In the immediate context, Zwingli used the dichotomy of soul and body to justify his preaching and the support given to it by the Council. By providing for the preaching of the Bible, the magistrates have met a basic human need. The establishment of the preaching office in November, 1522, extended this line of thought.

Zwingli next considered the assurance and strength of the scripture. The particulars of his discussion need not detain us here. He then repeated the warning voiced very clearly both in the *Apologeticus* and *Admonition* to Schwyz. Citing the example of the punishment heaped upon Israel by the Babylonians, he depicted the fate which awaited those who failed to heed God's word.[3] Finally he expounded upon the clarity of the Word by asserting that scripture was sufficiently clear to render human reason or authority unnecessary:

Tell me, wizard, which council or judge stipulated that he [Jacob] should accept the Word of God and should believe that what he heard was indeed God's Word? Look, you squabbler, the Word of God has brought its own clarity and illumination with it. . . . That the Word of God which is God himself illumines all men. . . .[4]

These remarks provided the magistrates with further assurance that the course they had followed since 1520 was sound and encouraged them to go on.

Zwingli criticized theologians and the church for subordinating the Bible to the judgment of men. God, not man, teaches and gives confirmation: "Hear what the schoolmaster's name is; [it is] not doctors, not fathers, not Pope, not throne, not councils; he is called the father

1. *Z*, I, 338, 8–9.   2. *Ibid.*, 349, 8–11; 352, 30–353, 5.
3. *Ibid.*, 360, 24–361, 7.   4. *Z*, I, 364, 13–16; 365, 31–32.

of Jesus Christ." Zwingli denied that an assembly of bishops had the Spirit of God, for, he said, they were too exalted and too far from it; the Spirit of God does not reveal itself through the spirit of this world. Their titles are from the world and not from God.[5] The implication behind these statements was that the bishops do not preach the Gospel and therefore do not have the spirit of God. The remainder of the sermon dealt with the same theme.

In one passage Zwingli referred to the church in the following terms: "Christ is the head of the Church, that is Christ is the head of His assembly or Church. . . ."[6] The equation of *versamlung* (assembly), with *kilch* (church) is important. It bears out the previous argument that the basic institution Zwingli thought of when he spoke of the church congregation was the political assembly of the city. It also reinforces the contention that he had no idea of a separate church congregation: the political assembly he had in mind was an assembly of Christians and hence a religious assembly as well.

The sermon *Concerning the Eternal, Pure, Maid Mary* was written to answer the charges of the Zurich monks, who accused Zwingli of neglecting and defaming the Virgin Mary, and to calm the fears of his family who were concerned by the rumours of his radicalism.[7] The concerns of the sermons are not pertinent to this study. It is enough to note in passing that he maintained the mediaeval conception of Mary as eternally pure, but re-cast her role so that her place of honour glorified, rather than obscured, Christ.[8]

By November Zwingli felt that it was time to begin the actual reform of the institutions and practices of the ecclesiastical establishment. Bishop Hugo's attacks upon his disciples in the fall and the outbreak of tithe agitation, inspired, in part, by the radicals, called for measures which would draw together the reform party and pacify the extremists. Before these matters are considered, Zwingli's response to a threat from another quarter should be touched upon. Zwingli and some of his friends believed that Christian renewal, both in Switzerland and Germany, was endangered by the activity of the Pope, Hadrian VI. Hadrian had called a reform council which met at Nürnberg on November 17. Michael Hummelberg told Zwingli that the assembly had been arranged to

5. *Ibid.*, 366, 26–7; 369, 16–25.
6. *Ibid.*, 366, 9–11.
7. It is believed that the Abbot of Fischingen in Thurgau, Johannes Meile, who had warned Zwingli that he was following an ill considered course of action, was his uncle (*Z*, I, 386).
8. O. Farner, III, 300–3; Oberman, "The Virgin Mary in Evangelical Perspective," *JES*, I, 281, 290.

achieve four things: an agreement between the Pope and Charles V; the extermination of Lutheranism; the reform of the church; and the prosecution of the war against the Turks. Hummelberg also erroneously informed Zwingli that the Pope had declared Erasmus a heretic.[9]

Zwingli feared that the Pope's real aim was to destroy Lutheranism by diverting attention to peace, reform in the church, and the Turkish war.[10] If the Pope succeeded, Zwingli knew his own movement would also be destroyed. To warn of the danger he penned anonymously his *Suggestion for Deliberation upon the Proposition of Hadrian at Nürnberg (Suggestio Deliberandi super propositione Hadriani Neroberge)* which was addressed to the German princes. Citing the papacy's previous record, he cast doubt upon the Pope's ability to make peace and pointed out to the princes that an attempt to suppress the Gospel by war would benefit only the Pope. He implied that the old faith, identified as it was with the secular power of the church, had little to offer the Empire. If the Pope should be victorious, Zwingli added, the result would leave him in control of the whole world: "If indeed it shall have been done, Rome has obtained not only the rule of all Germany but the monarchy of the Christian world."[11] The passage reveals the implicit connection between the Gospel faith, which was anti-hierarchical, and the growing national aspiration of sixteenth-century Europe. The Gospel offered freedom from Rome to the nations of Europe.

Zwingli then said that the Pope could solve the problem of reform very easily; all he needed to do was to order Christian doctrine to be preached "purely, faithfully, and consistently."[12] He proposed to the Pope exactly what he had to the Bishop of Constance, and his proposal, unrestricted preaching of the Gospel, again reveals the main objective of his programme for a rebirth of Christ. Everything else depended upon the right to proclaim the Good News. It also provides insight into his policy at Zurich; he could always afford to go slow with reform because he had already won the only concession necessary for success: the right to preach. Though the tract had much to say to the Germans in the Empire, it also reflected the problems Zwingli faced at home.

The pamphlet represented only one part of Zwingli's activities. At the same time as it appeared, the Council took measures to protect the city. As has already been noted, in November it forbade anyone to receive a foreign pension. Provisions were made for the youth of the city to receive proper religious instruction and, in keeping with Zwingli's

9. *Z*, VII, 607, 12–14, 19–20.
11. *Ibid.*, 438, 18–21; 439, 6–8.
12. *Ibid.*, 440, 11–12.

10. *Z*, I, 437, 6–13.

urgings, the morality of the people was more carefully supervised.[13] The fast laws were enforced, as Röubli learned to his dismay, and the nuns at Oetenbach were prevented from leaving the Cloister. Although the balance of the Council's commands appears to have been inclined towards maintaining the status quo, the city fathers were actually bent upon protecting and furthering the cause of reform. The conservatism of their policy can be easily explained by the hostility which Zurich faced on every side.

The Council's determination to aid Zwingli was soon demonstrated. Claiming that he needed more time to devote himself to the verbal and written proclamation of the Bible, he resigned from his post as People's Priest. The Council approved his decision and, in accordance with his own wish, requested him to continue to preach at the Grossmünster. At the same time, it instructed the Chapter of the Grossmünster to find another man to fill the position of People's Priest.[14]

The fact that the matter was arranged without referring to the Bishop indicates the extent of the Council's authority over the affairs of the church. The magistrate's right to supervise the appointment and dismissal of the clergy was well established. However, when the councillors asked Zwingli to continue to preach at the Zurich Great Church, they did something new. In effect they sanctioned the creation of an evangelical preaching office which eventually replaced the old priestly office.[15] The purification of the cult had begun.

In the past, the Council never would have taken such a step without first gaining the approval of the Bishop. But now, bolstered by Zwingli's conception of scriptural authority, the Council, which had given up hope the Bishop would respond to its April petition, felt free to act on its own. Though this did not lead to an immediate break with Constance, the decision implied that the councillors no longer accepted the religious authority of the established church.

The creation of the new office, which was in part the answer to the difficulties which the Bishop's alliance with the Confederacy made for the Zurichers, explains the restrictive measures which coincided with its

13. Staehelin, I, 252.   14. E.A., 290.
15. This is the interpretation given by Egli, O. Farner, Köhler, and Staehelin (Egli, 75; O. Farner, III, 318–19; Köhler, 92; Staehelin, I, 252). Köhler dates the move on October 10, rather than November 12. Yoder believes that this development may have marked the beginning of Zwingli's departure from his original conception of the Church. When he accepted an appointment directly from the Council, he may have "unconsciously" founded the State Church (Yoder, 165). It seems more likely that this step was consistent both with the policy and the ecclesiology that Zwingli had maintained from the beginning of his career at Zurich.

establishment. The efforts of the Confederates to stop Zwingli's reform
movement had set off a wave of discontent within the city itself which
made the Council sensitive to the existence of hostile elements there. In
order to keep control of the situation and still proceed with reform, the
Council had to be careful. Its policy tried to appease both sides: it
checked any manifestation of radicalism in favour of the reform movement, while it served the cause by creating the preaching office. Formal
adherence to the traditional practices of the old cult was maintained by
the proposal to appoint a new People's Priest who was never actually
appointed. In this way the Zurich government avoided giving further
offence either to the Confederates or to the conservative party in the city,
which could be expected to view the appearance of the new preaching
office with hostility.

If the unwise conduct of the enthusiasts could be stopped, the creation
of the preaching office itself left the opposition in the city and Zurich's
foes abroad fewer grounds for complaint. The priests remained and,
except for the elimination of the *Salve Regina* from the service and the
simplification of the breviary which had taken place in 1520, the services
of the church continued to be performed as they always had been. At
the same time, the foundations of the traditional cultus were being undermined. The new post freed Zwingli from the priestly functions required
of the People's Priest and left him more time to instruct his converts and
to win over the groups in the city which still remained unconvinced. His
work would be paralleled by his successor as People's Priest, certainly
a man sympathetic to reform. Though ostensibly employed to carry out
the responsibilities of the priestly office, which included saying the Mass,
he would be able to preach against abuses of the services which he
performed. Together, the two could prepare the way for the abolition
of the Mass. As the situation merited it, this solution was also applied
in the outlying district.[16]

The existence of two offices was only temporary, but it did allow the
work of reform to proceed without causing an open break with past
tradition. This was probably the most that the state of affairs in the
city permitted. It lessened the danger that events at Zurich would pre-
cipitate outside the intervention or domestic uproar. At the same time
the creation of the preaching office was an answer to the demands of
the radicals, who were using the tithe issue to press for a reform of the
cult. Without appreciably altering the externals, the creation of the
new post was an attack on the Mass, whose performance was the major
responsibility of the priesthood.

16. *E.A.*, 351, 360.

The method Zwingli employed did not go unnoticed by Grebel's circle. When, in the summer or fall of 1523, Grebel and Stumpf suggested that the shell of the old church be permitted to remain and a new believers' church, unsupported by tithes, be erected along side of it, they were only following the pattern of change used by Zwingli himself. The latter's initial decision to resign and devote himself to preaching had probably given Grebel and his friends the impression he had begun to move in the right direction. They may have hoped that further agitation on their part would bring him the rest of the way. This would explain their part in the anti-tithe demonstrations during the spring and summer of 1523. The logical sequence to their participation in the fresh outburst against the tenths was the proposal that a separate church be established.

Actually, the formalization of the scripture's authority implicit in the establishment of the preaching office was a major step in the direction that the radicals wished to take. If one were to criticize them, it might be said that they had their eyes too firmly fixed upon the externals and failed to see the reasons for Zwingli's continued caution. Once the preaching office was set up, an end to the Mass was bound to come. However, due to the opposition both within the city and throughout the Confederacy, the timing of this move involved a policy decision only the Council could make. If Zwingli is open to criticism for his conduct in this matter, his fault lies in his willingness to allow another to continue to perform services he considered abusive. Though his resignation left him better able to forward the cause of reform, it was not the most straightforward way to avoid a moral dilemma. The enthusiasts certainly had grounds for taking offence at this.

The creation of the preaching office was the prelude to the First Disputation. Both events were a direct answer to the internal tension within the city and the hostile policies of the Bishop and his allies in the Confederacy. They were also a defensive response to the possible outcome of the Nürnberg Reichstag which ended harmlessly enough in February, 1523.[17]

The interpretations of the Council's action in calling the Disputation have been varied.[18] This much can be said: the decisions reached in

---

17. Egli, 76.
18. Egli believed Zwingli viewed it as a gathering similar to the provincial synods of the ancient church. He added that, in its limitation to the canton, it carried with it the beginning of the Territorial Church ideal. The step was viewed with great seriousness by the town councillors, because, as a result, Zurich was politically isolated (Egli, 77). Staehelin notes the importance of the Council's claim to have the right to decide for or against the contenders upon the basis of Scripture (Staehelin, I, 260) O. Farner agrees with Staehelin. Up to this point, he argues,

January were long in the making. Their foundations rested upon the corporate nature of city government at Zurich and the control gained by the Council over the church prior to 1519. Zwingli's appearance on the scene enabled the government to gain full independence from the supervision of the hierarchy. He provided the government with a fresh conception of religious authority: the primacy of scripture. Thus, the Council, acting in accordance with the norms of Holy Writ, felt able to direct a purification of the cult. Its petition to the Bishop in April of 1522 shows that a break with the old tradition was already in the making. At that time it warned the Bishop that it would accept his response if it did not violate Christ's precepts as found in the Gospel.

The Council explained that it had summoned the Disputation in order to put an end to the unrest and division which Zwingli's preaching had caused within the canton. Its decision was taken at Zwingli's request: " . . . in order to stop great unrest and disunity, the honourable Council at Zurich has agreed and granted him a public disputation in the German language before the Great Council at Zurich. . . . "[19] As in the April missive to the Bishop, the Council accepted the authority of the scripture and promised to judge with the aid of "learned men" according to the truth contained therein. The decision issued after the Disputation reviewed the terms of the appeal to Bishop Hugo made in April, 1522, and noted that no answer had been received from him. As a result, disagreement in the canton had continued, and so the Council had been forced to take matters into its own hands and call a disputation. During the debate, no one had been able to prove with the aid of scripture that Zwingli was a heretic and, therefore, the magistrates explained, they had told him to continue his work. They also commanded the rest of the clergy to preach the Gospel and to refrain from abusing one another.[20]

There was no question in the minds of its members of the Council's right to act. It regulated the affairs of the church as part of its obligation to serve the common good, and Zwingli had provided the rationale for the "provincial church" undertaking the task of reform. There is no evidence that the Council viewed its deliberations concerning the fate

---

the general concept of papal authority as outlined by Boniface VIII had left the State subordinate to the Church. Though he admits the secular governments had a limited *ius reformandi* before the Reformation, it was used in the service of the church. What took place now was a complete change. The government claimed the right to decide between the authority of the Church and that of the Scripture. Once the Council decided for the authority of the Bible, it denied anyone the right to question its decision (O. Farner III, 332–4).

19. *Z*, I, 484, 11–14.
20. *Ibid.*, 467, 11–14; *E.A.*, 327.

of the religious establishment in a special category that implied the existence of a separate *Kirchgemeinde* (church congregation). The Council's role in the matter was another illustration of the unitary nature of city life in the sixteenth century. Church and magistracy were part of one Christian society, under the direction of a Council, elected by the political assembly of the citizens, which was the gathering of a Christian people. To be sure, the Council accepted the authority of scripture and consulted learned men when it dealt with religious questions. The magistrates respected the limitations imposed by scripture upon their authority, but this position does not exclude the possibility of an incipient separation betwen church and state. Zwingli certainly made a sharp distinction between the competence of the spiritual and secular authority; however, his theory of the division of powers was evolved to function within a corporate society governed by a representative magistracy.

The debate carried on during the Disputation expressed the position taken by Zwingli and the Council. Bishop Hugo's Vicar, Faber, led the conservative delegation. He refused to argue about matters that he said should be discussed by a general council or referred to the universities, and he warned that decisions made at Zurich might be contrary to the views held by other Christians. Finally, he assured the magistrates that the questions at issue would be settled at the General Council of the German Nation to be held at Nürnberg.[21]

Zwingli replied to Faber in detail. He declared that the present assembly was a *christliche versammlung* (a Christian gathering). The majority present wished to do God's will and therefore fulfilled the requirement for a Christian assembly that Christ had laid down in Matthew 18:20: " . . . where two or three are gathered in my name, I am in the midst of them. . . . " In comparison with a council of bishops, who are worldly princes and do not live up to the biblical requirements for the bishop's office, the men present at the Disputation are fitted by their learning and devotion to make decisions.[22] Zwingli criticized the higher clergy for withholding the scripture from the people and for behaving as if they alone could interpret the Bible. Reiterating the argument that he had already advanced in the *Apologeticus*, he maintained that there was no danger that the Zurich Disputation would reach conclusions contrary to the beliefs of other Christians.[23] If the truth of

21. *Ibid.*, 491, 3–6, 8–13, 24–492, 5.
22. *Ibid.*, 495, 10–17, 20–496, 8. Zwingli's definition of the Bishop's office was a repetition of the summary given in the *Sermon concerning the Choice and Freedom of Foods* (Z, I, 121, 8, 13–18).
23. *Ibid.*, 321, 35–6; 322, 1–3; 496, 8–9.

Christ is preached to all nations and is not withheld by papal, imperial, or episcopal mandates, all who hear it will turn away from human ordinances and agree upon those which are supported by the Word of God.[24] Zwingli was convinced that the Holy Spirit would bring unity to those who consulted the scriptures.

As far as Zwingli was concerned the focus of the Disputation was upon scripture and the gathering was in Christ's name. It is noteworthy that he applied Matthew 18:20 to claim that the meeting fulfilled the requirements for a proper assembly of Christians. In an earlier passage he had used Christ's words to define the church; here they served to validate the gathering which carried on the Disputation, as well as the decisions that it reached. The application of this definition to the assembly explains how Zwingli could later say that the Christian city was nothing other than the Christian church. On the other hand, his reference to both Matthew 18:20 and the argument that an assembly which included worthy, God-fearing pastors and consulted the scriptures, was competent to make decisions concerning matters of faith, could be used to justify the existence of a separate church capable of governing its own affairs without the support of government. The question of whether a group of Christians could gather for such a dispute without being summoned by the secular authorities was never raised. The fact Zwingli limited the clergy's task to the preaching of the Word and stressed that laws governing Christian conduct had to have the consensus of a Christian people make it unlikely that he could have conceived of this. The only assembly he knew was the political assembly of the city and its delegated authorities. In calling the Disputation, the Council acted in the same capacity as the emperors when they called the great ecumenical councils of the fourth and fifth centuries. Although the decisions of the Zurich gathering were reached by only a segment of the Christian community, this posed no problem for Zwingli because he believed that all Christendom would reach the same conclusions if it consulted scripture and was guided by the Holy Spirit. His argument was a break from past tradition and set the precedent for the right of a "provincial church" to reform itself. His answer to Faber was an appeal to the magistrates to guide the cleansing of the church that the scriptures demanded.

The remainder of the debate was an elaboration of Zwingli's original point. He cast doubt upon the outcome of the Council at Nürnberg because he claimed that the pope and the bishops would not permit a council to be held under the guidance of scripture. Then he rejected the need for referring the questions before the assembly to the universities

24. *Ibid.*, 496, 17–497, 7.

on the grounds that those present at Zurich were as able to interpret the Bible as the representatives of the universities.[25] There was no question in his mind that the Zurich gathering was guided by the Holy Spirit, and, consequently, the magistrates would judge the outcome correctly:

then there are in this gathering so many Christian hearts, without doubt taught by the Holy Ghost, of such honest understanding that they can easily judge and recognize according to the Holy Spirit, which party in their opinion presents the Scriptures rightly or wrongly, or otherwise forces them violently against proper understanding.[26]

There was no response to Zwingli's arguments and the assembly went on to consider other questions. The question of the validity of the councils was raised by one of the Bishop's representatives, Dr. Martin Blantsch from Tübingen, who defended their authority: "For the church, gathered through the Councils in the Holy Ghost, cannot err." Zwingli pointed out that councils have contradicted each other and concluded that the Holy Spirit could not always have been present when their decisions were reached. He maintained that it was not obligatory to obey the canons of a council reached in accord with human reason alone, but that those arrived at in accord with the Gospel must be followed.[27]

In pursuing the question Zwingli again discussed the nature of the church. He said the church had often erred. It had destroyed nations and peoples for the sake of worldly power and "without doubt not because of the command of Christ and his apostles."[28] The true church "is nothing other than the number of all the faithful gathered in the spirit and will of God, who also place a firm faith and an undoubting hope in God, her bridegroom." This church does not attempt to oppress or rule other Christians and does not err.[29] The picture of the true church presented here is a summation of the position Zwingli had been developing since the beginning of his career. His concept of the true church was a sharp weapon for the attack upon the institutions of the established church. But in the process of demolishing these institutions he neglected to make a clear statement concerning the structure of a reformed church. He obviously believed that the organization of the civic community provided a sufficient framework for the visible church. The only office the

25. *Ibid.*, 497; 10–12; 498, 2–9; 499, 2–7.

26. *Ibid.*, 499, 7–12. Yoder notes that Zwingli assumed that the legitimate representatives of the congregation were the magistrates. He sees in this assumption the basis for Zwingli's subsequent difficulties with the government (Yoder, 15). Yoder's description of Zwingli's assumption is correct, but it subsequently proved a problem not for Zwingli but for Grebel and his followers. Zwingli's position was the key to his success at Zurich.

27. *Z, I*, 534, 13–14; 536, 11–21.   28. *Ibid.*, 537, 11–17.

29. *Ibid.*, 537, 18–538, 6.

church needed was the preaching office which was supported by the community and not by a separate ecclesiastical organ.

Following the Disputation, Faber and Zwingli became involved in an argument over the articles, which Faber claimed he had just had time to read. Zwingli reiterated his views on scriptural authority and added one remark which is worthy of notice. He stated that in worldly questions he gladly accepted the judgment of the magistrates but in religious questions he would allow only the scripture, through which the Spirit spoke as judge.[30] This is the basis for the division between the work of the magistrate and that of the church in the Christian society upon which Zwingli developed his political theory. Worldly matters are judged by the magistrates; spiritual matters by scripture.

30. *Ibid.*, 548, 13–14; 557, 30–558, 5.

The Results of the
     First Disputation

THE YEAR 1523 WAS CRUCIAL. THE OUTCOME OF THE JANUARY Disputation had an immediate effect; between April of 1523 and the summer of 1524, Schaffhausen, Basel, Bern, Mülhausen, St. Gall, Appenzell, and the Toggenburg commanded their clergy to confine their preaching to the scripture.[1] Though this did not mean that the battle to introduce the Reformation into these regions was won, it did mean that the way was open for such a victory. At Zurich, the Council put an end to the last vestiges of the Bishop of Constance's jurisdiction in the canton in February.

The results of the Disputation caused renewed efforts to discredit Zwingli. Dr. Johannes Gebwyler, a professor at the University of Basel, accused him of fathering two illegitimate children. The Council showed its determination to defend Zwingli's good name by promptly complaining to the magistrates at Basel who compelled Gebwyler to send a written apology to Zurich.[2] Faber refused to accept his defeat and issued his own account of the Disputation, entitled *A True Account*, which claimed that he had won the debate. Zwingli's followers responded with a lampoon which made Faber look ridiculous and contributed to his difficulties in finding a publisher for his next attack upon Zwingli. Goaded by these setbacks, Faber urged the Confederacy to ally itself with Austria to suppress the Reformation by force, and warned Archduke Ferdinand that the House of Austria, as well as Christianity as a whole was menaced by Zwingli.[3]

The church's allies in the Diet were equally upset by the Disputation. When the Diet met on February 23, 1523, at Lucerne, Zwingli was burned in effigy.[4] The outbreak of tithe agitation at Zurich during the late spring and early summer gave rise to ugly rumours that convinced the majority of the Confederates that Zurich was gripped by a Lutheran heresy that threatened orderly government. The defence of the reform movement, published by Zwingli with the approval of the Council, and the Council's efforts to calm the fears of the other cantons had no effect.

1. *Z*, I, 450.   2. *E.A.*, 322, 335, 340–2.
3. *Z*, I, 447–8; Staehelin, I, 273–4.   4. Staehelin, I, 271.

Meeting at Bern on July 7, the Confederates decided to imprison Zwingli
if he entered their territories and considered expelling Zurich from their
ranks. Schwyz, Glarus, Schaffhausen, and Appenzell objected to the
Diet's policy but they were told to support the other cantons in the
campaign against Zwingli.[5]

Later in July Bishop Hugo seconded the Diet's action with a pastoral
letter to the Confederacy containing a copy of the imperial mandate
against Luther and Faber's new pamphlet, *The Shepherd's Letter*; the
Bishop's letter also warned the pious, under threat of punishment, to
stay clear of heretical teaching. The Zurich Council sent the Bishop's
letter back to him unopened. Along with it the magistrates sent an
epistle which stated that only the Gospel was preached at Zurich. They
also told the Bishop that if, as he said, heresy were being proclaimed in
the city, he should prove his charge and then they would deal with the
heresy as it deserved. To allay the Confederacy's fears about radicalism
at Zurich, the councillors had Zwingli's sermon *On Divine and Human
Righteousness* published and, at the same time, investigated those
responsible for sending false accounts of the events in the city to the
Bishop. The Bishop was furious at Zurich's response and reported to
the Confederacy that the situation in the city had become more
threatening.[6] Zurich representatives at the Diet denied this and defended
Zwingli.

The Confederates sought other means to stop the progress of Christian renewal at Zurich. Throughout the early months of 1523, they
intensified their efforts to arouse the discontent of the pro-mercenary
party within the canton. Reliable sources assured the Zurichers that the
Council had been bribed by the papacy to stay out of the French alliance.
Other informants announced that the Council's policy was so unpopular
that it would soon be reversed and that Zurich was about to join the
French alliance.[7] This propaganda was accompanied by the renewed
activities of French recruiting agents, who won an increasing number
of Zurichers for French service. There was a real danger that popular
opposition to the Council's policy of neutrality might cause a change of
government. A re-organized magistracy representing the interests of the
pro-mercenary party would certainly bring Zurich into the French
alliance and most probably remove Zwingli from office. Alarmed by the
growing disobedience to its policy, the Council held extensive hearings
in March and formulated a programme to avoid a domestic crisis.

Those who violated the law prohibiting service abroad for pay were

5. Egli, 91–2.   6. *Ibid.*, 92–3; *E.A.*, 386.
7. *E.A.*, 350, 351.

threatened with harsh penalties, but, as in the previous year, the penalties were not enforced. A month before the March hearings the magistracy had permitted Kaspar Röist, Burgomaster Röist's son, to remain in papal service.[8] By making this concession the government had prevented further friction with the papacy. The moderation shown by the Council in this case was extended to meet the general crisis. Real dissidents were allowed to join the French and thus prevented from causing further trouble at home. Those who wavered were kept at home by the threat of punishment. Only after the Reformation was consolidated did the Council enforce the law against mercenary service and pensions and use the death penalty upon violators like Jacob Grebel. There is a striking parallel between the policy employed to deal with the unrest over the question of mercenary service and that used later to handle the issue of the Mass and the images. In both, the Council made its aim clear but compromised until the aim could be achieved without running the risk of a domestic or foreign crisis.

The impact of Zwingli's preaching and the influence of Grebel's enthusiasts can be seen in the petitions of grievance which deluged the magistracy during the first six months of 1523. Directly or indirectly the petitions demanded purification of the cult. The Council's response to these requests indicated that it desired reform, but that it intended to proceed with caution. Although Zwingli and his allies in the government agreed with the radicals that the old cultus should be reformed, they disagreed with Grebel's faction about timing the procedure.

The Council's intervention in the controversy between the congregation at Wytikon and the Chapter of the Grossmünster which took place in March illustrates the magistracy's intention and the authority it exercised over the canton's churches. The parish of Wytikon, a filial of the Grossmünster, was involved in a dispute with the Chapter because it had appointed its own pastor, Wilhelm Röubli, and had refused to pay tithes. Röubli's appointment in this manner was of questionable legality and the refusal to pay the "spiritual" tithes, which supported those who performed the services of the old cult, could be construed as an attack upon those services, not the least of which was the Mass. The Council ordered Wytikon to resume tithe payments and allowed Röubli to remain until it could consider his case at the end of the year.[9] The fact that the villagers accepted the authority of the Council indicates that Wytikon did not ascribe to the principle of congregational autonomy. Moreover, as long as the government insisted that the "spiritual" tithes be paid, the economic foundation for the priest's office was maintained.

8. *Ibid.*, 343.   9. *Ibid.*, 351.

However, the fact that Röubli was allowed to stay in Wytikon meant that in effect a second pastoral office was created. This development paralleled what had taken place in November, 1522, when Zwingli resigned his position as People's Priest. The new post marked a step towards the full reform of all the services and the suppression of the Mass priests, but it was as far as the Council could go, for many still supported the mediaeval service. There is no mention of how Röubli was to be supported at Wytikon but it does not seem likely that he was supported by the tithes rendered by the village to the Grossmünster. No doubt the villagers themselves had to provide for him.

The Council followed a similar course of action with regard to the parish of Kloten. On April 11 the Abbot of Wettingen complained to the Council that the parish of Kloten was demanding a pastor who would preach the Gospel. The Council responded by upholding the Abbot's rights in the parish and by instructing the People's Priest at Kloten "to care for his charges as before, with preaching and other divine things." It also informed the villagers that they might also appoint the type of priest whom they wished to have, but that they would have to pay the cost "from their own funds."[10] The people of Kloten were not anxious to assume the financial burden which the Council's solution entailed, and on April 27 they appealed again to the Council. They requested that the Abbot use the tithes which they paid to him to provide them with a priest who would preach the Gospel. The Abbot objected to the request on the grounds that the present incumbent had served them well for twenty years. Another hearing was held on May 9. The Priest, Ulrich Kern, and the representatives of the parish and of the Abbot were present. The Council decided that the Priest should receive an assistant who would preach the Gospel to the people. The Abbot expressed his willingness to help and the magistrates said that they would hold him to the offer. They warned that if a proper aid for the Priest was not found, they would appoint a fitting person themselves; and, finally, they admonished Kern under threat of punishment to preach the Gospel as their mandates had prescribed.[11] The villagers' grievances and the compromise imposed by the Council indicates the nature of the magistracy's policy. The old Priest remained, while a place was made for a new appointee whose primary concern would be the proclamation of the Gospel. In this case, as in the case of Wytikon, the magistracy was the authority to which the people of Kloten and the Abbot of Wettingen appealed for a solution to their problem.

The government continued to receive complaints about the abuse of

10. *Ibid.*, 354.   11. *Ibid.*, 359–60.

tithes. The Canon Anselm Graf reported being criticized for not sharing the tenths he received with the poor.[12] Early in June the village assembly at Rümlang objected to paying the small tenths to the Fraumünster. The Council upheld the Fraumünster's right to the payments but invited all those who had been called upon to pay additional sums to present their case before the magistrates.[13] In this instance the government had no thought of ending the payment of tithes *per se*, but was quite willing to reform abuses.

The reasons for the complaints in these cases are of interest. When the magistracy ordered Wytikon to resume tithe payments it referred to the villagers' petition, which had expressed willingness to pay, except in the case where others were not obliged to do so.[14] The people of Kloten did not object to paying the tenths in themselves but demanded that their tenths be used to provide proper religious guidance for the congregation. In both instances the unwillingness to pay the fees which the law demanded reflected a demand for the improvement of the religious services rendered to the community. In the case of Anselm Graf and the petition of Rümlang social unrest and economic hardship were the apparent causes of grievance.

Widespread resistance to tithes broke out in the final weeks of June, 1523, and revealed that religious grievances were uppermost in the minds of the villagers who refused to pay their tenths. The villages of Zollikon, Riesbach, Fällanden, Hirslanden, Unterstrass, and Wytikon formally objected to paying tithes to the Chapter of the Grossmünster on June 22, 1523, because the money was misused by the canons. The petitioners could not understand how the payment of what the Gospel taught were gifts could be made obligatory, nor how the canons dared to squander money to which they had no right in the first place. The villagers also complained that they had to pay extra for the services of the canons at weddings, baptisms, funerals, and other occasions. The Council told the villagers to continue paying the tithes, but agreed to a revision of the payments imposed during the last 20 or 30 years. The magistrates also agreed to work out a solution to the other grievances in consultation with the canons.[15]

Neither Yoder nor Bender believed that there was any connection between this outbreak and the future Baptists.[16] Göters has provided

12. *Ibid.*, 355.   13. *Ibid.*, 365.
14. *Ibid.*, 351.   15. *Ibid.*, 368.
16. Yoder asserts that even the later *Täufer* felt that inherited obligations to pay interest should be honoured, though they believed Christians should not take interest (Yoder, 170–1). Bender claims that Grebel supported Zwingli's attitude towards the tithes in the summer of 1523 (Bender, 106).

another interpretation. As a whole the villages did not object to paying tithes. Their grievance was confined to the spiritual tenths which supported the parish clergy and the care of the poor. The object of their attack was the major ecclesiastical foundations of the city to whom the tithes were paid. What annoyed the petitioners was the fact that the money which they gave was not put to the proper use. Göters believes that the leaders of the radical faction, which had already emerged at Zurich, were directly involved in the agitation and sought to gain Zwingli's support for their activities. At the peak of the unrest over tithes, Stumpf, Grebel, and Manz proposed the creation of a separate church which would not be supported by the tenths. The abolition of the money payments was central to their project because it provided the occasion for a complete break with the ecclesiastical traditions of the past and would allow the introduction of a "pure cult."[17]

Except for the rumblings at Bülach in the fall of 1522, the actual connection between a call for an end to the Mass, the central ceremony of the old cult, and the abolition of the "spiritual" tithes was not openly expressed. The appeal of the villagers of Kloten that the Abbot of Wettingen use the tithes to provide a priest for them who would preach the Gospel illustrates this connection. Traditional worship centred in the Mass. The people of Kloten thought that the clergy's primary obligation was to preach the Gospel, not to perform ceremonies. Everyone agreed that their Priest, Ulrich Kern, carried out his traditional duties; but to those already influenced by the reform movement this was not enough. For this reason the villagers objected to the use to which their tithes were put. The tenths should support one who preached the Gospel. It is clear from this case that the "spiritual" tithes and the maintenance of the old service were intimately connected. The most the Council would do was to warn the Priest to confine his preaching to the Bible and to allow the appointment of a priest's helper who would preach the Gospel but would be supported at the expense of the villagers themselves. So long as the tenths were rendered, the old service and those who performed it were supported. It must have been obvious to anyone who was impatient for the final purification of the old cult according to the norms of the Gospel that the tenths were a barrier to such a change. Though Zwingli's preaching itself contributed to the unrest over the tithes, he recognized the right of the Council to maintain the practice. What he opposed was the justification of tithe payments on the basis of divine law. Apparently not everyone who heard what he said was careful to make the distinctions that he made when dealing with the matter.

17. Göters, 31–3.

Dissatisfaction with the tithe system had social as well as religious causes, as the case of Rümlang and Canon Anselm Graf's experience reveals. The feeling against the tenths was strong enough to offer those who were impatient with the slow tempo of reform sanctioned by the Council, and accepted by Zwingli, an opportunity to achieve a rapid and complete reform of the traditional pattern of worship by encouraging the demand that the "spiritual" tithes be abolished. If they were done away with, the economic support for the traditional cult would be removed and the way would be open for a far speedier implementation of Zwingli's reform programme.

A hearing held the day after the councillors considered the villagers' grievances reveals that the issue of the reform of the Mass was raised while the tithe question was at its height. A priest at the Grossmünster, Doctor Lorenz, who had been sent to preach at Zollikon, was criticized for preaching in support of transubstantiation. Among those who abused Dr. Lorenz were Jacob and Claus Hottinger. Jacob Hottinger told Lorenz he could not prove the real presence from scripture and said the sacrament ought to be given in both kinds. In reply, Lorenz noted: "Master Ulrich [Zwingli] is a clever, learned man; he is not able to accomplish it. What should I, then, do about it?" Lorenz's answer seems to have been directed to Hottinger's demand for the sacrament in both kinds. Hottinger's reply is significant: "if you can't effect it, then let me do it." The Council urged the brothers to be silent over the matter and to let others such as the clergy settle the question.[18]

The Hottingers' connection with radicalism at Zurich and their later activities as Baptists are well documented. They made no reference to the tithe issue when they accosted Lorenz but the fact that their opposition was voiced at this time is not without significance. The request for communion in both kinds made by Aberli, another member of their faction, during the spring of 1522, probably represents the desires of the radicals at this time. Of course, it did not necessarily mean the complete suppression of the Mass. By the time the Council permitted a modification of the Mass, the radicals regarded Zwingli's willingness to accept this concession in place of a complete revision of the service as a betrayal of the reform movement. The debate with Lorenz also demonstrates the Hottingers' independence of Zwingli. They had a solution to the problem of the Mass, even if Zwingli did not. The two brothers' attitude may well have represented the feelings of the extremists at this time.

Hearings to discover the cause of the outbreak against the tithes were

18. *E.A.*, 369.

held by the town fathers in July. The representatives of the villages cited the sermons of Wilhelm Röubli and Gregorius Lüthi of Richterswil in support of their refusal to pay the tenths. Lüthi had taken part in the fast violations of 1522 and, in the fall of 1523, inflammatory preaching cost him his post as People's Priest in Richterswil.[19] Röubli's expulsion from Basel, arrival in Zurich, and connection with the parish of Wytikon have been discussed; his role in the Baptist movement is well known.

Though Wytikon was one of the villages which objected to paying tithes, the report delivered to the Council did not mention what Röubli had said about tenths. Instead, it presented a graphic description of his criticism of the clergy and the secular authorities. According to the testimony presented to the magistrates, Röubli said that the clergy were "murderous," "heretical," and "thieving," and referred to the local vogt, burgomaster, and junker as "stinking Vogt," "stinking Burgomaster," "stinking Junker."[20] Röubli's views were certainly not shared by Zwingli, and his attitude indicated that at least one of the future Baptists had already begun to have doubts about the personnel of the secular government. His strong language is reminiscent of Grebel's remarks to the Council in July, 1522. The incidence of those associated with the fast violations, the tithe question, and the Baptist church is too high to justify Yoder's denial of a connection between early radicalism at Zurich and later Anabaptism. Although the evidence presented so far does not prove that the radicals participated in the tithe agitation in order to realize their own plan for reform, it does make it more likely.

Göters sees the proposals for the creation of a separate church advanced at this time by Grebel, Manz, and Stumpf as a part of their attempt to achieve a more rapid and complete break with the traditional cult, and he associates their programme with the tithe agitation of June, 1523; but the majority of modern scholars who have considered the question do not agree with him. Some admit that the first proposals may have been made as early as the summer of 1523, but deny that they represented a joint undertaking by Stumpf, Grebel, and Manz or that they had any connection with the tithe agitation. Stumpf may have acted independently in the summer, but they state that Grebel and Manz made their suggestions after the October Disputation, when the breach between their position and Zwingli's was becoming increasingly obvious. These scholars maintain that the account which Zwingli gave of the discussions in the hearings of April, 1525, reflects his impression of a series of

19. Göters, 32; *E.A.*, 378, 379, 427, 445, 479.
20. *E.A.*, 378.

conversations that were carried on between him and the future Baptists from the fall of 1523 to September of 1524.[21] Göters finds general support among the older generation of Zwingli scholars both for his assumption that there was an organized radical group in Zurich which contained

21. There is wide disagreement concerning the exact dating of their proposals. Bender, who denies the existence of a radical party until the summer of 1524, believes that, in the face of persecution, a number of diverse groups who had become disillusioned with Zwingli's policy drew together during the summer of 1524 and quickly recognized Grebel as their leader. Only after the October Disputation did Grebel and Manz begin to break away from Zwingli's inner circle. Bender does admit that Grebel was active with Aberli, Pur, and Hottinger, but he claims that there was no evidence of an organized connection beween them and Grebel. The proposals for a separate church could have been made at any time between the summer of 1523 and early September, 1524. He agrees that the first suggestions about a separate church were probably made in the summer of 1523, but he does not think that Grebel, Manz, and Stumpf co-operated with each other, or made their approach to Zwingli at the same time (Bender, 86, 88, 95–6, 104–5, 107). Blanke goes even further. Arguing that Grebel and Manz were among Zwingli's closest followers, he asserts that the plan for the establishment of a believer's church was first advanced by them after the Second Disputation. The crux of the proposition was that the old Council be replaced by a truly Christian one and reveals that Grebel and Manz saw the Council as the main obstacle to a further reform of the cult. Zwingli refused the suggestion and forced Grebel and Manz to think through their position once again. Grebel and his friends arrived at a fully articulated programme by the fall of 1524 when they wrote to Thomas Müntzer (Blanke, 10–12). Krajewski allows that there may well have been a small group of opponents to Zwingli's policy who later became *Täufer*, as early as 1523, but he does not believe that the group was fully organized until 1524. Noting that Grebel, Manz, and Castelberger were never mentioned in the records as a group, he argues that mutual disillusionment brought the three men together during 1524. The discussions with Zwingli took place before the question of Baptism became a central issue which would mean that they had taken place before the summer of 1524, or, more likely, the spring of 1524, when Röubli began to preach against infant baptism. He agrees that some of the conversations must have been held in the fall, if not the summer of 1523, but does not think that the proposals made to Zwingli represented a common undertaking. Though he maintains that there was already tension between Zwingli and the later *Täufer* before the October Disputation, he claims that Manz did not share such feelings and doubts that he was even present at the Second Disputation. He concludes that Manz took part in the discussions with Zwingli after Grebel and Stumpf had already presented their ideas. It is likely that Manz became involved only after Stumpf had left Zurich, and that the bulk of the conversations took place at the end of 1523 or the beginning of 1524. Krajewski (29–31, 37, 40–1). Yoder doubts Blanke's assumption that all the proposals were made after the October Disputation and asserts that at least some of them took place before Stumpf left Zurich at the end of 1523. He believes that all of them occurred between the fall of 1523 and 1524. The fact that the initial approach was made in 1523 indicates how close Grebel and his friends were to Zwingli's position. They believed that their proposals would win Zwingli's support and would put the whole church at Zurich on their side (Yoder, 29–30). Yoder's account appears to assume that the three men were working together when they made their suggestions to Zwingli.

among its members the future leaders of the *Täufer* church, and for his assertion that they advanced proposals for the creation of a separate church in the summer of 1523.[22]

When Zwingli gave testimony concerning the activities of Grebel and Stumpf during 1523 at the hearing held in April, 1525, the events he described must have occurred before Stumpf's expulsion from the canton in December, 1523. The problem with the entire testimony is that it was given almost two years after the events took place. Time, the emergence of the Baptist church, and the hostility its appearance evoked certainly coloured Zwingli's testimony. The Baptists had developed their programme by 1525, and Zwingli may have read elements of their present position into his recollection of the proposals made in 1523. According to Zwingli's testimony, Stumpf approached him and Leo Jud several times to propose the establishment of a "separate people and church" which would be made up of those whose lives were "blameless" and who were true to the Gospel. The members were to be free of any obligation to pay tithes and interest. Zwingli and Jud rejected the proposals in a friendly manner. After this Conrad Grebel came to Zwingli and advanced the same proposition which Zwingli rejected. Despite the fact that their proposals did not meet with Zwingli's approval, the supporters of this programme continued to meet at night and to plan for the creation of a separate church. Zwingli claimed that in another conversation Stumpf had suggested killing the priests. Stumpf subsequently denied Zwingli's report, but the latter described how he had confronted Stumpf with Leo Jud and Caspar Goodmann, who was the chaplain in the hospital run by the Dominicans, as witness and made him admit before them that he had made such a proposal. After that Stumpf once

22. Baur, II, 3–8, 11–20, 27–8, 47–8; Egli 86–91, 97–8; O. Farner III, 380–96; IV, 102–32. Baur says that the "radical agitators" Röubli, Grebel, and Stumpf openly expressed their dissatisfaction with Zwingli and his methods, especially his willingness to leave the implementation of reform to the government, after both the First and Second Disputations. He believes that the efforts of the "radicals" at Zurich "were first directed against the form of the cult." Though the "radicals" sought to increase the tempo of reform through the tithe agitation, Baur asserts that the opposition to tithes also had a social aim. The "radicals" sought not merely to alter the forms of religious life but also to change the social and political structure of the city (Baur II, 13–14, 16, 47). He does not specifically relate the proposals for a separate church with the tithe agitation. Oskar Farner connects Grebel and Manz with the original fast violators of 1522, and says that they met with others, including Stumpf, at the house of Andreas Castelberger, who expounded the letters of Paul to them. He places the conversations between Zwingli, Jud, Grebel, Manz, and Stumpf in the second half of 1523. He does not connect these proposals with the tithe agitation of 1523, though he does link the activity of the extremists with the outbreak against the tithes which took place in June, 1523 (O. Farner, III, 381, 386; IV, 114–15).

again came to Zwingli and told him he had informed the elders at Höngg, that they need not pay interest or tithes.[23] Zwingli maintained that both Grebel and Stumpf had urged him, "more than once," that all things should be held in common.[24]

Zwingli recorded a similar experience with Manz. Manz had once accosted him in the street before the house of Hans Huiuf, a goldsmith who was subsequently connected with the *Täufer*, and had spoken of the nature of the new church to which only those "who knew themselves to be without sin" should belong. Later he had come to Leo Jud's house while Zwingli was there, and had admonished him and his fellows to subject their sermons to the scrutiny of Manz's circle of friends.[25]

The next bit of testimony concerned a report from Bern that a man named Martin, who had been with the Baptists, had claimed that they were right in believing there should be no government and in advocating common property. It was also reported that Blaurock, one of the Baptist leaders, had said the *Täufer* would fight "my Lords" when they had gained a sufficient following. Taken in conjunction with recent statements made by Grebel that the Messiah was about to come, Zwingli said he was convinced that Grebel and his group sought to increase their numbers in order to free themselves from the magistracy. He accused the "rebaptizers" "of continually changing their minds." First they had sought to establish a separate church to which only those who knew themselves to be sinless could belong and then Manz had sought to subject the preaching of the city's pastors to the supervision of the *Täufer*.[26]

---

23. *Z*, IV, 169, 1–14; 170, 9–171, 8; *E.A.*, 692.

24. *Ibid.*, 171, 9–10. The report that Grebel and Stumpf had also demanded that all goods be held in common by the members of the church is difficult to connect with the initial programme attributed to them. Such a request would seem to relate to a later stage in the development of the *Täufer* movement. On the other hand, such an idea might have been advanced. If it were, it would raise the question of how well the radicals understood Zwingli's programme. Zwingli's response in the Archeteles to article forty-six of the Bishop's letter of May 24, 1522, to Chapter had contained the boast, that as result of the rebirth of Christ at Zurich, "all things were thought of in common." Cf. pp. 120–21; *Z*, I, 309, 2. He had qualified this remark by stating that no man thought of things as his own but rather thought and acted in terms of the interests of his fellows and the community rather than those of his own property. When taken in context, the statement cannot be interpreted as a call for Christian communism but rather as a claim that the proclamation of the Gospel had produced a Christian attitude among Zurich's citizens. However, if used carelessly, it could be employed to justify the advocacy of common property, and might have led Grebel and Stumpf to present Zwingli with such a demand. If so, the request only provides another example of the distance between Zwingli and some of his followers.

25. *Z*, IV, 171, 11–172, 8.   26. *Ibid.*, 172, 9–173, 11, 15–23.

The testimony given in 1525 gives every evidence of recording the progressive development of the Baptist position. It is indeed difficult to isolate the proposals made in 1523 from those made later by the Baptists, but it does seem that Zwingli identified both Stumpf and Grebel with the first approaches that were made to him. Some of Zwingli's subsequent references to the programme advocated by the Baptists are useful to anyone who seeks to discover the nature of initial plan that was presented to him. In *Who Causes Tumult*, which appeared at the end of December, 1524, Zwingli derided the *Täufer* for their inconsistency. To begin with, they were too much concerned with external matters and, in addition, they seemed to have difficulty making up their minds.

> Now they wish to have no government; then they desired the government; indeed [now] no one is a Christian who is a ruler. Now they wish to have their own church; afterward the government should not protect the preaching of the Gospel with force. Now, one should kill the false priests; then one should let them preach freely without the use of force.[27]

After this Zwingli complained about their opposition to infant baptism which also anticipated the final position taken by the *Täufer*.[28]

Against the Wiles of the Anabaptists, appeared on July 31, 1527. It was a major attack upon the Baptist position and in it Zwingli gave an account of the origin of the movement. The leaders, who were clearly "fanatical men," had approached Zwingli with all sorts of compliments. He said that he was suspicious of them from the start and knew that opponents of the Gospel would be found even among those who "gloried in the name of Christ." The precedent for what they requested was found in the book of Acts which recounts how those who truly believed had separated from those who did not to found their own church which soon attracted all who had faith. The leaders of the "sect" wanted the same thing to be done at Zurich and had assured Zwingli that a majority, whom Zwingli himself was to summon, would join the separate church and would elect their own Council. The leaders objected to the status quo in the city because there were many "godless" men in the present Council and in the existing "mixed church."[29]

Zwingli's answer to them was typical. Citing the parable of the wheat and tares to support his argument, he agreed that the godless, even among those who appeared to confess Christ, were always present; but he maintained that as long as their conduct was proper, the church could

27. *Z*, III, 404, 5–10.
28. *Ibid.*, 404, 10–13.
29. *Z*, VI, 32, 2–33, 6; 33, 8–11, 13–34, 1.

afford to have them as members. Zwingli hoped that by keeping the godless in the church many of them would be won over to the faith, and he said that in any case the pious were able to live with them. He feared that a separation would cause unrest and he denied that the example in Acts fitted the situation at Zurich. At the time when the incident in Acts took place, the separation occurred because many refused to recognize Christ; this was not the case at Zurich, where he was nominally recognized by all. The majority desired no division, and Zwingli was convinced that further preaching would increase the number of believers, without causing tumult, while a division of the "body" (*corpus*) would not achieve this result. Though he granted that the Council appeared to the early Baptists as devoted to worldly concerns, he refused to countenance any change in its composition. His reason was simple: the magistracy supported and advanced the proclamation of the Word of God, as Jehoshaphat had protected the priests and Levites both with the law and with armed force.[30] There was no reason to alter the membership of the Council.

When the leaders saw that they could not get anywhere with Zwingli, they chose "another way." In the ensuing passage Zwingli described their attack upon infant baptism, his attempts to meet with them to discuss the matter, and the friction which resulted. Ultimately he claimed that they fastened upon rebaptism which became a sign of "tumultuous" men.[31]

The main outlines of the plan advocated by Grebel, Manz, and Stumpf can be discerned. First, they sought the establishment of a separate church, and though the exact nature of the government's relation to the church cannot be determined, it seems that they sought to replace the Zurich Council with a magistracy recruited from the ranks of "true Christians."[32] Unless Zwingli's testimony is completely unreliable, it presents considerable evidence that the demand for the abolition of tithes was made as part of the original proposition for the establishment of a separate church. Zwingli stated that Stumpf and Grebel had desired the members of the believers church to be free of any obligation to pay tithes. Later in the hearing he returned to the same issue and said that Stumpf had boasted to him that he had told the elders at Höngg they need not pay tithes or interest. It also seems justifiable to conclude that Zwingli assumed those who approached him did so on behalf of an

30. *Ibid.*, 34, 2–36, 5.
31. *Ibid.*, 36, 7–43, 3.
32. Bender, 103–4; Blanke, 10–11; Yoder, 29–30, 167–8; Göters claims that the radicals probably hoped for a more "evangelical" Council but he is not sure of this because of their extreme statements concerning government (Göters, 33).

organized group "among those who gloried in the name of Christ," i.e., among his own followers.

Zwingli's remark that the *Täufer* first wanted government support and then rejected it indicates that they only later turned against the idea of government support for the Reformation. When Stumpf advocated killing the priests, he must have assumed that this action would be supported by the magistracy, for otherwise it could not have been carried out. The account given in *Against the Wiles of the Anabaptists* reveals that Grebel and Stumpf apparently thought a majority of the people would favour their entire scheme and that this majority would be able to replace the present Council with a "Christian" one. The conclusions that Zwingli drew from Blaurock's threat and Grebel's statement about the imminent coming of the Messiah, reveals that even after the emergence of the Baptist movement he feared that the *Täufer* had not given up their hope of winning support for their programme by using force and, possibly, by seizing control of the government. It also demonstrates that Zwingli felt Grebel and his circle still saw the advantage of winning a majority in support of a change of government, after their alienation from Zwingli and the magistrates. The final disillusionment of the *Täufer* with the secular power is reflected in the rumour reported from Bern that the *Täufer* wanted no government.

Zwingli's reply to the initial proposals of the radicals was consistent with his doctrine of the church as a mixed body, already developed by the middle of 1523. His desire to avoid tumult, to win further converts by continued preaching, and to avoid dividing the "body" of the people all follow from his assumption that society was a unified whole and that the Gospel was to be preached to the whole community. His defence of the Council because it aided the spread of the Gospel with law, and, where necessary, with force, reflects both importance of the Council in Zwingli's programme for reform and the reasons he relied upon it throughout his career. The account that he presented in *Against the Wiles of the Anabaptists* indicates that the discussions concerning the separate church took place before the issue of infant baptism became central.

However, despite the fact that Stumpf was exiled from Zurich by the end of 1523, the question of whether the proposals were in fact made at the height of the tithe controversy and how great a role, if any, the enthusiasts played in it, in order to expedite a reform of the cult, remains open. Even among those who deny the connection between the tithe agitation and the early Baptist movement, there is no universal agreement that the first proposals were not made in the summer of 1523.

Only Blanke places all of them after the compromise which took place in December, 1523; Yoder would place the first conversations in the fall of 1523, while Bender and Krajewski agree that the initial conversations probably took place in the summer.[33] The assumption which underlies the chronology adopted by this group is that there was little or no connection between Grebel and Manz and the enthusiast element at Zurich until after the break with Zwingli in December, 1523. Whatever suggestions were made before December could not be the result of organized action by a group of radicals, as has already been noted. If, as it seems more likely, there was a radical group which desired to speed up the tempo of reform, then its association with the tithe agitation would appear more plausible. Though it cannot be denied that conversations betwen the future *Täufer* and Zwingli went on between the fall of 1523 and 1524, it is difficult to say what was discussed by the participants. Zwingli gives the impression that the future *Täufer* made contradictory demands.

The major question is whether Grebel and Manz would have suggested either the creation of a separate church, or the substitution of a Christian magistracy for the present government after Zwingli's firm alliance with the existing Council had been so clearly established by the events of December, 1523. When Grebel wrote to Vadian on December 18, 1523, he accused Zwingli of neglecting "the divine ordinances against saying Mass" and claimed that he had followed a prudent course which was also "diabolical." Grebel also referred to the commission that had formulated the final decision on the question of the Mass as "bare faced scoundrels."[34] If Grebel meant what he said, it seems unlikely that he would have tried to win Zwingli, whom he identified as one of the "scoundrels," for his programme after that date: in view of Zwingli's expressed attitude this would have been a fruitless undertaking.

Blanke believes that Grebel, Manz, and Stumpf approached Zwingli after the Council's mandate of December 18 and that they suggested the Council be replaced by a truly Christian magistracy because they viewed the Zurich magistracy as the main obstacle to the further reform of the cult.[35] Blanke's interpretation underestimates the key position that the Council already occupied in the affairs of the Reformation. Unless the radicals felt strong enough to challenge the Council, which is doubtful, the only reason for them to advocate their programme was that they thought the Council might be amenable to it. Although the Council had

33. Cf. chap. X, n. 21.
34. *Q*, I, 8.
35. Blanke, 10–11.

restrained the progress of the reform movement throughout 1522, neither the full extent of its policy of caution nor of Zwingli's willingness to adhere to it had been realized by the spring and early summer of 1523. There was good reason for the radicals to hope that they would meet with success.

It is still possible that the radicals made their approach to Zwingli in the early fall of 1523; but when the Council issued its mandate which allowed for the appeal of grievances, while enforcing the continued payment of tithes, Grebel expressed his anger at this "tyrannical and turkish behaviour."[36] If Grebel had remained as close a follower of Zwingli as some modern scholars would have us believe, his angry response is all the more puzzling, especially in view of the positive attitude towards secular authority that Zwingli had already expressed in the sermon *On Divine and Human Righteousness*. However, if the question of the spiritual tenths and the plan for a separate church, as well as the proposal that the Council be replaced by a truly Christian one, were part of a general campaign mounted by the radical element in the hope that both Zwingli and the Council would greet them with favour, then Grebel's harsh words over the Council's action are quite understandable. They imply anger and disappointment with the government and with Zwingli who had failed to act in support of the radicals' plan.

It is true that Grebel's attitude toward the civil power was not completely clarified until after the final break with Zwingli in December, and it seems that he shared much the same opinion of the government's place in the task of reform as did Zwingli during the course of the Second Disputation. On the other hand, there were several exchanges between Stumpf, Grebel, and Zwingli during the Disputation that indicate that the radicals were already sceptical of Zwingli's policy and had begun to turn against the government. Though Zwingli denied it, Stumpf had questioned whether the Reformer was actually allowing the magistrates to decide the issue of the Mass and the images for themselves. Grebel had called for an immediate mandate to be issued listing the abuses connected with the Mass. Zwingli had agreed that there were several abuses involved in the ceremony but suggested that these be done away with slowly in order to avoid public turmoil. Grebel had then engaged Zwingli in a debate over the use of leavened or unleavened bread which Zwingli had maintained was not a central issue and should be left to each congregation to decide.[37] If the three men were in agree-

36. *Q*, I, 2; Göters, 34; *E.A.*, 419–20.
37. *Z*, II, 784, 10–14, 17–18; 786, 5–6; 789, 7–16, 26–30; 790, 17–20.

ment, it is hard to see why Grebel and Stumpf felt called upon to challenge Zwingli. It is possible, as some scholars have claimed, that the documents of the Disputation were altered to fit the terms of the compromise Zwingli subsequently accepted at the behest of the Council. This problem will be dealt with in the next chapter, but it seems unlikely that this was the case. If the leaders of the enthusiasts had already laid their plans before Zwingli and he had rejected them, then their motivation for questioning his stand and the extent of the magistracy's authority over the affairs of the church makes sense. They had begun to have their doubts about Zwingli and no longer trusted the magistrates. Thus, what took place at the Disputation marks a stage in the disillusionment of some of Zwingli's close followers and shows that they were already beginning to turn away from his policy.

The Council's decision to delay the removal of the images and the abolition of the Mass revealed that the Zurich government was determined to procede with caution, and also demonstrated that it was fully in control of the situation. Even if Grebel, Manz, and Stumpf had still hoped to win Zwingli for their programme between the end of October and the middle of December, what real prospects did they, or Zwingli, if he had agreed to their ideas, have of achieving their goal? There is no evidence that they proposed using force but short of this how could they, even with Zwingli's help, have hoped to take steps far more extreme than those which the Council had just refused to take. To gain their object at this time would have meant an open conflict with the established government and almost undoubtedly would have caused civil strife, if not civil war, in the canton. The programme suggested to Zwingli must have been formulated and forwarded at a time when the radicals believed that both Zwingli and the Council might be sympathetic to it, not at a time when the Council's attitude was clearly opposed to any such action.

Yoder claims that one of the major factors leading to Zwingli's conversion to the alliance with the magistracy at the end of 1523 was that the January Disputation had been won so easily. This convinced him that co-operation with the magistracy was the most advantageous method of achieving reform and led him to believe that the magistrates would follow his lead in carrying it out.[38] It is just as possible that his victory persuaded the radicals that their own hopes had good prospects. In the first half of 1523 the tide of reform seemed so strong and the Council so pliable to the wishes of those who stood for Christian renewal that it was conceivable for the enthusiasts to believe that the Council might sanction not only the creation of a "believers church" but also a

38. Yoder, 165.

reorganization of the government to bring its composition into line with the growth of the party which favoured the religious changes taking place in the city. Without some prospect of agreement with the Council the proposals of the enthusiasts were pointless.

At this time it was clear that the establishment of a separate church would have achieved a complete break with the traditional cult, and Zwingli himself obviously wished to achieve a thorough transformation of the old liturgy. In spite of Stumpf's desire to kill priests and the demand that tithes be done away with, the proposals of the radicals merely extended the logic of the policy Zwingli and the Council had pursued since November, 1522. The preaching offices set up with the Council's approval had created an institution rivalling the priestly office. The existence of two posts in the same church was transitional and prepared the way for the completion of Christian renewal at Zurich. The extremists did not demand the destruction of the old church. In effect they were asking that a second church be set up alongside the old one. Once the new church, which was untainted by any connection with the old cult, had won support, the old church would not long survive and it would also be possible to appoint a more truly Christian government.[39] However, the plan they supported provided for a more rapid transition from the liturgy of the old church to a reformed worship than did the Council's policy. The radicals were no doubt unduly optimistic about the number of sinless souls ready to join the new church and they differed with Zwingli in believing that external piety was a sure proof of sinlessness; but what they suggested was by no means entirely out of step with what had already been taking place in the city.

Grebel and his friends made their initial proposition in the late spring or early summer of 1523, when the chances for a favourable hearing were best, and probably repeated them after Zwingli had stated his own views in the sermon *On Divine and Human Righteousness*, delivered in late June and published on July 30, 1523. It is questionable if there was a strong reason for them to make any such suggestion to Zwingli after the end of September, when they began to become angry and disillusioned with his policy. If they did, it must have been with a growing sense of frustration.

If there was a fallacy in the thinking of Grebel's circle, it was their tendency to centre attention upon the progress of reform in Zurich. Even if the situation at Zurich merited the proposals they made, the demand for the creation of a separate church was dangerous. As a transitional measure it embodied the negation of the traditional view of a unified

39. Göters, 33–4.

Christian society. It was an attack upon the cultic practices of such a society and upon the economic basis for the cult, which involved secular and clerical interests. A separate church at Zurich, especially one supported by a newly appointed Christian magistracy, would have caused a violent reaction in the rest of the Confederacy.

At the very time Grebel, Manz, and Stumpf were making their proposals, the Federal Diet, alarmed at the revolutionary character of events in the city threatened Zwingli with imprisonment if he entered any of the other cantons. Further radicalism would have meant war.[40] The Zurich magistracy supported Zwingli because the majority of the councillors believed in his cause and because, for the sake of the future of Christian renewal, Zwingli was ready to temporize. If Zwingli had embraced Grebel's proposals, the magistrates would have been forced to abandon him in order to protect Zurich. Without them the entire reform party would have been crushed. Zwingli, who was already closely allied with the magistrates, had to reject the suggestions of the radicals.

The records from the end of June bear out the wisdom of his refusal. A hearing of the Council concerning a report given by Kaspar von Mülinen, an aristocratic opponent of church reform, to the Confederacy gathered at Bern reveals the impression that the tithe controversy made upon the conservative party at Zurich. The Council could not control the populace and men were not safe even in their own homes; farmers refused to pay tithes or interest; the city and countryside were divided against themselves.[41] In a letter written to Henrich Göldli at Rome, Canon Johannes Widmer described the anxiety of the conservative clergy: "We priests in the city really do not know whether we are safe." Widmer lamented that the common man no longer respected the Mass because it was openly called a fraud in the pulpit. He warned that if the papacy did not act to protect the clergy, they would be forcibly deprived of their faith and office by the people.[42] Widmer's account bears out the fact the anti-tithe agitation was accompanied by unrest over, and opposition to, the Mass. Such unrest inevitably aroused the other Confederates against Zwingli's programme and the city which supported it. The situation demanded caution on Zwingli's part.

Zwingli exercised restraint. The tithe controversy reached its height while he was still preparing the defence of the Sixty-Seven Articles. Two days after the six villages had presented their grievances to the Council, Zwingli delivered his sermon *On Divine and Human Righteousness*. Although it cannot be proven definitely that Grebel had called for the creation of a separate church either before Zwingli delivered the sermon

40. Egli, 92.　　　41. *E.A.*, 370.　　　42. *E.A.*, 372.

on June 24, or before he had published it in July, there is ample
justification to claim that Zwingli addressed his remarks to the men
around Grebel.[43] Even if there was no connection between the demand
for a separate church and Zwingli's sermon, the latter's difficulties with
the extremists culminated in the tithe agitation. The extremists were
exploiting genuine dissatisfaction over the misuse of tithes to force the
immediate completion of the reform of the church. A policy statement
that would calm the majority, who followed Zwingli, and, at the same
time, make his supporters aware of the difference between them and
Grebel's faction was needed. The sermon *On Divine and Human
Righteousness* achieved this, and, in published form, served to refute
the charges of radicalism levelled against Zwingli's reform party by the
Federal Diet. Shortly after its appearance the *Defence of the Sixty-Seven
Articles* was published. To understand what divided Zwingli from Grebel,
it is necessary to consider certain aspects of both works.

The letter addressed to Nikolas von Wattenwyl, Provost of the
Cathedral Chapter at Bern, which was prefaced to the published edition
of the sermon briefly described the relationship between the Gospel and
the magistracy that was the cornerstone of Zwingli's political theory. The
sermon itself was a long elaboration of this basic idea. As long as civil
government fulfilled the responsibility that God assigned it, the Gospel
supported the government. "The Gospel of Christ is not opposed to
government . . . but rather is a support to the magistracy . . . in so far
as it [the magistracy] acts in a Christian way, according to the standard
which God prescribes."[44] In the body of the sermon, Zwingli asserted
that the world was governed by a twofold righteousness.[45] The basis for,
and the limitation upon, civil government were found in the doctrine
of human righteousness. The major tenet of human righteousness,

43. Cf. p. 146–7 ff. Egli assumes that this was the case (Egli, 90–1). Schmid's
recent study of Zwingli's sermon asserts that it was directed to a particular group
which was responsible for stirring up the unrest over the tithes. Among its members he lists Simon Stumpf, Wilhelm Röubli, and Andreas Castelberger (Schmid
14–15). Their activity threatened the social structure of the city and allowed
Zwingli's pro-papal opponents, especially among the aristocracy, to win back lost
ground. Schmid does not associate the sermon with a response to Stump's and
Grebel's proposal concerning a separate church, but he does identify the group
which caused Zwingli problems at this time with the future *Täufer* (Schmid, 15,
17). Schmid has been sharply criticized by Yoder for associating the tithe agitation and Zwingli's sermon with a radical group which subsequently became the
cadre of the *Täufer* movement (Yoder, *MOR*, XXXV, 84–5).
44. *Z*, II, 473, 1–5.
45. The parallel between Zwingli's conception and that outlined by Melanchthon's theses concerning the twofold nature of government should be noted. Cf.
pp. 23–4.

established by God to govern the conduct of men in the world, was that each person must be given his due. Government existed to make sure that this exchange took place. The standard of human righteousness in the world was eternally challenged by the requirements of divine righteousness.

Divine righteousness was prior to and essential to human righteousness because it was part of God's nature. Although none could live up to its norm, God still demands those who wish to come to Him to do so. The apparent hopelessness of man's plight had been relieved by Christ; thanks to his grace, Zwingli asserted, men could find God. All those who hear and believe the Gospel, the message of grace, are made holy and are able to fulfil requirements of divine righteousness.[46]

Having made man's need for Christ clear, Zwingli spelled out exactly what divine righteousness was by comparing the standard of external conformity to God's law with what God's righteousness really demanded of men. For example, Zwingli said it was not enough that a man should not kill, or commit adultery. Those who were truly just would not only not kill or commit adultery, they would not be angry at others, or lust after another man's wife.[47] He concluded that all the commandments were contained in the words of Christ found in Matthew 22: 37-9.[48] The love commandment epitomized all others and was the sum of what divine righteousness required. Although Zwingli recognized the existence of human righteousness, which he identified with outward confirmity to God's law, his definition of true righteousness rejected an external standard of behaviour, by which a man could be adjudged truly just, and placed the criterion of judgment beyond the authority of any human institution. Only God knew what was in the hearts of men.

Once he had done this, Zwingli then discussed the application of his doctrine of righteousness to society. The law, like righteousness, is two-fold. One part of the law is based upon divine righteousness and applies to the inner man whom God alone judges; the other part is concerned with the external behaviour of men:

Therefore there are two kinds of law, just as there are also two righteousnesses: a divine and a human (law). One kind of law concerns only the inner man: how one should love God and ones neighbours. No one is able to fulfil this law; thus no one is righteous except the one God, and except

---

46. *Z*, II, 475, 5-9, 15-19; 476, 3-9; 478, 1-6, 19-28.
47. *Ibid.*, 479, 28-30; 480, 6-7.
48. *Z*, II, 482, 19-21; "37 Jesus said unto him, Thou shalt love the Lord thy God with all thy heart, and with all thy soul, and with all thy mind. 38. This is the first and great commandment. 39. And the second is like unto it, Thou shalt love thy neighbour as thyself."

he, whose redemption is Christ, and who, through grace, is made just by faith. The other kind of law concerns the external man; and consequently one may be outwardly pious and just, and, nonetheless be inwardly impious and damned before God.[49]

It was not for the pious that God ordained the law governing the external man, but to restrain the Godless who were capable of destroying individual believers and whole nations. The lesser law uses compulsion and can never make a man just before God; its inability to make men truly just is the ultimate proof of its inadequacy.[50]

The law founded upon human righteousness, which Zwingli said was summarized in the ten commandments, was established by God as a result of the Fall and made it possible for men to live together in peace. If men followed the love commandments the rest of the commandments would be unnecessary. However, Zwingli admitted that in the present situation they were essential and that it was the magistrates' task to administer the law founded upon them.[51] Therefore he concluded that judges and magistrates are the servants of God. because they enforce the commands of human righteousness through the law. Disobedience to their law is disobedience to God: "Therefore the judges and rulers are servants of God; they are the schoolmasters; and he who is not obedient to their justice acts also against God, be he priest or layman. . . ."[52] No statement could make clearer the basis for his justification of government, nor, for that matter, the position and positive function he gave to the government as the "schoolmaster."

To illustrate the relationship between the government and the twofold righteousness Zwingli presented a number of examples. Among others, he considered the question of usury. The place he assigned to government in the discussion actually left it to enforce a standard of behaviour even less rigorous than that enjoined by the dictates of human righteousness; it also appeared to contradict his subsequent identification of human righteousness with secular authority.

He argued that divine righteousness counsels men to give what they have to the needy without expecting repayment but that God has provided two other alternatives. If men fail to give away what is theirs, God has commanded that they at least loan money without interest. Failing this, God has provided the government, which allows interest to be given and taken and regulates the disagreements which result from

49. Z, II, 484, 15–24.
50. Ibid., 483, 16–21, 24–36, 30–2; 485, 22–30.
51. Ibid., 486, 20–21; 487, 4–9.
52. Ibid., 488, 4–6.

the practice. Those few who don't give or take interest are considered pious among men, but are disliked by the government because they do not. However, since they do not sell what they have and thus distribute it among the poor, they are not pious before God. As Zwingli saw it the gap between the two standards was very great.[53]

Zwingli went on to explain the relationship between divine righteousness and the secular authority. Divine righteousness must be expounded to prevent the ruler and his subjects from being satisfied with human justice, for if they were content with it, they would go astray.[54] These remarks were followed by a discussion of the relationship between human righteousness and secular authority. In the course of considering the matter, Zwingli denied that the scripture provided a realm of authority within the domain of human righteousness for the spiritual estate. Since it did not, he equated human righteousness with the civil government. "Human righteousness or government is nothing else than the regular authority, which we call the secular power; for the authority which is called spiritual has no basis in the Divine Scripture for its sphere."[55] The conclusions Zwingli reached clarify his conception of both the clergy's and the magistracy's role in society. The magistracy's policy and administration are concerned with human righteousness, while the clergy's concern is directed toward divine righteousness. In practical terms this meant that the clergy was denied any place in the affairs of government. Its role was to proclaim the norms of divine righteousness that made ruler and subject alike aware of how poor their law and justice were.

Yoder has criticized Zwingli's identification of human righteousness with civil authority as inconsistent with his previous assertion that human righteousness was a divine revelation.[56] It was natural for Zwingli to equate human righteousness with secular authority because he believed government embodied the norms of human righteousness sanctioned by divine revelation. The remainder of his argument make this clear.

After affirming that the spiritual rulers were God's servants appointed to serve the Gospel and that they had no right to exercise secular power, Zwingli discussed the subjects' obligation to obey the magistrate. His argument was based upon the assumption that human righteousness required that each man receive his due. Christ had commanded that men obey 'this human righteousness or government" and he had himself rendered unto Caesar those things which were due to him. Though he was not obliged to do so, Christ had paid his penny to avoid causing

53. *Ibid.*, 489, 15–27.   54. *Ibid.*, 494, 27–9; 494, 12–18.
55. *Ibid.*, 497, 28–31.   56. *MQR*, XXXV, 83.

tumult and had thus set an example for all Christians. The Christian was
to be obedient to whatever ruler was placed over him, be he emperor or
king. However, no one was required to render to the clerical estate the
obedience to the secular authority that God expected from the faithful.[57]
According to Zwingli, all rulers were established by God and therefore
even a bad ruler was entitled to obedience, because he fulfilled God's
purpose by punishing the sins of his people. Those who presumed to
disobey him went against the divine order. However, Zwingli did set
limits to the authority of the ruler. He cannot rule his subjects' consciences, for conscience is known and governed by God alone. If a
prince or ruler, after the manner of Nero and Domitian, or the defenders
of the pope seeks to govern the conscience of men, he should not be
obeyed.[58] No prince has the right to order that which is contrary to the
Gospel or to command that the Gospel be preached according to the
whim of men. Quoting Acts 4:17 and 5:29, Zwingli admonished his
readers to remember that in such a case, they should obey God rather
than men.[59] The reasoning that he pursued at this point provided the
basis for his doctrine of the right of resistance to tyranny, but he did not
develop the idea further in this section. He merely went on to note that
the ruler's inability to control the conscience of his subjects revealed the
weakness of human justice. Unless an evil conscience manifests itself
by punishable behaviour, the justice administered by the ruler is unable
to govern it:

That evil consciences, which are not evident can not be punished by the
rulers, for they cannot recognize them until they are manifested by
works. . . . And from this it is seen that human righteousness is a poor
righteousness, although one is as needful of it as of eating.[60]

In the same section, Zwingli returned to a matter he had touched on
earlier in the sermon. He stated once again that the ruler, as well as the
citizen, profited from hearing the Gospel. In both cases the hearers were
reminded of the inadequacies of human righteousness. On the other
hand, the ruler gained from hearing the Gospel because it informed him
about good and evil and enabled him to raise the administration of
justice beyond the norm of human righteousness: "but rather it brings
the ruler [as well as] the subject to inward piety and greater perfection
than human righteousness requires. . . ."[61] This passage established the

57. Z, II, 497, 31–498, 2, 6–11, 13–20; 499, 28–9.
58. Ibid., 500, 12–14; 501, 5–6; 502, 18–20, 27–9, 33–503, 2.
59. Ibid., 503, 5–9.
60. Ibid., 503, 29–31, 33–504, 2.
61. Ibid., 504, 12–16.

connection between the two levels of righteousness in the world. Both were known to the ruler; their juxtaposition created a tension and forced the magistrate to exceed the standard maintained by enforcing the dictates of human righteousness. Although Zwingli never said that the divine standard could be fulfilled, he assumed that the knowledge of it would affect the conduct of the citizenry and would cause the government to better its administration of justice. The combined result would be an improvement in the general level of life and conduct in society.

Zwingli next considered the subjects' obligation to support the magistrate with taxes. Those who maintained the standard of human righteousness are the servants of God, and taxes paid for their sustenance are a fair return for the contribution they make to society.[62] His comments upon the citizen's obligation to pay taxes were followed by a reminder that he was also required to pay the "spiritual" tenths.[63] He justified the payment on the grounds that the magistrate had the right to command it: "But concerning the tithes which are of the clergy. . . . What indeed may a government do there . . . I say this; each is obliged to render them, as long as a government orders everyone to do it."[64] Those who refuse to pay deserve to be punished, because those who withstand the law of the magistrate resist God's law. No private individual has any right to attempt to take action on the matter, lest he be considered a thief. The supervision of the payments and the correction of abuses is to be left to the magistrates; abuses are not to be ended through disorder, but by "careful consideration."[65] This was Zwingli's answer to the radicals. It reflected not only his conception of the magistrate's right to administer the law of human righteousness, but also his understanding of the situation in the city. Long before he arrived in Zurich, the magistrates had gained control over the financial affairs of the church, including the supervision of the tithes. It was impossible for Zwingli to change this without alienating his closest allies.

Having clarified his attitude on the tithe question, Zwingli reconsidered the limits of the magistrate's authority. He began with a rhetorical question. Did his position on the question of the spiritual tenths mean that the magistrates also had the right to force men to believe that the Mass was a sacrifice, and that it was necessary to "run" to priests to obtain forgiveness of sins, or that the Gospel must be preached according

62. *Ibid.*, 509, 27–30.
63. Zwingli said that he did not wish to consider other types of tithes and ground rent payments and passed on to the question of the "spiritual" tenths (*Z*, II, 512, 10–13).
64. *Z*, II, 512, 14; 513, 3–5.
65. *Ibid.*, 512, 5–6, 13–15; 513, 21–514, 3, 7–9.

to the wishes of the pope. The answer was no, because, as Zwingli explained, the ruler had no power over the Word of God or Christian freedom.[66] If the secular power sought to exercise such control, those who preached the Gospel would oppose it. Zwingli repeated what he had said before: men should obey God rather than men. What God expected was clear enough: he had commanded that his Word be preached and had forbidden men to be silent concerning it.

If Zwingli had ended the sentence which asserted that God had commanded his Word to be proclaimed at this point, it would have rounded out a passage denying the magistracy the right to prevent a further reform of the cult. Instead, Zwingli qualified what he had said with the phrase, "however at the proper time."[67] He then moderated his statement concerning the right to resist the civil authority by shifting the question of justified resistance from the issue of the Mass and other ceremonies to what he apparently considered was a more basic one. The real test of a magistracy's attitude was its willingness to let the Gospel be preached and to let it affect society.

Thus, if your rulers wish to be Christian, they must allow the clear word of God to be preached and afterward let it work. . . . Furthermore, let us notice well, that the authority which the government has over our temporal goods and bodies cannot extend over the soul.[68]

Zwingli noted that these restrictions upon the magistrate do not free men from the payment of interest, usury, and the like, because such matters fall within the administrative competence of the government.[69] The preceding section is of considerable significance. In it Zwingli clarified his position on the problem of the spiritual tenths and concluded that the government had the authority to regulate them. The juxtaposition of his views on this question, and his remarks upon the government's authority over the Mass and the confessional, does not appear to be accidental and it gives added support to the supposition that the agitation against the spiritual tenths was closely connected with an attempt to bring about a purification of the cult. The way in which Zwingli dealt with this issue of further reform is crucial. When he stated that the government had no right to coerce the people and to maintain the traditional view of the Mass and other ceremonies against the

66. *Ibid.*, 514, 11–19.
67. The Latin equivalent given in footnote sixteen for the words "doch zu rechter zyt" is "opportune tamen omnia peragamus," "however let us accomplish everything seasonably."
68. Z, II, 514, 30–515, 3, 5–7.
69. *Ibid.*, 515, 7–10.

authority of the Gospel, until it saw fit to change the usages, his position appears to agree precisely with that Grebel took during the Second Disputation. But Zwingli did not stop there. First, he added a limiting phrase to what seemed to be a call for the immediate abolition of abusive practices condemned by scripture: "however at the proper time." Then, in effect, he explained why he did not push for these changes and oppose the wishes of the government: the real test of a regime was its willingness to let the Gospel be preached and to let it work upon society.

When the policy pursued by the magistracy since the mandate of 1520 is considered, the reason for Zwingli's reluctance to press for the modifications the Gospel called for is clear. The Zurich government had done all that was possible to forward the proclamation of the Gospel and had given it time to take effect. Therefore, there was no reason to oppose it because it had already fulfilled the essential requirement for a "Christian" magistracy. In so doing, it had recognized the limits of its authority and was not attempting to impose beliefs contrary to God's Word upon the people. What remained to be done had to be carried out at the proper time, and it was within the right of the magistrates to determine what that time was. The way in which Zwingli defined a truly Christian magistracy could lie behind his reasons for rejecting Grebel's plan for a separate church and the appointment of a truly Christian magistracy.

The passage explains the nature of Zwingli's alliance with the civil authority, as well as his attitude toward the timing of the changes that the study of scripture made inevitable; it also foreshadows both his willingness to delay the transformation of the Mass at the end of the Second Disputation and to accept a further compromise on the matter in December, 1523. At that time, there was no question that the Council agreed to what the Gospel required. The problem was that the city fathers did not feel that the time was right for change; the full effect of Christ's teaching had not yet been felt in the countryside. When this section of the sermon is considered, it is surprising that some argue that Zwingli and Grebel were at one until after the October Disputation. Zwingli had already taken a stand in the sermon which Grebel, during and after the Second Disputation, made clear he did not accept. The grounds for the break between the two were already clear in July of 1523. It is not correct to say that Zwingli had a sudden change of mind in December.

Zwingli repeated the main themes of his exposition in the summary of the sermon. All men are obliged to follow the norms established by the divine righteousness, but, because they cannot, a lower level of righteousness, the equivalent of natural law, has been established to maintain society. Guardians, whom Zwingli identified with the ordinary magistrate, have been appointed to enforce the standards of human righteousness:

These guardians are the regular magistracy, which is none other than that of the sword, to wit: the one which we call the secular authority, whose office is to carry out all things according to the divine will, and, if this is not possible . . . to carry out all things according to the divine command.[70]

Zwingli's description of those who were the "guardians" left no doubt that he excluded the clergy from the exercise of authority in the world. Those who wielded the sword, the magistrates, were the sole possessors of this power. His conception of the government's task also emphasized the relationship between the two levels of righteousness in the world. The absolute norm for the rulers was the divine will, but since most people were unable to fulfil it, God had provided commandments, i.e., the law of human righteousness, which the magistrate was to enforce. The knowledge of God's will for men, i.e., divine righteousness, obliged the magistrate to strive for a standard beyond the minimum enjoined by the law of human righteousness. To avoid any doubt about the inter-relationship between the two standards, Zwingli warned that the existence of a lesser law allowing men to live together in peace did not free them from the obligation to act according to the norm of divine righteousness. He added that the punishment imposed by the civil arm was directed against outward misdeeds. Nothing the ruler did could make a man inwardly just or unjust, for only God could do this. For this reason, a little later, he told the magistrates that they should not punish anyone because of the ceremonies, whose abolition many demanded, or for anything which was a matter of conscience and concerned the inner man. He reminded them that God alone was able to judge the conscience of men. However, he did not deny that the magistrates had an important task to perform: they punished disobedience and were responsible for removing "all that is against the Divine Word."[71] The problem of doing away with all that was against the Word was very much on Zwingli's mind and he closed with a warning to the magistrates that when the abuses revealed by the Gospel "are not removed by a timely expedient" the anger of the oppressed might become dangerous to the ruler.[72] It is significant that the problem of the abolition of ceremonies and the government's relationship to it, and

70. *Ibid.*, 522, 2–6.
71. *Ibid.*, 523, 4–6, 9–11; 524, 12–14, 30–525; 4, 10–13.
72. *Ibid.*, 525, 14–16.

not the tithes, are the matters touched upon in the conclusion. This fact lends greater weight to the assertion that the tithe issue was intimately connected with a campaign, carried on by a radical group among Zwingli's followers, for a speedier transformation of the cult. Zwingli's problem and attitude are also clear. He wishes to restrain the extremists, but to do this the government had to proceed with a programme of reform. Hence his appeal to the government to abolish the abuses by a "timely expedient." Otherwise, the radicals might win a strong following and attack the magistracy.

The sermon *On Divine and Human Righteousness* made explicit what had been implicit in Zwingli's co-operation with the magistracy throughout his ministry at Zurich. He believed that human life was subject to divine authority and that its purpose was to fulfil God's will as revealed in scripture. The co-operation of the pastor and the magistrate was essential to God's plan. In making these assumptions Zwingli re-asserted the mediaeval conception of society's purpose: life in the world was to be organized to help men reach the Heavenly City. The main difference between the mediaeval conception and Zwingli's was that he replaced the authority of the church with the authority of the scripture.

It is significant that Zwingli never mentioned the church in the sermon. He spoke only of the two offices which governed society and whose functions were defined by the twofold doctrine of righteousness. The strict limitation of the clergy's function to the spiritual realm reflected both the influence of the Erasmian reform programme and the actual situation at Zurich before the Reformation. Zwingli gave the magistrate control over the spiritual tenths because the support of the clergy was a secular matter. For the same reason he later allowed the magistrates to control the ban and to supervise baptism. These were matters of external behaviour and came under the laws of human righteousness.

The attitude expressed in the sermon follows logically from Zwingli's conception of the true church as a spiritual body known only to God. A Christian society might hear the Gospel and strive to move beyond the level of human righteousness, but it remained a mixed body and could never become a true church. Adherence to the externals of church life and confession of the faith made a citizen just in the eyes of the world; only grace could make him just before God. Zwingli's conception of civil power allowed the magistracy to supervise the external life of the church. It did not allow the government to replace or judge God's authority. The theory of the Christian society and the functions imparted to its officers by God was Zwingli's answer to the individualism of the radicals. The radicals may have accepted the same view for a time, as

Yoder suggests, but they later became disenchanted with the Christian magistrates.

The uniqueness of Zwingli's doctrine requires notice. Luther published his *Von weltlicher Obrigkeit Wie weit man ihr Gehorsam schuldig sei (On the Worldly Magistrate; How Far One is Obliged to Obey Him)* in March, 1523. The similarities between the two documents are marked, and Zwingli may have read Luther's tract before he wrote his own. The letter to Blarer in 1528 criticized Luther's conception of Christ's kingdom and demonstrates Zwingli's awareness of Luther's views.[73] Nevertheless, it is difficult to say when Zwingli became familiar with these opinions. Assuming Zwingli had not read Luther's exposition before he published his own views, the best explanation for the similarities between the two is found in the influence exercised upon both men by Augustine, late mediaeval philosophy, and the Erasmian tradition.

Luther did not speak in terms of a twofold righteousness, but his doctrine of the two kingdoms and their guardians who wielded the two swords paralleled Zwingli's. Like Zwingli, he argued that the Fall had made the establishment of secular government necessary. The prince, who presided over the kingdom of the world, derived his authority from God's ordinance. The prince was to punish the wicked and protect the upright, and he achieved this through the administration of the law, which restrained evil-doers and prepared men to receive grace by making them aware of their sinful state. The temporal power was also to protect the people from false doctrine. Luther and Zwingli agreed that the authority of the prince extended over the bodies, goods, and external affairs of men but had no power over the conscience, which was the domain of the spiritual kingdom. The Christian prince carried the sword not for his own benefit but for the sake of his subjects. In so doing he fulfilled the requirements of the love commandment, the norm for those who belonged to the kingdom of God. Luther stressed the importance of the love commandment in the prince's administration of justice as he felt that the mere application of legal principles contained in the law codes was not enough. True justice, which revealed the prince's adherence to the Gospel, required implementation of the love commandment.[74]

It is at this point that Luther's and Zwingli's attitudes differ the most. Although Luther does say that the prince's administration of justice should be influenced by the love commandment, he is neither as specific

73. Z, IX, 452, 15–17.
74. L, XI, 247, 21–7; 257, 27–258, 11; 250, 10–34; 268, 4–21; 271, 27–272, 24; 278, 12–279, 14.

nor as optimistic about what the prince's government can achieve as Zwingli. Because of the corporate nature of the society in which the latter worked and thought, he came to believe that "when the Gospel is preached and all, including the magistrate, heed it, the Christian man is nothing else than the faithful and good citizen; and the Christian city is nothing other than the Christian Church."[75] Zwingli assumed that the secular arm was subject to the norms of divine righteousness, the knowledge of which would not only improve the quality of the justice rendered by the magistrate but would also make possible a constant improvement in society. Therefore it was natural for him to assign to the magistracy familiar with the Gospel a positive function in regulating the affairs of a Christian society. Guided by the Gospel, the magistrates would be able to bring even the external practices of their Christian commonwealth into a closer, though never complete, harmony with the standards of divine righteousness. Unlike Luther, who declared that the kingdom of Christ is not external, Zwingli maintained in a letter to Ambrosius Blarer, written in 1528, that both Christ and the Apostles made decisions about such matters as sabbath observance and circumcision because, he asserted, they were external questions of religious observance and were therefore the responsibility of a Christian magistracy.[76] Citing, in the same letter, the example of the Council of Jerusalem, which had contained lay advisers, he refuted Luther's claim that Christ's kingdom had nothing to do with the external affairs of religion and justified the right of a city council acting with the consent of the people, to abolish the Mass and the images.[77] For Zwingli the Gospel was the norm for government and ultimately ruled over both the inner and the outer man and his society.

Although Luther certainly recognized the right of the prince to direct the initial organization of the territorial church, it is sometimes forgotten that he objected in vain to the interference of the secular arm in the external observances and discipline of the regional church. He wished

75. Z, XIV, 424, 12–22.
76. Z, IX, 452, 16–17; 453, 30–5; 454, 14, 16–17; 455, 24–30.
77. *Ibid.*, 455, 30–456, 2, 30–5; 457, 34–458, 3. Locher explains Luther's attitude in terms of his deep sense of human selfishness which led him to divide sharply the two Kingdoms and to assign to the secular power the essentially negative task of keeping order. Luther did not believe that the world could be improved and saw the task of the Christian to pass through it as best he could. For Luther the Kingdom of God had nothing to do with external things; it was governed by the Gospel "of forgiveness and love." Zwingli believed that the Kingdom of God was concerned with external affairs and, because of his great faith that the "truth and Spirit of God" could not be resisted, assumed that all aspects of society as well as individual existence could be influenced by the Gospel (Locher, *Reformatio*, I, 207, 210).

to place them under the supervision of some kind of ecclesiastical body.[78] His basic understanding of the ruler's function was negative: the ruler was to allow the Gospel to be preached and to permit Christians to live in peace by restraining evil-doers. His conception of the prince's justice left a place for the realization of something more than the mere letter of the law, but he did not believe that society as a whole could be improved. In comparison with what Zwingli said about the relationship between the government of the magistrate and divine righteousness, Luther's advice to the prince appears as little more than an appeal for the rigour of the law to be tempered by mercy. His view of society was static, while Zwingli's was, within limits, dynamic. Whatever the cause of the differences between the two men, the uniqueness of Zwingli's views is apparent.

In general, Luther and Zwingli shared a similar conception of the Kingdom of God and its guardians, the clergy, whose task was to preach God's Word. Both agreed that the spiritual kingdom was superior to the secular because membership in it made men just before God. Zwingli was one with Luther when he said that society was a mixed body in which the members of the Kingdom were scattered among the rest and they agreed that the godly had no need for the law but still were obliged to obey it. However, while Luther advocated passive resistance to a prince who attempted to rule the consciences of his subjects, Zwingli left a greater place for active resistance to tyranny.[79]

Zwingli's exposition of the role of church, the pastor, and the magistrate in the *Defence of the Sixty-Seven Articles* added little that was new to the position which he had already taken in the sermon *On Divine and Human Righteousness*. He discussed the church in article eight, where he stated that the German word for church, *kirck*, or *kilch*, referred to the house in which men gathered to hear God's Word, to have baptism, and to partake of the Lord's Supper, and that it was not an adequate translation of the Greek, Hebrew, or Latin terms that referred to a gathering of the people. In view of the actual meaning of the word he said that where the term "folk" is found in the scripture, it should be rendered as the *gemeind*, i.e., congregation or assembly.[80] This conclusion explains why Zwingli was able to identify the political assembly of the city with the church, as does his definition of the Church Universal which followed. The Church Universal was "the community of all elect believers,"

78. Bornkamm, "Das Ringen der Motive in den Anfängen der reformatorischen Kirchenverfassung," *Das Jahrhundert der Reformation*, 204, 217–19.
79. *L*, XI, 258, 12–30; 251, 12–31; 267, 14–29.
80. *Z*, II, 56, 6–14.

founded upon faith in Christ, joined together by the Spirit, and known only to God.[81] It followed from this that a gathering of self-professed Christians at Zurich, or elsewhere, would be a mixed body and therefore subject to the laws of human righteousness administered by the magistrate.

While discussing the nature of the Church Universal, Zwingli mentioned the place of baptism in it. Baptism, as he conceived of it, was twofold. Baptism with water was an outward sign. Only when the baptized was granted faith did baptism with the Spirit, which initiated him into the Church Universal, accompany the outward sign.[82] He developed the same theme in article eighteen which elaborated his memorialistic doctrine of the Eucharist. Neither Baptism nor the Eucharist were more than outward signs unless the Spirit of God moved the heart of the participant to faith in Christ.[83] By implication, the two-fold nature of both sacraments left the supervision of the outward sign in the hands of the magistrate who was responsible for regulating external expressions of piety. These passages indicate that Zwingli spoke of baptism as an outward sign before the question of rebaptism was raised by the *Täufer*.

Zwingli also made a number of other remarks about the practice of infant baptism in the section concerning confirmation included in article eighteen. His comments reveal a willingness to accept the present practice, if certain changes were made, and demonstrate once again his moderate approach towards the issues of reform. To begin with, Zwingli explained that infant baptism had led to a custom of confirmation which served to provide the child with an understanding of the faith that his parents and godparents had attested for him when he was baptized. In earlier times children had first been instructed and then, when they understood what the faith was and could say that they felt they possessed it, they were baptized. Zwingli did not object to the present practice of infant baptism, but he expressed the hope that the old practice of instructing children properly on the faith would be revived, so that they would be able to receive the Word of God. If it were not, the young would be greatly harmed. Then he alluded with pride to the steps taken the year before at Zurich to provide the correct instruction for the children, so that they would be able to affirm the faith into which they had been baptized when they reached the age of reason. This was, Zwingli said, what confirmation was supposed to achieve.[84] He definitely

81. *Ibid.*, 56, 17–19, 32–3; 57, 15–19.   82. *Ibid.*, 57, 29–32.
83. *Ibid.*, 122, 5–6; 143, 4–6, 15–16, 19–26.
84. *Ibid.*, 123, 4–9, 12–30, 33–124, 3.

did not reject infant baptism, as long as proper religious instruction was given to the young after it had taken place. At Zurich the provision for such training was the responsibility of the magistracy.

Another cursory reference to baptism was made at the end of article sixty-seven in which Zwingli defended himself against those who had charged he had said that unbaptized children were not damned. All that he had really said was that it was more likely that a child of Christian parents, who died unbaptized, would not be damned, than it was that he would be. He maintained that God alone could judge these cases and objected to the practice of preventing unbaptized children from being buried in consecrated ground.[85] The references to infant baptism found in the exposition of the Sixty-Seven Articles are not made, as Yoder implies, to question the practice but to connect it with a sound programme of religious instruction and prevent a man-made legalism from governing the burial of the unbaptized children of Christian parents.[86] Taken as a whole, his views on the subject are consistent with his general attitude of moderation; infant baptism was regarded by him as an external sign of membership in a Christian society.

Having formulated his definition of the Church Universal, Zwingli discussed the second use of the word "church." It referred to a "particular gathering" which, he said, "we call a parish or church congregation." A little later he stated that these gatherings could also be termed "assemblies," or "a general gathering" and, as was fitting, these "assemblies" were referred to as churches and were all members of the Church Universal, which was one in Spirit.[87] By definition, the local churches, gathered to hear the Word and joined by the Holy Spirit to the Church Universal, which consists of all who have faith in Christ, are mixed bodies. It is also manifest that the terminology he used to designate the local church could also be applied to the political assembly of a village or city.

Zwingli considered the character of the priesthood in articles sixty-one, sixty-two and sixty-three. He denied the mediaeval definition of the priest's character and asserted that the priest's honour came not from ordination but from the proper performance of duty.[88] His duty was to

85. *Ibid.*, 455, 18–20, 25–456, 3.
86. Yoder believes that Zwingli himself had led some of his younger followers who became *Täufer* to doubt the validity of infant baptism (Yoder, 33, 43–4, 160–2). This is possible but the passages referred to above make it a questionable assertion. By attributing the main lines of the *Täufer* position to Zwingli, Yoder denies them the credit which they deserve for evolving a truly unique conception of the church and what its religious practices should be.
87. Z, II, 58, 9–15, 20, 26–31.
88. *Ibid.*, 438, 17–25; 439, 4–12, 16–18.

preach the Gospel and care for the poor: "[the clergy are those] who teach in the church; who proclaim God's Word; who translate the Greek and Hebrew language; who distribute help and alms to the poor . . . for this whole part belongs to the Word of God."[89] He also stressed that the congregation "is obliged to give sustenance" to its pastor, a point relevant to the tithe agitation at Zurich.[90]

In articles thirty-four to forty-three Zwingli had discussed the magistrate's office and the subject's obligation to the magistrate. What he said represented an expansion of the basic concepts found in the sermon *On Divine and Human Righteousness*. He denied the clergy any part in the exercise of secular power and asserted that clerics were subject to the civil magistrate. Quoting the words of Christ in Matthew 22:21, he justified the magistrate's function and reminded Christians of their obligation to obey the ruler.[91] He maintained that the good magistrate was a Christian, and that, as a Christian, he sought to promulgate laws "in conformity with the Divine will." Although the righteousness the magistrate served was a mere shadow of true righteousness, the laws he made "have something of the form of Divine law and will."[92] Zwingli went on to consider the right of the magistrate to execute criminals, to demand economic support from the people, and, finally, to lay down the conditions under which an ungodly governor could be removed. Citing the example of Israel, he concluded that obedience to Christ's teaching was the best support for a nation and its ruler.[93] He had no doubt that the magistrate carried out God's purpose in the world. The doctrine of the two-fold righteousness on which he developed the rationale for the ruler's task allowed him to speak of an externally pious Christian city, which as the same time was a mixed body in the eyes of God.

Zwingli reviewed the various aspects of the tithe question in the first section of article sixty-seven. He began denying that he had ever advocated refusing the payment of interest. As long as the government permitted interest, those who have contracted to pay it must do so. All that he had sought was to reveal to pious consciences how they should deal with the matter in order not to anger God. He said, as he had before, that he was unwilling to consider the general question of tithes, some of which were now paid to laymen, and confined his remarks to the spiritual tenths which were rendered to the church. It is possible that Zwingli was considering some compromise on the subject. However,

89. *Ibid.*, 441, 7–12.
90. *Ibid.*, 444, 14–19.
91. *Ibid.*, 304, 10–15; 305, 1–7; 310, 6–16; 319, 10–12.
92. *Ibid.*, 330, 10–14.
93. *Ibid.*, 346, 18–21; 347, 3–7, 20–1.

the position he took was similar to that of the magistracy which refused to remove the obligation to pay but was willing to reduce the burden in some cases and to see to it that the money was put to the proper use. Zwingli's answer to the question whether Christians were obliged to pay tithes by either "divine or human laws" was equivocal. He stated that the clergy had often been deprived of the support to which it was entitled and suggested that a fair proportion of the tithes, but not necessarily the whole amount, be restored to them so that they could enjoy a proper living.[94] The nature of his answer indicates he believed that proper financial remuneration was due to the clergy, according to the laws of human righteousness. Therefore the magistracy which administered this law had the right to enforce the payment of funds sufficient to maintain the clergy. The attitude toward magisterial authority expressed in the sermon *On Divine and Human Righteousness* remained unchanged in the *Defence of the Sixty-Seven Articles*.

Many scholars cite Zwingli's discussion of the ban in articles thirty-one and thirty-two to prove he was a proponent of congregational autonomy. Any reference to the question of an autonomous congregation has to be read within the context of the corporate political structure that influenced Zwingli's thought and made congregational autonomy impossible. Zwingli said the ban must be imposed by the congregation and the pastor of the culprit's home parish. In order to deny a bishop or the pope the right to excommunicate, he defined very carefully the nature of the institution which should impose the ban. As the Universal Church is never visibly gathered together and is known only to God, the individual gatherings of Christians called "church congregations" are the agents of excommunication. If the pastor of the congregation should hesitate to act, the other members are obliged to take the requisite steps, for the responsibility rests with all. He denied that the ban could be laid upon anyone because of debt. Financial questions and other similar matters were to be referred directly to the magistracy. According to Christ's command, excommunication should be imposed only upon those whose offences might infect the entire congregation. These included adultery, blasphemy, seduction, gluttony, false witness, spreading malicious rumours, mercenary service, pimping, lying, and all things causing unrest among Christians.[95] Even these crimes were considered civil offences. When, in 1520, the Zurich Council issued a list of those who should be deprived of alms, every type of offender whom Zwingli said was worthy of the ban had been enumerated. A clear distinction between

94. *Ibid.*, 454, 14–23, 27–455, 4–11.
95. *Ibid.*, 276, 25–8; 278, 12–15; 281, 6–20, 24–30; 282, 5–13; 286, 13–18.

civil offences and private license or immorality was not made; the punishment of all these offences was the responsibility of the magistrate. The way was open, from the first, for the magistrate as the delegated authority of the assembly to control the ban. When the councillors made formal what was implicit and took over the administration of excommunication, they supervised it in co-operation with the marriage court and later the synod. This meant they acted with the advice of the clergy. Thus, through its representatives, the local congregation retained control of the ban. The magistrates' part in the excommunication of offenders did not violate the procedure Zwingli advocated, nor did it mark a departure, as some believe, from a principle of congregational autonomy. Zwingli had never been an advocate of congregational autonomy.

11 The Open Split between Zwingli and the Radicals: August 1523 to December 1523

THE LAST FIVE MONTHS OF 1523 WERE A DIFFICULT TIME FOR Zwingli and the Zurich government. The coterie around Grebel used popular discontent with the old cult and the economic abuses involved in it to forward their reform programme. The successful exploitation of discontent at Zurich by the radicals made the city's position in the Confederacy more difficult, and the situation was further complicated by the preparations of the French for a new campaign in Italy. During August and early September the Council attempted to restrain without causing further unrest, those who wished to serve the French.[1]

Zwingli, in co-operation with the Council, sought to alleviate grievances and to satisfy the average citizen that further reforms would be forthcoming. Official policy tried to differentiate between those eager for additional reforms and the extremists who desired a dangerously swift completion of Christian renewal. As the Council removed one set of grievances, Grebel, Manz, Stumpf, and their following sought to exploit others. The Council thwarted them and they were gradually driven into isolation.

The reforms introduced by the Council reveal the connection between the tithe agitation and demands for a purification of the old cult. A German version of the baptismal service was introduced at the Grossmünster in August, and Zwingli published a preliminary suggestion for the revision of the Mass, *De Canone Missae Epichiresis*. The suggestion, like his early preaching, prepared the people for the next stage of his programme. His proposal, which envisaged the retention of the Latin chants, the priests' vestments, and the liturgical prayers of the old service, was clearly intended to provide for an interim compromise on the question of the Mass and indicated his cautious approach to the sensitive issue of its reform. It evoked sharp criticism among some of his followers, which Zwingli answered in an *Apology*, written on October

1. *E.A.*, 395, 398, 407–8.

9, 1523. He explained that his concern for the weak and uninstructed had dictated the nature of the reform scheme, and he expressed his willingness to set aside both the Latin chants and clerical vestments used in the service. He was not, however, prepared, as his critics demanded, to suppress all the liturgical prayers, except the Lord's Prayer, because they were not scriptural.[2] He did not specify who the dissidents were, but the excessive literalism of their criticism and Zwingli's appeal to all who were Christian to avoid strife provides some grounds for the belief that the *Apology* was directed to the radical element among his followers. His initial plan for the revision of the Mass in the *Apology* reveals his desire to meet the demand for further reform without causing undue unrest in the city, or arousing the hostility of the Confederacy. Thus, the way for the gradual reform of the cult which had been under way since 1520 was to be kept open.

In the meantime, the Council was putting the finishing touches upon an investigation, begun in late June, of the abuses practiced by the Grossmünster Chapter.[3] The conclusion of the investigation was timely, for although the major outbreak against the tithes was over, isolated protests continued.[4] A mandate concerning the tenths, issued by the Council shortly before the reform of the Chapter in September, indicated how much the recurrent protests contributed to Zurich's difficulties with the rest of the Confederacy. Although the magistrates promised that they would deal with genuine grievances concerning the tenths, the mandate, to which Grebel objected with great passion, warned that refusal to pay tithes was not merely a domestic issue; the Confederacy might use it as an excuse to go to war with Zurich: "and our confederates . . . might find cause to wage war against our lords, the city, and the country, which would bring great harm. . . . "[5] If nothing else, the Council's statement refutes Yoder, who claims that there was no real danger of war until the "old order was menaced in a previously unheard of way" by the attack upon the images.[6]

The reform of the Chapter followed close upon the mandate. Zwingli informed the Council that the canons were ready, with the help of the magistracy and the guidance of the scripture, to reform themselves. He also told the magistrates that they were not willing to give up the tithes due the Chapter. The details of the reform were worked out on September 29. Charges for the services of the clergy at weddings, funerals and the like were abolished and the Council promised that, in return for

2. *Z*, II, 6, 617–18; Yoder, 18.
3. Egli, 99.
4. *E.A.*, 376.
5. *Ibid.*, 420; Göters, 34.
6. Yoder, *MQR*, XXXII, 134–5.

tithes, the people would be properly served by the clergy. The number of clergymen supported by tithes was diminished, while a portion of the Chapter's income was assigned to support the education of pastors and a school for boys. The filial churches of the Chapter, Albisrieden, Wytikon, and Schwamendingen, were provided with pastors at the Chapter's expense. Funds not otherwise assigned were set aside for the hospital and the deserving poor. Titles and distinctions separating the canons and the chaplains were abolished; both were to have the same title and function.[7] This change hastened the transformation of the priestly office into a preaching office, and foreshadowed the end of the Mass. Many of the old grievances against the tithes were removed by the Council's action, and the way was open for further reform.

Even before the reform of the Chapter took place, the radicals had shifted the focus of their agitation. On the day the Chapter was reorganized the Council set up a commission to consider the problem of "the images and other such matters."[8] The commission was necessary. During September, Zwingli and Jud had preached against the images and their sermons had been followed by attacks upon the statues of saints in the churches of the city and outlying districts.[9] This was not what Zwingli and Jud had in mind. They had merely begun to prepare for change by their preaching. The Council, however, imprisoned Lorenz Hochrütiner, Wolfgang Ininger, Hans Ockenfuss, and Claus Hottinger for their part in the outbreaks of iconoclasm.[10]

The Council discovered that Hochrütiner and Ininger had been encouraged by Andreas Castelberger. When Hochrütiner and Ininger reported their action to Castelberger, he told them not to worry about what they had done because they had done it publicly. The magistrates also learned that Castelberger had been holding a "school" for the benefit of those who shared his dissatisfaction with the practices of the old church that were still tolerated.[11] In his lectures on Romans to the members of the school Castelberger expressed hostility toward tithes and rich men, because they caused the poor to suffer.[12] The fact that he taught that neither spiritual or secular persons should have anything to do with interest, prebends, or the like, may provide a link between his teaching and the proposals advanced to Zwingli by Grebel and Stumpf: that the separate church should be unsupported by tithes or interest.

7. *E.A.*, 426.   8. *Ibid.*, 425.
9. *Ibid.*, 414–16, 421–2.   10. *Ibid.*, 415, 421.
11. *Ibid.*, 415; Göters, 31.
12. *E.A.*, 623. Egli dated this hearing on January 20, 1523, but because one of the chief witnesses, Lorenz Hochrütiner, was exiled from Zurich in November, 1523, it is clear that the hearing refers to events which took place in the early fall of 1523 (O. Farner, III, 595).

Castelberger's influence also may be reflected in Claus Hottinger's testimony. He explained to the Council that he had taken part in the destruction of an image in order to sell the wood from the statue for the poor.

The names of those who came to Castelberger's gatherings included Heini Aberli, Lorenz Hochrütiner, Wolf Ininger, and Bartholomew Pur.[13] After Hochrütiner's expulsion from Zurich, Grebel wrote Vadian and commended him as a brother from God in Christ 'with whom he had heard the word of God,' which makes it more than likely that Grebel had attended Castelberger's school with Hochrütiner.[14] Oskar Farner also believes that both Grebel and Manz had attended Castelberger's school.[15] Aberli and Pur, as well as Claus Hottinger, who was not directly associated with Castelberger's school in the hearing, had been reprimanded along with Grebel by the Council in July of 1522.[16] The information at hand gives strong grounds for identifying Grebel with Castelberger's school and with those who took part in the attack upon the images. The correlation between the men involved in the iconoclasm of September and in Castelberger's school is high enough to indicate that Castelberger played a part in causing the outbreaks. Every one of the men involved in the attack upon the images had taken part in the fast controversy of 1522. This is more than a coincidence. It represents as good a proof as can be found that there was a radical faction at Zurich which probably formed late in 1521 or early 1522 and continued to be active throughout the next two years. If Grebel was not actively involved in the events of September, he was certainly sympathetic with those who were. Although the Council's records do not mention him by name, its hearings refer to "a monk from Swabia" who preached at Höngg in support of those who removed the images. The editor of the Actensammlung, Egli, inserts Stumpf's name in brackets followed by a question mark. Stumpf was originally a monk from Franconia and became pastor at Höngg in 1520. The reference to the "monk from Swabia" most certainly would apply to him, though technically he was from Franconia. Stumpf was cited before the Council on November 3, 1523, and deprived of his parish.[17] It does seem justifiable to number him among those who encouraged the iconoclasts. The evidence presented contradicts Yoder's claim that the iconoclasts were followers of Zwingli.[18] A radical party in disagreement with Zwingli's policy was present at Zurich before the Second Disputation.

The vandalism that occurred in September was, to some extent, a result of the sermons preached by Zwingli and Leo Jud, but it was not

---

13. *Ibid.*, 623.
14. Göters, 31.
15. O. Farner, III, 381.
16. *E.A.*, 269.
17. *Ibid.*, 422, 441; Z, VII, 195.
18. Yoder, *MQR*, XXXII, 130.

done at their behest. A hearing held by the Council considered Thomas Kleinbrötli's charges against Jud and Zwingli. He said that they were responsible for the outbreaks: "Leo wished the images struck from the altars with an axe . . . Zwingli has caused much unrest in this city."[19] On the other hand, the report of the destruction of the crucifix at Stadelhofen reveals the gap between the extremists and those who supported Zwingli. The miller at Stadelhofen, Heini Hirt, reported that Claus Hottinger came and asked him when he was going to remove his false god, the crucifix. Hirt answered that the matter should be left to the government: "he wished to let my lords deal with the matter, for he was not learned in Scripture and had no understanding of the thing." Hottinger then said a good Christian would do away with the idol as scripture commanded.[20] Hirt's position follows the one outlined in Zwingli's sermon *On Divine and Human Righteousness*; the removal of the images is a question for the government. Hottinger's stand mirrors the view of the extremists; the images must go immediately, because the scripture commands it. The two positions reveal the division between Grebel's following and Zwingli's.

Zwingli's attitude to the iconoclasts and to the place of the Council in the reform of the Church are revealed in a letter he wrote to Ambrosius Blarer on October 9, 1523. Referring to the recent outbreak against the images, he admitted that it "doubtless" appeared "more terrible among outsiders than among us" and informed him that the Council had appointed a commission in order to settle the matter.[21]

. . . the senate has given four [men] from its order and just as many from the lesser order, who are called the two hundred by us, who with the three bishops, who are in the city, may examine diligently the passages of Scripture concerning the images and afterwards deliver a *summa* to the senate of the two hundred; this is the highest authority among us: In the meantime those private persons who have contended in battle with the images are held in prison.[22]

He closed the letter by explaining that he lacked the strength to write more and then added a postcript:

I send the decree of the senate, which, as I hope will give an example to many free cities, just as the discussions of the Gospel which was held at the end of January. Nor should you wonder that general matters are thus dealt with here. Everything is right with us, but not even by a moment is it given to relax labour and vigils.[23]

---

19. *E.A.*, 416.
20. *Ibid.*, 421
21. *Z*, VIII, 124, 2–4.
22. *Ibid.*, VIII, 124, 4–9.
23. *Ibid.*, VIII, 124, 14–18. The editor of volume VIII says that the decree of the senate probably refers to the plan approved by the Council for the reorganization of the Chapter (*Z*, VIII, 124).

The letter leaves no doubt that Zwingli wanted something done about the images and shows that he was not without sympathy for those who had acted against them. But his sympathy was qualified, for he still employed the adjective "atrox" to refer to what the iconoclasts had done, and did not criticize the continued imprisonment of those "private persons" who had assaulted the images.

When considered together with the postcript, the description of the steps the Council had taken to consider the matter reveals that he approved of them, as well as of the general role which it was playing in the direction of the reform movement. The closing phrase of the passage relating the Council's action demonstrates his recognition and acceptance of its authority: "This [i.e., the Council of 200] is the highest authority among us." The postscript shows that he was clearly pleased with the reform of the Chapter and the outcome of the First Disputation, which had been held under the auspices of the magistracy. It is significant that he believed that the way in which the reform was being carried out with the aid of the "highest authority" should be an "example" to other "free cities."

In comparison with his approval of the Council's action and his expression of contentment over the progress of his programme of Christian renewal, Zwingli's brief references to the individuals who had acted against the icons on their own initiative explain, at least in part, why he still felt the need for vigilance. He did not approve of the conduct of those who had destroyed the images on their own initiative, for their action ran counter to his desire for an orderly reform and disregarded the wishes of the "highest authority" in the city. Up to this time the alliance with the civil power had been the key to his success and he had no reason to applaud the behaviour of those who endangered it. In view of the opinion that he expressed in his letter, it is difficult to accept the view that in a few weeks he was to compromise his programme for the sake of an alliance with the state. The alliance was already firmly established and was the pre-condition for the Reformation in a city with Zurich's constitutional traditions.[24]

The letter also demonstrates how Zwingli's doctrine of biblical authority enhanced the position of the Council (which had already attained a semi-sacral character before the Reformation began) in

24. Yoder in particular misunderstands the significance of the corporate tradition at Zurich He sees Zwingli's acceptance of the idea that the government represented the congregation in religious affairs, which he says was manifest during the First Disputation, as the cause of Zwingli's subsequent difficulties over the Mass, and the contributing factor to the break between Grebel and Zwingli (Yoder, 15). The nature of Zwingli's relationship with the Council since 1520 and the terms of his letter to Blarer make this interpretation highly questionable.

dealing with religious questions and complemented the corporate tradition that underlay the nature and extent of the Council's power in the canton. It was now able to deal with a religious question by appointing a mixed body of clergy and laymen to consult the source of religious authority, the Bible. Once the teaching of the God's Word on the issue had been summarized, the Council would have access to the information necessary to formulate a policy regarding the images.

Though to an observer not familiar with the traditions of government at Zurich the Council's action and the composition of the commission might appear as an example of undue interference in spiritual matters by the civil arm, the course of action taken was consistent with the argument that Zwingli had repeatedly advanced: a local assembly which consulted the Bible would be guided by the Holy Spirit to make a correct decision. Zwingli had defended the gathering of the First Disputation in this way and he was soon to justify the competence of the Second Disputation in the same manner. The commission the Council appointed followed this pattern in miniature and its composition prefigures that of the marriage court and the synod.

It is interesting to compare the composition of the commission with that of the purely clerical group that the Council had consulted on the question of the fast in April of 1522. At that time, past tradition had been strong enough to limit the membership to the Provost and the three People's Priests. Now, a year and a half later, it felt able to appoint a mixed body; the fact that the Provost of the Chapter was conspiciously absent reflects the impact of the Reformation and the more active role that the laity was permitted to take in religious affairs. Zwingli had every reason to be satisfied with the course of events at Zurich.

The mixed membership of the commission also represented both the corporate nature of Zurich's government (for the councillors chosen were selected from those whom a Christian people had delegated to rule) and the result of Zwingli's attack upon the clergy's status as the sole guardian of religious authority. The Bible was open for consultation and interpretation to the clergy and laity alike. The Council did not then presume to appoint a purely lay body to determine what scripture said, nor did it ever do so: it recognized the need for guidance from those whom God had appointed as the guardians of the spiritual kingdom, the realm of divine righteousness, and who were especially trained to expound God's Word. The inclusion of the three People's Priests, whom Zwingli refers to as "the three Bishops who are in the city," implies a recognition on the part of the Council that it was not empowered to govern the spiritual realm. The desire of the government

to discover what the Bible said about images and to base its policy upon
that source of authority for religious questions provides further evidence
of the magistracy's willingness to accept the limitations God had placed
upon its authority. The Council acknowledges a division of labour in the
society, but neither its members nor Zwingli questioned the fact that it
alone was empowered to execute the policy that scripture, properly
expounded, called for.

Instead of presenting the Council with a *summa*, the commission
suggested a disputation to ease tension in the city and to clarify the
question of the Mass and the images.[25] On October 12 invitations to a
disputation on October 26 were issued by the Council to the Bishops
of Constance and Chur, the Confederates, and the prelates, administrators and clergy of Canton Zurich. The purpose of the disputation was
clearly defined: "That they may hold a discussion and help to make
a decision from . . . the Old and New Testaments about what they
should do."[26]

Many who were invited did not attend. No bishop appeared and of
the Confederates only representatives of Schaffhausen and the city
of St. Gall came. The unwillingness of the other Confederates to take
part in the discussion made Zurich's isolation in the Confederacy all
too clear and explains the Council's cautious policy at the end of the
disputation.

Although some scholars have questioned whether the Second Disputation served the same purpose as the First, Zwingli's introductory
statement to the delegates indicates that he believed it did.[27] He offered
a definition of the nature of the church in support of the assembly's
authority, and he referred to Matthew 18:19, which promised that those
who gathered in Christ's name and sought God's help would receive
it. On the previous day "the whole company of our Christian people"
had gathered together in the "temples" and beseeched God's help.
Although it was not possible for those present at the Disputation to
kneel in prayer, Zwingli asked each person to call upon God for guidance
in his heart.[28] What he requested was that the assembly fulfil one of
the major biblical requirements for a proper gathering of Christian

25. Egli, 101.
26. *E.A.*, 430.
27. Egli claimed that the First Disputation was concerned with the formal
principle, the authority of the scripture, and led to immediate decisions, while the
Second was called to hear what scripture said, but not to reach a decision (Egli,
102). Yoder says that the Second, like the First Disputation, followed the general
pattern of Reformation disputations which were called "when a move of major
political significance was to be made" (Joder, *MQR*, XXXII, 133).
28. *Z*, II, 680, 12–23.

people. Tacitly assuming that this had been done, he proceeded to justify the competence of those present to interpret the scripture for the benefit of the government. His explication of the assembly's authority in reaching the decision that followed was based on the assumption that it spoke for the "whole company of our Christian people." This "whole company" was identical with the political assembly of Zurich.

Zwingli used the twofold definition of the church first formulated by him in the summer of 1522 and expounded further in the *Defence of the Sixty-Seven Articles*. The true church "was the whole number of all believers which is alone known to God" and will be gathered visibly before Christ at the last judgment. This is "the holy Christian church" built upon Christ.[29] As he had done before, Zwingli explained the second meaning of the word "church" in greater detail. According to scripture, "church" could be used to refer to a congregation in a particular place such as Bern or Zurich. Christ assigned to local churches the task of disciplining sinners because the Church Universal could never be gathered on earth. It was true that the word "church" meant nothing else than an "assembly" or "gathered throng" and could be used to designate meetings other than those of Christians, but in this instance the other definitions did not apply. This was gathering of Christian people. Zwingli defended its validity by denying that the assemblies of bishops and popes, or Councils, fulfilled the biblical norm for a church. They did not represent the Church Universal, for they included unbelievers and, at the same time, they did not constitute individual congregations either.[30]

Zwingli showed how the Zurich assembly was a church competent to make decisions governing religious observance. The argument he used presupposed the relationship between the Council and the assembly that lay at the heart of the Zurich constitution. It also assumed the division of powers between the spiritual and worldly sphere outlined in the sermon *On Divine and Human Righteousness*. Zwingli asserted that the "gathering" at Zurich was an infallible assembly because it essayed neither to establish nor to deny anything, but sought only to discover what God's Word said about the Mass and the images. He left no question that the purpose of the assembly was to advise the magistrates. It was convened before them and once it had clarified the meaning of the scripture, the representatives at the gathering would advise the councillors about their conclusions.[31] He obviously believed

29. *Ibid.*, II, 681, 26–30; 682, 4–6.
30. *Ibid.*, II, 682, 19–683, 6.
31. *Ibid.*, 683, 18–24.

that the Council, acting as delegates of a Christian people, would then decide how to bring present practice into conformity with the requirements of the Word.

The passage makes clear what had been implicit in Zwingli's thought from the very beginning. The local church was identical with the political assembly of the city, which is why Zwingli later said that the Christian church was nothing more than the Christian city. Actually, at Zurich, this meant that, when the congregation or its representatives were gathered, such a gathering constituted a provincial church because of the control that the assembly, via the magistrates, exercised over the whole canton; but Zwingli did not argue along these lines.

Zwingli's attack upon the councils of the mediaeval church contradicted his earlier acceptance of canons framed by a council, such as the Council of Gangra, in accordance with the Gospel and the teachings of the Apostles. The logic of his attack also invalidated the authority of the Zurich assembly, for it did not represent the Church Universal, and the presence of representatives from beyond Canton Zurich made it impossible to claim that the gathering was a congregational meeting. However, Zwingli avoided this difficulty. While proving that the "old" church did fit the scriptural definition of a church, Zwingli had considered the historical precedent of the Council of Jerusalem. He maintained that the Council of Jerusalem did not grant a biblical precedent confirming the authority of Councils or of a church dominated by bishops and the pope. The Council of Jerusalem was made up of representatives of the congregation at Jerusalem, with no more than two representatives from Antioch: "for the same was nothing more than the congregation at Jerusalem and there were no more than two representatives from Antioch."[32] Like the Council of Jerusalem, the gathering at Zurich represented the local congregation and contained only a few delegates from other regions. It fitted the biblical definition and had the right to seek to discover what the scripture required.

Any study of the Second Disputation must consider a question raised by Yoder. Yoder claims that the official record of the Disputation does not give an accurate account of what took place. He asserts that Zwingli, Grebel, and Stumpf were in agreement throughout the disputation. The evidence he cites for this is a letter of Viet Suter, who was apparently a Habsburg agent, written on October 31. The letter indicates that the Council decided to retain the Mass and images because it feared the Confederacy would attack Zurich if any further changes in the cult were made. According to Suter's letter, Zwingli opposed the Council's decision

32. *Ibid.*, II, 683, 6–9.

and denied that the Zurich authorities had the right to delay further reform. When a fresh outbreak of agitation calling for the end of the Mass broke out in December, 1523, Yoder says, Zwingli made it known that regardless of the Council's decision he was determined to institute the Lord's Supper by Christmas. However, during the week of December 10 to 18, Zwingli is said to have surrendered to the wishes of the Council, while Grebel maintained the stand they had both held.[33]

How reliable is Suter as a source? Is Suter's account consistent with the internal evidence found in the documents of the Disputation? The section of Suter's letter which Yoder quoted was taken from Oscar Vasella's very brief article, "Zur Geschichte der Täuferbewegung in der Schweiz," which appeared in Vol. XLVIII of the *Zeitschrift für Schweizerische Kirchengeschichte*. Vasella gave very little evidence concerning Suter's reliability as a witness. He merely said that Suter was by no means unfamiliar with the situation at Zurich, and indicated that he was writing to Innsbruck.[34] Vasella does not explain who Suter was or what he was doing at the Disputation, and Suter's name does not appear in any other material concerning the Zurich Reformation.

Vasella made several suggestions that Yoder incorporated into his article. He said that the evidence in Suter's letter indicates that the political situation at Zurich thwarted Zwingli's plans for an immediate reform of the cult and that Zwingli's willingness to accept the delay caused the break between him and Grebel. Enough time had elapsed before the official version of the Disputation was approved by the Council for publication to permit documents indicating Zwingli's opposition to any further delay to be altered to fit the Council's wishes.[35] Yoder adds no further information in support of Suter's validity as a source. He cites the fragment from Suter's letter that appeared in Vasella's article, and gives no indication he himself read the letter.

If Suter's account is trustworthy, it means considerable portions of the official record of the Disputation were revised. Suter's quotation directly contradicts Zwingli's remarks at the start of the Disputation. At that time Zwingli justified the right of the assembly to decide what the scripture says and the Council's right to decide how the dictates of scripture were to be carried out. Suter's version gives the impression that the Council ignored what scripture said in order to follow an

---

33. Yoder, *MQR*, XXXII, 134–5, 136–8. Although he dates Zwingli's surrender to the state during the Second Disputation, Williams advances the same argument (Williams, 90). Though he does not acknowledge it, his position is basically that of Bender (cf, Bender, 253).

34. Vasella, *ZSK*, XLVIII, 184.

35. *Ibid.*, 184–5.

expedient policy. However, more than one citation is necessary to prove that, after more than three years of close co-operation with Zwingli, the Council completely repudiated the principle of religious authority basic to its support of the rebirth of Christ and the Gospel.

One bit of evidence bears out Yoder's contention that Zwingli and Grebel were in agreement until the end of the Disputation. After the first day's debate, Sebastian Hofmeister, who presided during the Disputation, summed up the findings. He said the purpose of the debate was to consult scripture to find out if the Mass and the images should remain. The evidence, Hofmeister concluded, indicated they should not be permitted to remain. On the basis of these findings he requested, in the name of the clergy, that the Council deal leniently with the iconoclasts and release them from prison.[36] His request can be taken as an indication that Zwingli supported the iconoclasts' behaviour. This would lend credence to Suter's report about Zwingli's position on the Mass.

The exchange that took place early in the Disputation between Konrad Schmid of Küsnach, the Commander of the Knights of St. John, and Zwingli also appears to support Yoder's interpretation. Schmid had advocated caution in abolishing the images. He maintained that before it would do any good to remove them the idolatry in the hearts of men should be done away with and replaced by the teachings of the Word of God. To this he added what he considered an even more practical objection to immediate action. He warned that it was unwise to remove the crutches of the weak before they had something else to lean on. The images should remain untouched until the people had received sufficient biblical instruction to be willing to give up the external support that images provided for their faith.[37]

Zwingli's response was sharp, and Schmid apparently felt that he had misunderstood him and had taken his words as a criticism of his diligence in preaching the Gospel for he interrupted to assure Zwingli that he had not intended to reproach him. Zwingli said that he understood what Schmid wished to say. What he objected to was that Schmid had spoken of the idols as supports for those who were weak in faith. Images were not non-essentials like the fast; God had forbidden them. Those who relied upon them were not merely weak in faith, they were "Godless."[38]

Zwingli admitted that Paul had allowed Timothy to be circumcised, but he also said that Paul had forbidden it in the case of Titus, because

36. *Z*, II, 730, 17–731, 13.
37. *Ibid.*, II, 704–24–33; 705, 18–23.
38. *Ibid.*, II, 708, 13, 16–18, 21–4; 709, 29–30.

the time had come to end the abuse. However, as far as Schmid's proposals were concerned, if one waited to put away the images until all the idols in men's hearts were broken, they would never be abolished. Both the images and the Mass have been forbidden by God and must be abolished. Schmid did not object to what Zwingli said but exclaimed that he was "well pleased" with his words.[39]

It is possible to see this passage as proof that Zwingli was determined to demand an immediate abolition of both the Mass and the images. However, on the other hand, he did not ignore the Pauline precedent in the question of circumcision and he certainly agreed with the need for instructing the people properly before any action was taken. What he seemed most anxious to maintain was the principle that the Mass and the images were an offence to God and, as such, should be abolished. Schmid appeared to share Zwingli's feelings about this principle. Although the latter was apparently inclined to think that the time was right for further change and clearly opposed undue delay, his response to Schmid did not exclude the possibility of a further period of preparation, as long as the necessity of removing the Mass and the images was recognized.

Any assessment of Zwingli's intention must take into account his attitude towards the role of the civil power in implementing further reform. The letter to Ambrosius Blarer on October 9 indicates that he recognized the Council as the supreme authority in the city. Neither the letter nor the bulk of the evidence found in the extant records of the Disputation offer solid grounds for believing that Zwingli said the magistracy had no right to impose a further delay in the removal of the abusive ceromonies, or that he opposed the government's decision.

On the second day of debate Schmid again took the podium to complain about those who said that the Mass and the monastic orders were the creation of the devil.[40] Zwingli responded to him by explaining that he was responsible for such statements, because he had preached that what did not come from God, the author of all good, came from the devil. But he denied that he approved of the "sundry indecorous ones" who said that the monks and the Mass were the creation of the devil. To make his own attitude plain, he declared that he had never allowed such remarks and called for the punishment of those who had made them. His hope was that the clergy would preach the Word so constantly "that all sects, rabble, and orders together with other abuses would be put aside."[41] This is the position that he had taken towards

39. *Ibid.*, II, 703, 34–710, 10, 18–24, 29–30.   40. *Ibid.*, II, 739, 2–6.
41. *Ibid.*, II, 739, 17–27; 32–740, 2.

those who acted upon their own initiative in favour of the reform movement since the beginning of his career at Zurich. They were, he felt, as great a problem as the orders and he advocated the proclamation of the Gospel to silence them as well as his conservative opponents. The specific reference to "sects" and rabble indicates that he recognized that there was an organized extremist element at work in the city. The reference to the rabble in conjunction with both sects and orders may refer to those who, as in the case of the tithe agitation, could be goaded into tumultuous behaviour by either group. The only faction or "sect" that I have been able to discover is the one including Conrad Grebel among its members.

The debate concerning the Mass was carried on during the second day and provides little evidence to support Suter's report that Zwingli's willingness to delay reform fomented his break with Grebel. When the Prior of the Dominicans spoke in favour of letting the Council decide what should be done about the Mass, Zwingli agreed, but said he considered the magistracy bound by the requirements of scripture: "My lords should also prescribe no law other than from the holy, unerring writing of God." He warned that if the magistrates recognized another law in this matter he would use the Bible to preach against them.[42] According to Hätzer, who recorded the debate for publication, "there were some who wanted to follow the command of the Zurich magistrates and pay no heed to the command of God. . . ."[43] Zwingli was indeed concerned about the eventual outcome of the debate, however, the attitude he expressed was consistent with his general policy. As long as the magistrates recognized the authority of scripture and worked out a policy consistent with its norms, he would be satisfied. If they did not, he would be obliged to preach against them.

The argument that broke out between Grebel, Stumpf, and Zwingli at the end of the second day of the debate also gives little support to Suter's account and Yoder's interpretation of it. Grebel demanded that a decision be made about the Mass before the Disputation considered the question of purgatory, which was next on the agenda. Zwingli answered that the magistrates would decide how to deal with the question: "My lords will recognize with what propriety the Mass should be used from now on."[44] Stumpf rose to deny Zwingli the right to leave a matter already decided by the Spirit of God in the hands of the magistrates. Zwingli denied that there was any question of the magistracy judging the case. The Disputation had been called because the

42. *Ibid.*, II, 775, 12–16.   43. *Ibid.*, II, 775, 17–19.
44. *Ibid.*, II, 784, 8–9.

magistrates wanted to find out whether or not the scripture said that the Mass was a sacrifice. The magistracy's task was to discover a "suitable way" for the results of the Disputation to be carried out without causing "tumult."[45]

Yoder believes that Zwingli and Grebel were in agreement on many points, including the right of the individual congregation to make its own decision about the Mass and the images. He also says that the major difference between the two lay in Zwingli's willingness to wait until the people were in agreement with the changes which he proposed.[46] Although he does criticize Zwingli elsewhere for assuming that the government represented the church congregation, here he appears to take the view that Zwingli believed that the church congregation and the political assembly were separate entities, and consequently this commentator misses the nature of the magistracy's relationship to the assembly of the Christian people. He also underestimates the importance of the difference in attitude between Zwingli and Grebel. The ultimate success of Zwingli's programme depended upon the support of the government, and he could not ask it to follow a policy which might endanger the city and which the magistrates did not yet believe had sufficient popular approval. These considerations do not seem to have remained central ones in Grebel's view of the problem, or in his conception of the means by which it could be solved.

Zwingli's answer to Grebel and Stumpf followed from the position he had already taken. It was the question of the timing of the abolition of the Mass that divided him from them. Grebel and Stumpf wanted immediate action. When Zwingli said that the magistrates should arrive at "a suitable way" to implement the decisions of the Disputation without engendering "tumult," he left it up to them to decide how and when the change was to be made. There was no question in his mind that the magistrates accepted what the scriptures said. This was not the issue. Of course it is possible that the record of what Zwingli really said was altered, but this seems unlikely in view of the consistency between his statements at this juncture and his previously expressed attitude towards the Council. A basic disagreement over the tempo of reform had separated Zwingli from the enthusiasts since the fast controversy. Those eager for more rapid change were never satisfied with less than a major step forward. Zwingli was invariably willing to accept the compromise solution government policy required because he considered the support of the government essential. In general, the dis-

45. *Ibid.*, II, 784, 12–15, 19–26.
46. Yoder, 25.

agreement at the Second Disputation provides another example of the tactical questions that divided Zwingli and Grebel.

October 28, the third day of the Disputation, was the feast day of the Apostles Simon and Judas, and, in honour of the occasion, Zwingli preached a sermon on the pastor's role in the church, entitled *The Shepherd* (*Der Hirt*). The sermon was later printed in March, 1524, at the request of the people of Appenzell and was dedicated to Jacob Schurtanner, who was a champion of the reform movement in that district.[47] It is difficult to say how much it was altered to fit the requirements of those who struggled on behalf of the Gospel in the district of Appenzell, but it does give an impression of the general line of thought that Zwingli followed at this time.

It is likely that Zwingli's discussion of the pastor's task was influenced by his argument with Grebel and Stumpf. He defended the right of the pastor, or shepherd, to protect his flock against tyrants and he reminded rulers that they were not to be tyrants: "Seneca too calls royal power: a service; that is, the Kingdom or government is an office of doing good."[48] In order to prevent his harsh words about tyrants from being taken as an attack upon civil authority, whose functions he had already justified earlier in the sermon in terms of a lesser righteousness, he said: "It is well known that one owes the government something. But we speak here against the tyrannical offenders, in whom there is no fear of God and no love, and indeed, no respect for the neighbour."[49]

The pastor was obliged to criticize the conduct of all, even princes, and Zwingli likened their role to that of the Spartan ephors, the Roman tribunes, and the chief guildmasters in many German cities who prevented the government from misusing its authority. If the shepherd's warnings went unheeded, then the welfare of the whole people was endangered and a fate like the Babylonian captivity of Israel awaited them. Lest his conception of the pastor's function be misunderstood, he hastened to add that his role was to admonish but not to compel men to faith, nor was he to be concerned with the things of this world.[50]

Zwingli employed the same twofold definition of the church he had elaborated at the beginning of the Disputation to discredit the representatives of the old church and to prove that the congregation of Appenzell, which was a rural canton, fulfilled the biblical requirements for a valid Christian church. Every congregation has certain obligations and among them Zwingli listed the duty to support a pastor from

47. *Z*, III, 1.   48. *Ibid.*, III, 27, 13–19.
49. *Ibid.*, III, 24, 15–19; 27, 19–22.
50. *Ibid.*, III, 36, 7–12, 20–6; 38, 11–16.

"interest and tithes."[51] These words to the congregation leave no doubt about his positive attitude towards tithes, when they were properly used, and it also provides further evidence that the Christian assembly at Appenzell to which he addressed his remarks had worldly, as well as spiritual, responsibilities. The administration of the tithes definitely lay within the competence of the political assembly and its representatives, the magistrates.

The final question that Zwingli considered in the sermon illustrates his conception of the relationship between the assembly of a Christian people and the magistrates. How was a false prophet to be removed? Zwingli first explained that no Christian had the right to kill a false prophet without the express command of God. Once the entire parish, *gantz kilchhöre*, recognized that its pastor was false, it should have him removed but leave it to the "administrators who bear the sword" to decide whether or not he was to be executed. If, however, the magistrates share the same faults as the pastor and do nothing about him, the people are to suffer as if they were in a "Babylonian captivity until God rescues us with his own hand." Eventually, Zwingli assured his readers, Christ will come to them and arm either the ruler or the people for revenge.[52]

Zwingli then interjected an appeal to false shepherds. If there was an ounce of humanity in the heart of the false shepherd, Zwingli begged him for the sake of God, human society, and the "poor people" to free the people from captivity. To assure the common man that his sufferings at the hands of a false prophet would not go on indefinitely, and to remind the ruler that he could not resist the will of the people by protecting an evil pastor, Zwingli stated that secular authority was derived from the people. A ruler was able to support a false pastor only as long as he had the help of his people. Once they have discovered the truth and are won to the Gospel, no secular authority will be able to defend a shepherd who oppresses them, for the Gospel will protect the people until God finds a way to deliver them.[53]

The sermon is consistent with the position that Zwingli had taken in the past and reaffirms his denial of the magistrate's right to judge the Word of God, as well as the pastor's obligation to oppose a tyrannous government. As he had maintained throughout his years in Zurich, the pastor spoke for the well-being of society as a whole. If the pastor's

51. *Ibid.*, III, 48, 13–15; 54, 8–10.
52. *Ibid.*, III, 63, 28–30; 64, 6–8, 22–6, 65, 16–18.
53. *Ibid.*, III, 66, 31–67, 6, 16–30.

words were not heard, the people would suffer as the Israelites had at the hands of the Babylonians. His appeal to the false pastor to free the people for the sake of God and "human society" bears this out.

In view of the charges that Zwingli compromised his ecclesiology for the sake of the support of the secular arm in December, 1523, if not earlier, his conception of the pastor's obligation and of the effect that his preaching would have upon the society is of particular significance. This must have been the position which he had taken during the Disputation, for if he had compromised his original ecclesiology in December, 1523, it hardly seems likely that he would have added these portions of the sermon when it was revised for publication in March, 1524. If anything, he would have deleted the section which discussed the tyrannical magistrate, the pastor's duty to oppose him, and the consequences to society if the pastor were ignored.

Zwingli's definition of the church and its obligation to support clergy with tithes had already been clarified before the Second Disputation. He added nothing new in the sermon. When he considered the removal of the false pastor, he assumed that the secular rulers would be present to act as the executors of the congregation's will. This is the position that he took during the Second Disputation and it represents the key to the magistrates' power at Zurich: they were the delegated authorities of the people. The distinction that Zwingli made between the proper function of the government and the rule of a tyrant, and his words concerning the subject's obligation to the civil power, only emphasize the fact that he valued the co-operation of the secular authority.

Zwingli certainly called for restraint when he considered the possibility that the magistrates might not follow the will of the congregation and retain an undesirable pastor. In this case the people would have to suffer. But he qualified this statement almost immediately by warning the secular ruler that his authority rested in the people and that he could not resist their will indefinitely. The Gospel had been provided for such contingencies and God would redeem his people. In saying this he revealed his faith in the power of the Gospel to produce a state of mind among the people and their governers that would lead to a reform of abuses.

If one considers this passage in relation to the issue of the Mass, it explains why he was willing to delay the abolition. The government was not defending a false pastor who would not preach the Gospel. The councillors put no obstacle in the way of those who preached the Gospel. The magistrates were only retaining an abusive ceremony until they felt the time was right to remove it. The faith that once the Gospel was widely understood there would be ready popular acceptance of the end of this ceremony gave Zwingli good reason for patience, and there was nothing new in this attitude.

The sermon, then, gives little evidence that Zwingli changed his view of the magistracy and its relation to the church and the problem of reform between October, 1523, and March, 1524. Though it was certainly altered to fit the needs of those who were fighting to introduce the Gospel in Appenzell, and much of what Zwingli said about the connection between the false prophet, the magistracy, and the people applied to the situation there, the sermon continues the general line of thought that Zwingli had pursued throughout his career at Zurich. It probably reflects his state of mind during the Second Disputation and makes Suter's account seem unlikely. It also weakens Yoder's claim that Zwingli surrendered to the magistracy in December.

On the final day of the Disputation the question of purgatory was shelved and the debate over the Mass continued. Grebel attempted to expand the scope of the debate and suggested that since all were agreed that the Mass had no basis in scripture, the individual abuses in the service should be considered. Balthasar Hubmeier, a future Baptist, seconded Grebel with a list of specific criticisms and demands for their alteration.[54] Zwingli agreed that additions to the service such as the clerical vestments and singing during the Mass, that had not been instituted by Christ, were an abuse, but he warned that they could not be removed all at once. Each had to be done away with at the proper time in order to avoid "tumult" and "disunity among Christians." Before anything could be done, the people must receive proper instruction: "The people must be instructed beforehand with the Word of God. . . . When the people are prepared, then these things may be abolished without rebellion."[55] Unless the entire account of the Disputation was altered radically, it appears that Zwingli, like Schmid, saw the need for a cautious approach to further reforms.

A debate followed between Grebel and Zwingli on whether leavened or unleavened bread should be used in the communion. The argument illustrates the difference in temperament between the two men. Grebel said scripture called for leavened bread and Zwingli responded by asserting that the use of unleavened bread was not a major issue. As long as the essentials of the service prescribed by God's Word were not changed, an individual congregation (*kilchhöry*) could decide for itself what kind

54. *Z*, II, 786, 1–787, 27.
55. *Ibid.*, II, 788, 15–17; 789, 7–14, 21–3.

of bread to use.[56] Grebel held a rigid, literal position, while Zwingli was flexible about "non-essentials."[57]

As the afternoon's proceedings drew to a close, Konrad Schmid made a number of suggestions that the Council subsequently followed. Schmid agreed that the Mass and images should be done away with but he disagreed with those who called for their immediate suppression. To do this without instructing the people further would hinder the Gospel. He advised the Council to issue written instructions to the people and clergy concerning the images and the worship of Christ. After the people have been educated, the images could be removed, and, in this way "all abuses can be reformed and changed without riot and reluctance."[58]

Schmid stressed the need for government action to support the dissemination of Christ's teaching: "The worldly power must act, that Christ may remain upright and supported; I mean his Word and teaching."[59] He cited the precedent of Paul, who was protected from the high priests by the Romans, and described the current corruption of the clergy. He charged that the churchmen were so involved in deriving economic benefit from their prebends that they failed to preach the Gospel. For this reason, he said, the magistracy is obliged to take a hand in the affairs of the church: "If the clergy should not wish to help with it . . . it will be necessary for the secular authority to undertake it."[60]

56. *Ibid.*, II, 790, 18–21. The reference to the right of an individual congregation to make a decision should be read within the context of the Zurich constitution.

57. Yoder sees Grebel's demand for the use of unleavened bread as an example of the same biblical literalism that led Zwingli to demand that the clerical vestments and the singing during Mass be done away with because they were not established by Christ (Yoder, 25). There is a difference between the vestments, and the singing, and unleavened bread. Zwingli objected to the singing because neither the common man, nor many of the priests understood what was sung (Z, II, 788, 19–22). He believed that an understanding of what was going on was essential for the service to benefit the congregation. Incomprehensible singing could not help anyone and hindered the major aim of his programme: to preach the Gospel so that all would understand it. There was good reason to stop the singing and there were even better reasons for his objection to the wearing of clerical vestments during the Mass. The clothes were worn to help convey the impression that the Mass was a sacrifice (Z, II, 789, 2–6). This was opposed to what Zwingli believed the Scripture said the Eucharist was. Unleavened bread neither stood in the way of the clear proclamation of the Gospel, nor gave the impression that the Mass was a sacrifice. In discussing Zwingli's literalism, Yoder tends to ignore the distinction that he made between the sense and the letter of the Word (cf. Z, I, 294, 22–4).

58. Z, II, 793, 20–6; 794, 3–18; 795, 4–8, 796, 6–9, 11–14.

59. *Ibid.*, II, 796, 29–30.

60. *Ibid.*, II, 796, 33–797, 22, 31–798, 1.

The latter part of his speech may have been an attempt to reason with Grebel and Stumpf, who believed control of the reform was being surrendered to the magistracy.

Schmid's plea echoes the positive role that Erasmus assigned to secular authority in an era when the clergy had failed in its spiritual duties. His general appeal for the co-operation of the secular arm in the course of reform coincided with Zwingli's view of the matter. Zwingli had opposed the activities of "sundry indecorous ones" during the fast controversy, the crisis over the tithes, and in his own statements during the Disputation. The reason for this was clear: it was up to the magistracy to discover "a suitable way" to initiate reform without causing "tumult." The letter of October 9 to Blarer shows that his approach to the question was conditioned by the place that the government occupied in the constitutional structure of the city and also reveals that, up to the time of the Second Disputation, Zwingli was satisfied with the councillors' policy towards the reform movement.

Zwingli's final statements reveal that he desired God's commands to be obeyed in spiritual questions, but that he repudiated disobedience to the magistrates, whom he admitted had had to bear much adversity for the sake of God's Word.[61] Assuring the assembly that God would not leave "his own" in need forever, he appealed to them in the name of heaven to let "My Lords" rule. Then he repudiated a rumour apparently spread about the night before, that now the body and blood of Christ would be used as a "nightcap."[62] In closing, he warned against rash action on the part of individuals: "Let no one wish to do something upon his own authority, as has now occurred with the images."[63]

Vadian's summary of the debate stated that the scripture called for an end to the Mass and the images, but left no doubt that it was up to the magistracy to find the means to remove them without tumult: "Here, noble lords, we refer the discussion which has now been heard to your wisdom, to consider and to judge it . . . to submit and present the means and the way, through which the Word of God . . . will be administered and preached, and in addition the abuses . . . remedied and removed in your territory without wounding the weak."[64]

Mayor Röist's speech, which followed Vadian's, expressed both the magistracy's willingness to acept the authority of the Bible and its doubts

61. *Ibid.*, II, 799, 5–9, 10–12.
62. *Ibid.*, II, 799, 12–17. Yoder claims that this passage makes it impossible to say that Zwingli favoured a policy of delay and was willing to leave the question of introducing further changes to the magistrates (Yoder, 24).
63. *Ibid.*, II, 800, 17–18.
64. *Ibid.*, II, 801, 13–21.

over exactly what should be done. He asserted that the councillors would seek to serve the best interests of all as far as they were able, and he admonished his fellows in the Council to accept the Word of God "boldly, manfully and without any fear." Though Röist himself confessed that he did not know what to say about the question, he stated that he did believe the Word of God had to be acknowledged, and he prayed to God that all would go well.[65] His remarks leave no question that the government recognized the authority of scripture as the norm for religious life in the city but they do reveal that in this case the civil rulers were not sure about how to carry out the commands of God. Just before the meeting broke up, Vadian, followed by the Abbott of Kapel and seconded by the Provost of the Chapter and the Komtur, Schmid, asked the Council to release the iconoclasts.[66]

Suter's report of the outcome of the Disputation creates a major textual problem. The published records of the assembly and the printed version of *The Shepherd* are rendered useless as source material. Zwingli's argument with Grebel and Stumpf must be an official forgery. The records should show that Zwingli, Stumpf, and Grebel defended a common position against someone else, possibly Schmid. However, an extensive revision of the records would not have gone unnoticed. Rumours concerning the alteration of the documents would have come down to us, and such rumours do not exist. Neither Stumpf nor Grebel questioned the official version of the Disputation.

If Suter's letter and Yoder's interpretation of the Disputation are correct, it would mean that the Council presumed to judge religious questions on its own authority. There is no evidence that the Council ever did this, either before or after the beginning of the Reformation. Yoder's conclusions also indicate that Zwingli's view of the Christian magistrate's function changed suddenly in the midst of the Second Disputation. There is no other proof to support this conclusion.

It is more likely that Suter did not understand Zwingli's position or was not well informed about the Disputation. His report may have been influenced by sources favourable to Grebel who were anxious to prove that Zwingli and Grebel agreed. It is tempting to suggest that a garbled version of Zwingli's argument with Grebel and Stumpf at the end of the second day of the Disputation lies behind the account which Suter sent to Innsbruck. The documents give an accurate account of the Second Disputation. The Disputation was carried on under the shadow of a rift within the reform party. If this were not the case, there would

65. *Ibid.*, II, 801, 35–7, 39–802, 8.
66. *Ibid.*, II, 802, 13–18, 28–31.

have been no reason for Grebel and Stumpf to question Zwingli's policy during the debate. Grebel's angry reaction to the Council's decision concerning tithes, which was reached on September 26, shows that the extremists had begun to lose patience with Zwingli and no longer shared his trust in the magistracy. In the fall they had launched a campaign against the images and Mass that further complicated Zurich's foreign policy and also threatened to cause a domestic crisis. The Second Disputation was an attempt to head off the zealots and to find a way to continue the purification of the church without endangering the security of the city. The appeal that moderates like Schmid made on behalf of the prisoners at the end of the Disputation bears this out. It was a gesture of conciliation to the men who had sided with Grebel. The moderates still hoped the disagreements between the two factions might be settled. The attempt to mollify the radicals does support Yoder's contention that the final break between Zwingli and Grebel came later. However, it does not prove there was no divergence of opinion between them before or during the Disputation.

After the conclusion of the Disputation the Council set up a commission to study further the question of the Mass and the images. The commission followed Schmid's suggestion and advised against any action until the people in the countryside were fully instructed. The Council approved its advice and asked Zwingli to write an educational pamphlet, which appeared on November 17, bearing the title *Eine Kurze Christliche Einleitung* (A Brief Christian Introduction).[67] The pamphlet was sent to the clergy of the canton, accompanied by an order that it was to be used to enlighten the people.[68] To expedite the education of the country people, the Council implemented another of the commission's proposals and ordered the Abbot of Kappel, Konrad Schmid, and Zwingli to preach in the various districts of the canton. The Council's command gave Zwingli the chance to continue preaching against the Mass and the images and reveals that it did not seek to oppose what the Gospel taught, but to encourage it. These measures were followed by a mandate forbidding anything to be done about the Mass and the images "until a further decision, which, if God wills it, will be given shortly on the basis of the Word of God." However, individuals who had put statues or pictures in the churches were allowed to remove them, as long as it caused no tumult.[69] The senators did not presume to make a theological decision; they promised one would be forthcoming from the Word of God. In the meanwhile, for the sake of order, nothing was

67. Egli, 108.   68. Z, II, 628, 23–8.
69. E.A., 436; Egli, 108.

to be done until the people had received further instruction. This action taken by the magistrates conforms to the function Zwingli assigned them in the sermon *On Divine and Human Righteousness*.[70]

The Council took up the case of the iconoclasts on October 29 and again on November 4. Klaus Hottinger was exiled for two years while Ockenfuss was warned and forced to pay court costs. Lorenz Hochrütiner, who had already been in difficulties with the Council, was banished from the canton.[71] Both Zwingli and Grebel wrote on his behalf to Vadian at St. Gall. Zwingli's letter of November 11 is important for the light that it sheds upon his attitude towards the government and the iconoclasts a few days after the close of the Disputation. He thanked Vadian for the part he had played in the Disputation, and he advised him: "Accept those things which have followed after."[72] The comment indicates that Vadian, who had previously been impatient with the slow pace of reform at Zurich, may have been disappointed that the Council had decided to delay any action upon the Mass and the images. Zwingli then described the measures the government had approved for the further education of the people in the countryside, and he seemed pleased that the Council had been satisfied with the introduction (*Einleitung*) he had written at the behest of the commission.[73] The letter gave no indication that Zwingli was unhappy about the course of action that the Council had chosen to follow, nor is there any evidence that he questioned the Council's right to delay the abolition of the Mass and the images.

When Zwingli discussed the treatment Hochrütiner had received at the hands of the Council, he explained his own reasons for accepting the Council's decision. Hochrütiner had been dealt with very strictly, " . . . why that is you yourself know."[74] His behaviour had frightened those who were, as yet, too attached to the traditional forms of worship to understand the reason for his action; to them he had opposed Christ. In order to prevent this element from turning away from the Gospel, it was necessary to make allowances for their weakness:

> But yet it has not been done contrary to reason, for you are not unaware that men are accustomed to fear such people, not because of the thing itself but because of the glory of Christ. For there are some who would turn away from the Gospel of Christ, unless you give in to their infirmity a little.[75]

---

70. Yoder agrees that the Council's behaviour seems to justify "the confidence placed in it to deal, not with the question of principle, but with applications" (Yoder, *MQR*, XXXII, 136).

71. *E.A.*, 438, 442; O. Farner, III, 454.   72. Z, VIII, 129, 4–5.

73. *Ibid.*, VIII, 129, 5–130, 9.   74. *Ibid.*, VIII, 130, 12–13.

75. *Ibid.*, VIII, 130, 13–17.

The reason that Zwingli accepted the policy laid down by the civil authorities is clear. He realized that many people were not ready for removal of the images and the suppression of the Mass. To guarantee final success of his plans, he felt that it was necessary to make concessions to those who were not yet prepared for change. Consequently, he opposed what Hochrütiner had done because it alienated those whom Zwingli hoped to win for the Gospel. The willingness to compromise which is apparent in the letter renders Suter's report concerning what Zwingli wanted during the Disputation even more doubtful. It also offers strong grounds for questioning whether the documents of the Disputation that went to press on December 8 were altered to fit the requirements of the decision imposed by the government at the end of the Disputation. The position Zwingli took on November 11 was the same one which he had maintained both before and during the debate.

The remainder of the letter shows that although Zwingli repudiated the methods employed by Hochrütiner and the other enthusiasts, he sympathized with what they sought to achieve, and, in the case of Hochrütiner, was willing to do all that he could to help him: "For these reasons I think that Lorenz Hochrütiner, a good man, by Hercules, has been dealt with a little more firmly not to say harshly. Because, so far, he has been more outspoken, he has been punished exceedingly severely"[76] Zwingli expressed the hope that there would be another opportunity to restore Hochrütiner when, as he said ironically, "we shall have been taught better by the people," by which he meant when he had had time to instruct the people. Meanwhile, since Hochrütiner wished to come to St. Gall and had asked Zwingli to commend him to Vadian, Zwingli appealed to Vadian to be his patron there, until the storms had quieted down in Zurich and Hochrütiner could go free.[77] Zwingli's desire to win all parties for Christ, which confirms the evidence that he supported a policy of compromise, was expressed at the end of the letter: " . . . for you know that I [like St. Paul] burn with the scandals of all and desire all in the bowels of Jesus Christ."[78]

Though, as far as the final goal of the reform movement was concerned, there was, at this time, certainly a fairly close agreement between Zwingli and the extremists, the difference in method and the attitude towards the society and its rulers which this difference implied was of crucial importance. Seen from this perspective, Zwingli and the radical element were deeply divided. Zwingli was still committed to his alliance

---

76. *Ibid.*, VIII, 130, 17–20.
77. *Ibid.*, VIII, 130, 20–131, 9.
78. *Ibid.*, VIII, 131, 9–10.

with the government and defended a policy of compromise. Though the radicals may have accepted his methods and tolerated his willingness to compromise for a while, they had never done so wholeheartedly or consistently, and now, in fact, the time was almost passed when they would be able to maintain even a semblance of agreement with him. The contrast between Zwingli's reaction to their behaviour, and his personal interest in them and sympathy for their ultimate goals, must have confused and angered them.

There was a fresh series of demonstrations against the Mass on December 10. The Chaplain's helpers at the Grossmünster objected to holding the service any more because the people mocked them. At the same time, vandals mutilated several of the service books. Yoder says that Zwingli was behind this outbreak, for, by instigating it, he hoped to force the Council to proceed with the reform of the cult.[79] This is possible, but, like the fast violation, the vandalism could have been engineered without Zwingli's knowledge. The conservative party around canons Hofmann and Widmer might have caused it to embarrass Zwingli and frighten the Council, and Grebel and Stumpf were capable of starting trouble to forward their own cause. The Council consulted the People's Priests and reissued the November mandate. To make sure that the mandate was obeyed, violators were threatened with prosecution.[80] The commission set up after the Second Disputation was reconvened and asked to submit written proposals concerning the abolition of the Mass. Three suggestions were put before the Council by the commission. The first, the work of Heinrich Engelhard, Zwingli, and Jud, called for the introduction of a service in keeping with "the institution and usage of Christ" on Christmas Day. At one point in the proposal Jud and Zwingli said, "We intend to begin the said usage . . . on Christmas Day."[81] Yoder cites this passage to prove that Zwingli intended to introduce a communion service, regardless of the Council's wishes. When the proposal was put before the commission, Yoder says, the other commissioners forced Zwingli to compromise.[82]

Yoder's interpretation is misleading. The passage to which Yoder refers does open with the words: "We intend to begin . . ." but it goes on to state the grounds upon which Zwingli was willing to defer his decision. If the request for the institution of a communion service could not be granted, Zwingli and the other clergy asked for the right to give communion in both kinds: ". . . and if one does not permit us the same,

79. Yoder, *MQR*, XXXII, 136.   80. *E.A.*, 456, 458.
81. *Z*, II, 809, 6–8.
82. Yoder, *MQR*, XXXII, 136–7; Yoder, 26.

we must give both the body and blood, bread and wine, to those who desire [it], or appear untrue to the Word of God."[83] The concession Zwingli sought was that which Hottinger had called for in his argument with Dr. Lorenz some six months before. However, by this time the men around Grebel were no longer willing to be satisfied with such halfway measures. They wanted the Mass done away with, not modified. Assuming that Hottinger's demand represented the aims of the radicals earlier in the year, it would seem that their position, rather than Zwingli's had changed. They had become more extreme in their demands and less willing to compromise. This was probably a major reason for the open split with Zwingli.

In the next to the last paragraph, Zwingli and his friends again considered the possibility that the Council would refuse to accept their suggestion. To meet this contingency they added a second request which, like the first, formed part of the compromise that the commission worked out: "Therefore, we beg your honourable wisdom, that they may at least consider that no one may compel any priests to perform the Mass."[84] In other words, the least they asked was that no clergyman be compelled to perform the Mass. The first proposal does not bear out Yoder's interpretation. Zwingli, Engelhard, and Jud obviously expected their demands would meet with difficulty. They expressed their desire to end the Mass, but indicated a willingness to compromise on something less. The final decision in this question, which was essentially a matter of procedure, was left to the magistrates.

The full commission presented to the Council a formal statement that Zwingli had composed, and which incorporated the compromises suggested by the People's Priests. Although the commissioners agreed that the reforms desired by Zwingli and the other People's Priests conformed to scripture, they took the same position Zwingli had taken in his letter to Vadian on November 11. So many were still "stupid," i.e., uninstructed and sympathetic with traditional usage, that "it will be necessary to give way somewhat" to them.[85] The commission's report advised the Council to permit the clergy to give communion in both kinds to those who requested it and stated that no priest should be forced to say Mass. Above all, the commission urged that the clergy avoid causing further tumult by confining its attention to preaching the Gospel. The report suggested that individual parishes be left free to replace the Mass, as long as the change did not cause disorder.[86] The commissioners left it up to individual priests to decide how they would

83. Z, II, 809, 9–11.   84. Ibid., II, 810, 5–7.
85. Ibid., II, 811, 1–3, 6–8.   86. Ibid., II, 812, 16–813, 10.

carry on the service and stated that since the Bible taught that "the Mass is not a sacrifice" the clergy would know what to do.[87] As far as the images were concerned, the commissioners maintained that the Council's decision about them should remain in force, but that no further use of them should be made in the service. Those of the clergy who ignore scripture and defend traditional attitudes towards the Mass and the images were to be admonished and, where necessary punished or deprived of their prebends.[88] The images were not removed from the churches for another five months.

Yoder claims that the Council rejected the advice of the commission on December 19.[89] The mandate issued by the magistracy on that date did not ignore the commission's advice. The Mass was retained, but, in keeping with the commission's directive, no cleric was forced to say Mass. Those who desired to perform the service were to be allowed to do so "in the form, that is closest to the will and the Word of God," and, as the second proposal had suggested, they were not to be abused and called "those who eat the Lord God, or God's butchers."[90] Nothing was said of the right of individual congregations to keep or abolish the service, and the Council specifically forbade that the communion was to be given in both kinds. The supporters of the Roman tradition in the city were once again given the opportunity to defend their faith before the Council.[91] To gain time and to pacify the conservatives in the city, the mandate also promised that copies of Zwingli's *Christian Introduction* would be sent to the Bishops of Basel, Constance, and Chur, the University of Basel, and the cantons of the Confederacy. These authorities were to be asked if Zwingli's views contradicted scripture. The Council awaited a reply by Pentecost and promised that the matter would be taken up again at that time.[92] Zwingli raised no objections to the mandate.

Yoder interprets Zwingli's acquiescence as the turning-point of the Reformation. For the sake of unity in the community, he had compromised his reform programme and abandoned his original doctrine of the church; his betrayal convinced Grebel he was a false prophet and the break between the two was complete.[93] Grebel's angry letter to

87. *Ibid.*, II, 813, 11–14.
88. *Ibid.*, II, 814, 3–11, 15–815, 2.
89. Yoder, *MQR*, XXXII, 137. Egli says that the second proposal concerning the Mass was completely accepted (Egli, 111). It may have been in practice, but formally it was not.
90. *E.A.*, 460; *Z*, II, 812, 10–12.
91. The conservative defence was presented on January 13 and 14, 1524.
92. *E.A.*, 460.
93. Yoder, *MQR*, XXXII, 138–40.

Vadian, written after the mandate appeared, indicates that he was thoroughly disgusted with Zwingli and there is no reason to deny that the breach between the two became final at this time. The main fault with Yoder's interpretation is that it fails to recognize the evidence linking Grebel to the radical faction from the summer of 1522. Grebel's letter to Vadian marks the culmination of a rift which had been almost two years in the making.

Zwingli recognized the sound political reasons behind the Council's refusal to sanction the formal suppression of the Mass. In return for the concessions the Council did grant, he was content to wait. The changes permitted by the Council deserve notice. When it stated that no priest was obliged to say Mass, it granted the minimum concession that the three People's Priests had requested and it recognized the authority of scripture, for it freed the clergy from the necessity of performing a ceremony contrary to the teachings of God's Word. By doing this, the government actually ceased to enforce the maintenance of the old service without formally abolishing it. Political considerations, as the appeal to the rest of the Confederacy, the three bishops, and the University of Basel for a judgment concerning the scriptural validity of Zwingli's *Christian Introduction* reveals, dictated both the councillor's willingness to permit those who wished to do so to continue to say Mass and the specific injunction that the sacrament was to be distributed in the customary way which prevented a communion in both kinds. The request for a judgment from the hierarchy and the other cantons was a delaying tactic designed to prevent the forces in the Confederacy opposed to the Reformation at Zurich from urging immediate action against the city now that it was ready to set aside the Mass. At least formally, the Mass had to remain until the government received replies from these sources. This is what the mandate itself said.

Nevertheless, by permitting some to continue to say Mass the government presumed to oppose what the Bible taught. Therefore, it would appear that Yoder is correct when he says that the "state acted against the Reformation" and thus "the problem of the State as an opponent of his programme was posed" for Zwingli who did not combat what amounted to the take-over of the church by the state.[94] However, those who were allowed to continue to say Mass were not given complete freedom. The government told them to say it "in the form that is closest to the will and Word of God."[95] What did this mean? The Disputation had agreed that the Mass was not a sacrifice and that God had forbidden men to make sacrifices to him. This decision was a rejection of the doc-

94. *Ibid.*, 138.   95. *E.A.*, 460.

trine of transubstantiation. When the magistrates told the adherents of the traditional service that they must follow the form "closest to the will and Word of God," they forbade any reference to the Mass as a sacrifice which emasculated the Mass.

Thus, although the outward forms of the service, which Zwingli had said were an abuse and should gradually be abolished, were retained until the spring of 1525, the doctrine that the Mass was a sacrifice that those forms expressed was denied.[96] By so doing, the government obeyed the Word of God and did not presume to oppose the Reformation. Thus Zwingli had no cause to object to what had been decided. His own expressed opinion on how the abusive practices connected with the Mass should be slowly done away with was followed.[97] Though he probably hoped for more, he had achieved his basic aim: the magistrates had begun to bring the major cultic practices of the church into line with the teachings of God's Word.

The changes which had now been sanctioned in effect altered the traditional form of the Mass. A reformed sermon was preached and all references to the Mass as a sacrifice were deleted; but the outward forms of the old ceremony, which included the use of Latin, clerical vestments, and the withholding of the cup from the laity, were, at least in theory, retained.[98] To a conservative, the suppression of any reference to the Mass as a sacrifice amounted to its abolition.[99] It was no doubt with this in mind that Zwingli later accused the *Täufer* of causing difficulties over external matters, for, after this change only the outward shell of the old ceremony remained.[100] What was lacking was a service that would replace the Mass, but the time was not right to introduce it. In the interim, provision had been made to prepare the clergy and the people of the canton for the final abolition of the Mass and the institution of a reformed version of the sacrament. At this time the Council also sanctioned a simplification of the Christmas service.[101] The magistracy's behaviour, though marked by caution, leaves no doubt of its support for Zwingli's programme. But if this was the turning-point of the Reformation for Grebel and his followers, it was not for Zwingli and the majority of his supporters.

96. Blanke says that all reference to the Mass as a sacrifice was removed and the remainder of the service retained (Blanke, 10).
97. Z, II, 789, 7–11.
98. Blanke, 10.
99. What was done was not unlike the policy adopted towards the Mass in the Second Edwardian Prayer Book which at the time marked a great advance of Protestant influence in England and was considered by many to be very radical.
100. Z, III, 404, 4–9.
101. Egli, 113.

Four years later Haller and Kolb at Bern experienced similar difficulties over the delay of the abolition of the Mass and wrote to ask
Zwingli's advice. Zwingli based his answer to them, which was framed
on October 11, 1527, on what had happened at Zurich, where even
after the Mass had been abolished, some had petitioned to be allowed
to hear the service in one of the city's churches. This petition was
rejected but, until after the disputation at Bern in 1528, such persons
were permitted to attend Mass in two villages outside the city and at
Baden and Einsieden outside the canton where it was still held. After
that all citizens were forbidden to attend Mass.[102] Zwingli advised Haller
and Kolb to prepare the way for change but to delay any major action
until the time was right for complete suppression. He warned that, if they
proceeded to celebrate communion before the Mass was officially done
away with, there was real danger that the conservative element would
petition for, and receive, permission to hold Mass in "some corner" or
"chapel." The result would be the toleration of two usages, one "apostolic," the other "anti Christian," which was what had occurred in
Bohemia where various Eucharistic practices were tolerated.[103] Zwingli
obviously believed that such diversity in religious practice was detri-
mental to the well-being of the community.

If the letter reflects accurately what had taken place at Zurich, it
indicates that a "reformed" and a "traditional" service were actually
performed between 1523 and 1525. In the proposals concerning the
Mass and the images, composed by Zwingli for the Council at the end
of May, 1524, he had noted with concern that priests followed one
usage and the laity another with respect.[104] Though in view of the
Council's official decision, it is difficult to understand exactly what he
meant, it does seem that members of the clergy who were conservative
went on saying Mass, while others, with lay support, were following, if
not exceeding, the directions of the Council concerning the service. The
fact that the diversity of practice worried Zwingli, and that he asked that
only the usage that conformed to the Word of God should be followed,
would tend to indicate that this was what was happening.[105] It would
appear that the Council was lax in enforcing its decision upon either side
and actually permitted a form of celebration that conformed more closely
to the commission's proposal for a reform of the Mass than the Council's

102. O. Farner, III, 515–17; Bullinger, I, 265.
103. Z, IX, 281, 13–282, 6.
104. *Ibid.*, III, 123, 13–15.
105. *Ibid.*, III, 123, 16–20. If this is the case, and it cannot be definitely proven,
then Egli's interpretation was the correct one after all. The second proposal about
the Mass was accepted.

formal proclamation allowed. If this was the case, it further explains Zwingli's willingness to accept the delay in formal suppression and renders the accusation that he betrayed his original position less tenable.

The letter to Haller and Kolb warned that such a premature development would leave the way open for a permanent concession to the traditionalists. They had advanced a petition for just such a concession when the Mass was set aside in April of 1525. Zwingli's backing from the Council was strong enough to prevent them from gaining the right to hold and to attend Mass in the city, but, for the moment, the Council had allowed them to go elsewhere to participate in the service.

Zwingli must have felt that what had taken place was a warning from God against any premature change which threatened to prevent unified religious observance in the society. The compromise and the delay he had accepted enabled him to prevent the adherents of the old service from retaining some sanctuary in the city where they could hear Mass, but just barely. Access to the Mass elsewhere was still possible when Zwingli's letter was dispatched. In retrospect, he must have felt a sense that God had indeed guided him in this matter and that his aid had averted a permanent compromise which would have prevented the achievement of the cultic unity he believed necessary for a healthy civic body. As he points out in his letter to Haller,

> The lord revealed this advice to us when we were in the process of abbrogating the Mass and, if we should not have acted in this way, the opposition would have obtained permission for them to say Mass in some recess. But once however it [the Mass] was rejected by public authority, no one now is allowed to undertake anything of this kind.[106]

The importance that he attached to the full support of the Council in order to prevent an undesirable compromise follows from his own experience at Zurich. It was quite natural for a man concerned with the reform of the church to view his success as the result of divine guidance.[107] If anything, the letter to Haller and Kolb indicates that Zwingli regretted having pushed for the final abolition of the Mass before the time was right; his implication is that they pursue an even more cautious policy than he himself had followed at Zurich.

The Council's decisions freed Zwingli from the moral dilemma that his resignation as People's Priest and re-appointment as People's Pastor had forced upon him. For over a year he had been freed from the

---

106. *Ibid.*, IX, 281. 7–11.

107. Yoder interprets Zwingli's reference to the advice which God revealed to him as an indication that Zwingli felt the need to justify his decision to delay the introduction of the Mass by basing it upon a divine revelation (Yoder, 27–8; Yoder, *MQR*, XXXII, 139).

obligation of conducting the Mass, while his friends and supporters among the clergy had to continue taking part in the service. Now at last, they were also free from an odious burden. The events that took place in December fulfilled the requirements of Zwingli's political theory. The government had accepted the prophet's interpretation of the Word and the prophet had acquiesced to the magistrates' authority in the sphere of human righteousness. At their behest, he waited until the spring of 1525 for the formal suppression of the Mass.

Grebel maintained his old position. The commands of the Word were clear; they had to be obeyed regardless of the consequences. The decisions reached in December allowed the Mass to continue and were a betrayal of the reform programme. Neither Grebel nor his friends could accept the tactics that Zwingli employed, and this was the last time they could tolerate his hypocrisy. True to their own understanding of God's command, the radicals turned away from Zwingli and his ally, the magistracy. When they did this, they rejected the ideal of the *corpus christianum* which dominated the political thought of the era. They came to believe in a church without state support. Zwingli's theological vision as well as his temperament and training prevented him from sharing their belief. He could not conceive of acting without the Christian magistrate, and, in the context of his time, he was right. Christian renewal at Zurich would have failed without the backing of the magistrate.[108] Both he and Grebel were true to what they believed the scripture required; each employed the tactics he assumed were fitted to fulfil God's command. Zwingli's were in keeping with the times, and brought him success. Grebel's were ahead of his time and brought persecution to his followers. Zwingli's policy during December, 1523, was consistent with his aim: the reform of the *corpus christianum*. Yoder does Zwingli less than justice when he claims that he abandoned the church to assure unity in society. As Zwingli understood the problem, church and society were one: to maintain the unity of the commonwealth was to defend the church.

108. Von Muralt states that Zwingli pursued this course of action because he recognized the critical nature of the situation which the people of Zurich faced and knew that the path followed by the *Täufer* would destroy the Reformation (von Muralt, *ZWI*, VI (1934), 79–80).

12 Developments at Zurich Subsequent to 1523

ONE PROBLEM REMAINS. IT CAN BE DEMONSTRATED THAT Zwingli's conception of the role of the magistrate and the pastor was consistent during the first years of his ministry. But many scholars assert that the combined pressures of the conservative opposition and the emergence of the *Täufer* (Baptist) church forced him to alter his views. Some say that after 1523 Zurich became a theocracy, and others say a state church was set up. A number of major developments are referred to as proof. In 1525 a marriage court, made up of two People's Priests and four other judges, two from the Small Council and two from the Great Council, was established and, by 1526, the Council took control over the excommunication of those found guilty of adultery by the court.[1] A synod, consisting of all the pastors of the canton and two lay representatives from each congregation, was created in 1528 to report on marriage problems, keep track of the enforcement of the laws against the Baptists, advise the Council, and censure and guide the clergy. Zwingli's part in its founding has been interpreted as an effort to guarantee the church some protection against the encroachments of the magistracy.[2] In the same year Zwingli became a member of the Secret Council, an emergency executive organ instituted by the Council in periods of tension. His participation in the Secret Council is said to mark the merger of the pastoral and magisterial office and is cited as the final stage in the creation of a theocracy at Zurich.[3] The *Sittenmandat* (morality ordinance) of 1530, issued by the Council in conjunction with the Synod, is also often used to prove that Zurich had become a

1. Ley, 48–50; Alfred Farner, 110. The composition of the court follows the pattern set by the Council in appointing commissions to deal with the problems of reform during 1523. As his letter to Blarer on October 9, 1523 reveals, Zwingli accepted this practice. The mixed character of the court should be noted. Ley says that the Council was responsible only for the physical punishment of the guilty and assumes that the spiritual punishment was carried out by barring the condemned from the communion. He believes that the Council took over this responsibility because the church congregation was also the political assembly and physical punishments were the concern of the civil authority which represented the assembly (Ley, 48–9).

2. O. Farner, IV, 400, 402.   3. Alfred Farner, 123–4.

theocracy. This point has been stressed because although the mandate recognized a distinction between the realm of faith and that of the secular power, it enforced compulsory church attendance and imposed not only the ban, i.e., exclusion from the communion, but also civil punishment upon those who failed to obey. At this point the magistracy acted both for the physical and spiritual well-being of the citizens. After Zwingli's death the citizens were also compelled to take communion. Thus participation in both sacraments was enforced by the secular arm.[4]

A good deal of the discussion concerning the changes in Zwingli's thought and attitude, as well as the claim that Zurich became a "theocracy" during the last years of Zwingli's ministry, ignores the position that the Council had occupied in the city before the Reformation. In the broadest sense of the term, city government could be said to have been dominated by a theocratic ideal before the sixteenth century began.[5] The urban magistracy already had a semi-religious character and exercised its power for the benefit of both the temporal and the spiritual well-being of its people. Its function was justified by the assumption that it governed to fulfil the will of God. The Reformation, whether at Zurich or elsewhere, did not change this. However, the terms in which the magistracy's role was explained were conditioned by the theology of the reform movement. The development of Zwingli's thought at Zurich provides an example of this. From the beginning, his ideals were worked out within the context of a pre-existing "theocratic" theory of government.

Brockelmann has provided an answer to those who see these developments in terms of an emerging theocracy. According to Zwingli, the elect are known only to God. Therefore, society is a mixed body; both the church and the community are judged by the standards of human righteousness administered by the magistrate.[6] When he permitted the Council to enforce church attendance and the use of the sacraments, he did not violate the tenets of his twofold doctrine of righteousness. The magistrates had every right to require outward conformity to the Christian religion. In fact, they were obliged to do so.

None of the developments between 1525 and 1531 abrogated the distinctions that Zwingli had made between the spiritual and secular realms. He allowed the Council to control the ban because the church at Zurich was a mixed body, subject to the norms of human righteousness. The position that he outlined in the sermon *On Divine and Human Righteousness* made this development the inevitable result of the consoli-

4. *Ibid.*, 127; Ley, 115.   5. Cf. Introduction, xii.
6. Brockelmann, 34–9.

dation of the reformed church. Moreover, the Council had issued and enforced morality ordinances long before the Reformation began.[7] The use of the ban to assure compliance with the law provided the government with a more efficient means of fulfilling a traditional responsibility. Nor was the control of baptism by the Zurich government unique or radical. At this time infant baptism throughout Europe was in some way supervised by the secular arm,[8] and when Zwingli said that partaking of communion was an outward sign, it was to be expected the magistrate would supervise it, as in the case of baptism.

There is a parallel between the function of the Synod and Zwingli's participation in the Secret Council. Though the Synod may have been created as a defensive measure, another interpretation is possible. The composition of the Synod provided the Council with a mixed representative body capable of advising it on theological questions. The lay element carried with it the consensus on religious issues of the assemblies in the city and countryside, while the clergy provided men competent to interpret the scripture. The Synod fulfilled the requirements Zwingli had laid down for a valid assembly of Christians. Its creation may reveal the Council's desire to have a standing gathering to advise it on spiritual questions, for the existence of the Synod freed the Council from the necessity of summoning frequent disputations. If so, it proves that the Council had no wish to violate the division between spiritual and secular authority. In practical terms, the Synod offered the government a means of keeping in touch with public opinion on religious matters, and of using the lay element in the body to consolidate public opinion behind its religious policy.

Similar arguments can be advanced for Zwingli's membership in the Secret Council. In the sermon *On Divine and Human Righteousness*, he had said that the magistrates should seek to raise the level of their government towards the norms of divine righteousness. It was the pastor's responsibility to inform the Christian ruler of God's will. As the leader of the reform movement in the city, it seems logical that the magistrates would seek Zwingli's advice on the religious implications of their policies. The fact that he sat with the Council and advised it does not mean he violated the limitations of his office and actually became a secular magistrate. The facts so often adduced to prove that Zwingli was unable to maintain a sharp division between secular and religious authority in his last years at Zurich may just as well prove that he consistently upheld it.

7. O. Farner, IV, 388.
8. Blanke, 17.

Scholars have referred to Zwingli's printed works to prove he was inconsistent. The crises he faced from 1523 on did drive him to elaborate his views more thoroughly, but the elaboration only continued, or clarified, what he had already said about the division of powers in the *respublica Christiana*. His periodic discussions of the issue only show how he applied his conception of the properly ordered Christian society.

A few of Zwingli's sermons and tracts from 1524 to 1531 should be considered. He re-stated his definition of the church in *The Reply to Hieronymus Emser*, which was issued during August, 1524. He began by reviewing the ecclesiology he had presented to Melchior Fattlin in 1522. Membership in the church constituted belief in the heart, an internal state, and confession with the mouth, an outward sign. Drawing upon both Old and New Testaments, he stated that the church on earth was a mixed body. In the Old Testament the church was the whole people of Israel; the pious and the impious. The church, as it is mentioned in the New Testament, includes all who confess Christ, but "truly the faithful are few." Even though the name church is used, wherever there are Christians, this does not mean the members belong to the Church Universal, which is "without blemish"; they are known only to God.[9] As long as the church on earth was a mixed body, the only standards of behaviour applicable to its members were those of human righteousness. For this reason the magistrate was the only authority who had the right to supervise the congregation's adherence to the standards of membership in the church.

By the end of 1524, Manz, Grebel, and their following had become advocates of adult baptism.[10] The treatise, *Who Causes Tumult*, dispatched by Zwingli late in December, 1524, to the congregation at Mülhausen, discussed the factions at Zurich who continued to cause difficulty. His criticism of the Baptists was particularly revealing. They caused trouble over externals and sought to establish a separate church without the protection or support of a government.[11] The Baptists had, by the end of 1524, moved beyond Zwingli's conception of Christian society, and their advocacy of adult baptism caused him to clarify his views on baptism. He had already propounded a dual doctrine of baptism in the *Defence of the Sixty-Seven Articles*, and he now spoke of both communion and baptism as external signs. Of course, he believed that the outward sign was paralleled by the working of the Spirit on the heart of the believer, but it is also clear that he viewed the perform-

9. *Z*, III, 253, 16–19, 24–31; 261, 4–8.
10. O. Farner, 112, 117.
11. *Z*, III, 404, 4–9.

ance of the sacraments as a sign of membership in the mixed body of the earthly church.

Zwingli admitted that the New Testament neither forbade nor commanded infant baptism, and he argued that from the time of Abraham some outward sign of faith had been given to children. In the Old Testament it had been circumcision and, citing Paul, he asserted that baptism had taken the place of circumcision, because it served to indicate that those who shared the same faith were one. He agreed with the Baptists that no sacrament removed sin, but he claimed that baptism and the elements of the communion were signs given by Christ for men to see.[12] The two sacraments were visible signs, expressing the unity of a Christian society. His position, presupposed the identity of the visible church with the populace of a Christian city or state. The assumption of this identity was the basis of his programme for Christian renewal at Zurich.

In his major theological treatise, *De Vera et Falsa Religione*, printed in March, 1525, and dedicated to King of France, whom Zwingli hoped to win for the Gospel, Zwingli again commented upon the sacraments and spoke of the magistrate's duties. He maintained that a sacrament was a pledge to become a soldier of Christ. Baptism represents a pledge that one's life will be formed according to Christ's rule, while communion reveals the participant's belief in Christ's death and unites those who share this belief. Both sacraments represent the transformation of the signs that expressed Israel's unity in the world, circumcision and the Passover, through Christ.[13] This interpretation of the sacraments clarifies the line of thought developed in the *Reply* to Emser of 1524. The people of Israel were a mixed body, but all shared in the outward signs of God's grace. Since the church, like Israel, was a mixed body, it could be co-terminus with a city state, in which all shared the outward signs of grace. When in *Who Causes Tumult* Zwingli termed the two sacraments, "signs of the elect,"[14] he spoke of them as the symbols of unity for a chosen people.

Zwingli carried this idea further when he discussed the magistrate's role in society. He sought to disprove the Baptist claim that a Christian could not be a magistrate, and he repeated the argument in favour of the Christian ruler in the sermon *On Divine and Human Righteousness*; no man could be a proper magistrate if he were not a Christian. The aims of the church and magistrate were the same as far as external

12. *Ibid.*, III, 409, 27–30; 410, 4–16; 411, 16–18.
13. *Ibid.*, III, 761, 24, 34–8; 803, 1–2, 11–17, 25–7.
14. *Ibid.*, III, 410, 27.

matters were concerned. Both sought unity, obedience to the laws and the common, rather than private, good.[15] The church provides what the secular power lacks because it engenders love of one's neighbour and drives out love of private gain, so that men obey the law naturally. This is why the city needs the Gospel and the good magistrate must be Christian. The magistrate without fear of God is a tyrant, but a ruler who fears God keeps the law and is a father to his people.[16] Thus far, there is no sign that Zwingli departed from the division of powers set forth in the sermon *On Divine and Human Righteousness.*

Some have tried to interpret the views Zwingli expressed between 1528 and 1531 as a rationalization for the creation of a theocracy at Zurich.[17] Neither his letter to Ambrosius Blarer at Constance in 1528, nor his *Introduction to Jeremiah,* dedicated to Strasbourg in 1531, support this claim. The two pieces mark only a further elucidation of the position taken before 1523. The letter to Blarer justified the right of the magistrate to make laws governing fasts and other religious observances. Certain elements at Constance, claiming government regulation of religious practices injured the consciences of the weak, objected to the magistrates' control. Zwingli attributed the discontent of these people to the influence of Luther, who taught that "the kingdom of Christ is not external." Although he did not deny that the New Testament offered ample precedent for Luther's opinion, he demonstrated that Christ was concerned with non-spiritual matters.[18] The precedent for the magistrate's right to supervise religious observance is found in the decisions and composition of the Council of Jerusalem. The Council abolished circumcision, an outward symbol of religious observation, but retained the laws against eating polluted meat. Both Christ and the Apostles made decisions which, in the present day, are the concerns of government. If they act with the consent of the church, magistrates who are Christian have the same right.[19]

Zwingli affirmed that the Council at Jerusalem consisted of pastors and men of age and wisdom who served the church exactly as a council of magistrates serves a city:

They have not properly understood the "presbyters" in the Scriptures, when they have taken them only as those who preside over the Word, for they may also be taken as; senators, decurions and those who deliberate. . . . For it is certain enough that those who are called presbyters in this passage

15. *Ibid.*, III, 867, 12–13, 17–20; 868, 15–18.
16. *Ibid.*, III, 868, 22–34, 38–9; 869, 1–4.
17. Alfred Farner, 112–14, 130, 132, 134.
18. Z, IX, 451, 17–18; 452, 16–17, 23–453, 10.
19. *Ibid.*, IX, 455, 21–30, 456, 30–1.

were not servants of the Word but men, venerable in age, prudence and faith, who, in directing and carrying on affairs, were to the church what the senate is to the city.[20]

In a world where the Christian magistrate was a reality, the officials of a representative government, like Zurich's or Constance's can care for the external affairs of the church. In so far as it was Christian and had the consent of the people, the Council at Constance had every right to issue commands "in a matter which pertains to religion, as long as it is external, even if not a few may be offended." However, he added that the decisions should be weighed "according to the standard of the Divine Word."[21]

Later in the letter Zwingli returned to the question of the magistrate's right to govern the externals of the faith. Some denied the Senate of Constance the right to act because it was not the whole church. Zwingli reminded them that most cities consult the *curiata comitia*, the representative assemblies of its districts, which, individually, are called the guilds. He argued that the decisions of the *curiata comitia* constituted an adequate consensus of the church, and he defended this opinion by stating that, with the agreement of the church, authority to solve a difficult problem could be delegated to a few. As he had done at the beginning of the Second Disputation, he based his stand upon the example of the Council of Jerusalem. In view of the biblical precedent, he concluded that there was nothing to prevent a city council, the delegated authority of a Christian people, to vote to remove images or to suppress the Mass. This was consistent with his doctrine of divine and human righteousness, for the implementation of changes in the externals of cultric practice that the teachings of scripture demanded fell under the laws of human righteousness. Lest any doubt remain, he found further precedent for the work of the magistrate in the life of Christ.[22]

When he spoke of the districts as guilds, Zwingli no doubt had in mind the situation at Zurich. The Great Council received its authority from the city assembly, i.e., the biannual of citizens, which, like the Council itself, was dominated by the guilds. This argument also applied to a majority of the south German cities, including Constance, whose councils were controlled by the guilds.[23] The reference to the decisions of the *curiata comitia* as providing an adequate consensus of the church again illustrates the assumption that the city assembly was a gathering of a Christian people.

20. *Ibid.*, IX, 455, 33–5; 456, 5–8.
22. *Ibid.*, IX, 456, 27–458, 6, 13–15.
21. *Ibid.*, IX, 455, 30–5.
23. Moeller, 64–5, 67.

The crux of Zwingli's position, that authority delegated by consensus to a smaller group still represented the agreement of the whole, is a reflection of the corporate theory of government that dominated the political thought of cities like Zurich and Constance. He clearly believed that Zurich's constitutional traditions paralleled the polity of the early church. The citizens of Zurich were a Christian people governed by a Christian magistrate, and the structure of the Christian community was one and the same with that of the visible church.

In a city state permeated by a corporate view of society, Zwingli's conception of the church made it possible for the magistracy to complete the process of absorbing the outward structure of the church into the framework of civil society. One of the major pre-conditions for his success at Zurich was a doctrine of the church that would make the fulfilment of what was implicit in the corporate nature of the Zurich community possible. This doctrine was present from the very start of Zwingli's career in the city. It antedates the split with the radical party and helps to explain why this division took place.

The other major pre-condition for Zwingli's success in the city was a willingness to accept the place that the magistracy already occupied in the affairs of the church. He had no qualms about this. When, throughout the letter to Blarer, he talked about the Christian magistrate and the Christian people, he made the same assumptions that Erasmus did in the *Education of a Christian Prince*. The Christian magistrate will not exceed the limits of God's will because, as a Christian, he is bound by the precepts of the Bible.

The *Introduction to Jeremiah* only brought the concept of the Christian society that had made Zwingli's work a success at Zurich into clearer focus. The letter to Blarer emphasized the rights of the Christian magistrate, while the *Introduction to Jeremiah* concentrated upon the function of the prophet. Taken together the two treatises represent an epilogue to the sermon *On Divine and Human Righteousness*. Zwingli began his exposition by applying the anthropology of the day, which divided man into body and soul, to churches, kingdoms, and republics. The carnal desires of the body politic, like those of men, require intelligent control to guarantee law and order, which is vital to human existence. The only source for such control is in heaven, because neither wisdom nor prudence can be found among men. If men fail to look to heaven and have no reverence for God, they return to a chaotic animal state, where each seeks his own ends to the detriment of the others. Religion sets aside selfishness and causes men to serve their neighbour.

For society to benefit from religion, agents representing it must be present, and the prophet and the magistrate were the agents provided by God.[24] The prophet taught heavenly wisdom, while the magistrate corrected the foolish deeds performed by the men who lacked it: "The prophets who teach heavenly wisdom, the magistrates who correct the wicked works of wisdom, that is; those which are not rightly but foolishly done."[25] Both the prophet and the magistrate are necessary because many men are restrained from evil out of fear of ignominy, rather than the love of virtue which the prophet teaches.[26] Zwingli, near the end of his career, still assumed Christian society was a mixed body.

He did not believe that either the prophet or the magistrate could give the spirit of true religion to others, but he said that Holy Spirit ruled all through the ministry of the prophets; and thus, when the prophet taught faithfully, all of society was benefitted. If the prophet failed to do so, the people suffered and the magistrate, deprived of religion, was likely to become a tyrant.[27] The best way for society to enjoy the unity God can give is for the magistrate and the prophet to co-operate: "Therefore it is certain that in no thing are peace and harmony provided to the church and the people of the city more greatly than in the office of the prophets and the magistrates."[28] A healthy balance between the two offices leads to true tranquility. The first place in society belonged to the prophet because his teaching was the guide for the magistrate's correction of the citizenry.[29]

Zwingli explained in detail the kind of a person a prophet should be: he must demonstrate that he loves God and his neighbour, and that he is the example by which the people and the rulers should be formed. One of his chief responsibilities is to recall the magistrate and the people from bad conduct and thus to preserve the health of the whole body of the church and the republic.[30] Zwingli noted the effect on the world of Rome's false teaching and poured contempt upon the rulers loyal to the pope who cited biblical passages enjoining people to prevent reform. He reminded his readers that the prophets, Elijah and Jeremiah defied their rulers so that true religion could be taught.[31] He then compared the failures of the old church with the hopeful signs of reform at Strasbourg.

24. *Z*, XIV, 417, 7–14, 21–3, 25–418, 11.
25. *Ibid.*, XIV, 418, 11–13.
26. *Ibid.*, XIV, 418, 13–16.
27. *Ibid.*, XIV, 418, 16–22, 33–6; 419, 9–13.
28. *Ibid.*, XIV, 420, 4–6.
29. *Ibid.*, XIV, 420, 9–12.
30. *Ibid.*, XIV, 420, 12–13, 22–4, 30–6; 421, 8–10.
31. *Ibid.*, XIV, 422, 8–13, 17–20.

The improvement is so great that one can view the Christian man as the faithful citizen and the Christian city as the Christian church:

Thus, your princes do not swell up with pride and your prophets teach fitly, faithfully and wisely; and thus a tranquil people accept doctrine and authority, and there is no reason for embarassment now over former statements that the Christian man is nothing else than the faithful and good citizen; and the Christian city is nothing other than the Christian Church.[32]

Zwingli's words represent the picture of a society enjoying harmony based upon the proclamation of God's Word. When, thanks to the co-operation of the prophet and the magistrate, the community is pervaded by divine teaching, the entire society is transformed, the Christian man is a good citizen, and the Christian city is the Christian church. What Zwingli idealized here was not a theocracy or Caesaropapism in the modern sense; it was simply the proper co-operation of the ruler and the priest, who drew their strength from God to rule a unified Christian commonwealth according to the divine purpose. This is what Zwingli set out to achieve at Zurich; nothing more and nothing less.[33]

32. *Ibid.*, XIV, 424, 17–22.
33. Locher maintains that Zwingli pursued this goal throughout his career at Zurich. He sought to renew the whole of society at Zurich and did not surrender the church to the state. For him church and state were not divided; together they formed a single unity, like the body and the soul (Locher, *Reformatio*, I, 209–10).

13   Conclusion

THE ORIGINAL PURPOSE OF THIS INVESTIGATION WAS TO discover the place Zwingli assigned to the magistracy and the clergy at Zurich to realize the rule of God. To understand Zwingli's theory of government it was necessary to consider his education and early career, as well as the political traditions at Zurich that contributed to the development of his ideas. Zwingli was forced to elaborate his views on the function of the magistrate and the pastor as his programme for Christian renewal was put into practice. Before any conclusions concerning his blue-print for the administration of Christian society could be drawn, the challenges which Zwingli faced and his response to them demanded clarification.

Zwingli began his public career as a patriot opposed to Swiss participation in the Italian wars, except to defend the pope. Before he came to Zurich, his personal experience and the influence of Erasmus and of the Bible altered his opinions. He became a convinced neutralist, but this was not the most important change which took place. He now believed the political ills of the Confederacy were the symptom of the clergy's failure to preach the Gospel to the people. If the Gospel were preached, the political difficulties that plagued the Confederacy would come to an end. The desire to insure the Gospel its rightful place in the life of the community is the key to understanding Zwingli's attitude toward government.

The programme he advocated was influenced by his study of Erasmus. Erasmus, like Occam and Marsilio before him, believed that the corruption of the church was due to the clergy's possession of wealth and secular power. He despaired of the church's ability to reform itself and looked to the Christian prince as the only agent capable of achieving reform. Erasmus believed that wealth and secular power should be removed from the clergy and given to the prince. This, he believed, would free the clergy to perform the function God had assigned to it: the proclamation of the Gospel. In a society where the magistrate and the priest performed the tasks God had given them, the divine purpose would be carried out.

Although Zwingli accepted Erasmus' basic assumption, he applied it

within a very different context. At every point, the development of
Zwingli's political thought, which was an integral part of his theology,
was conditioned by a corporate theory of society. The Zurich constitution presupposed this idea: the magistrates were the delegated authority
of the whole people, their power was sanctioned by the consensus of
the community. In theory at least, there was no limit to it. Indeed, as
far as Zurich and for that matter the majority of south German cities
were concerned, only the magistrates had the power to guarantee the
Gospel a central place in the life of the community. Zwingli's willingness
to accept the presuppositions that underlay the magistracy's authority
in the city and the place that the government already occupied in the
constitution became the foundation on which he built his political
theory; it also explains his close co-operation with the civil power, as
well as the success of his programme of reform at Zurich. A close and
harmonious relationship with the city councillors was doubly necessary
for Zwingli because he regarded the reform of the church at Zurich as
only the first step in his plan to win the Confederacy, and ultimately all
of Europe, for the cause of Christian renewal. Zurich was to be the
model which would help to win acceptance for the Gospel among the
European nations.

In keeping with the unitary structure of the community implied by the
corporate conception of society, there was, in the early sixteenth century,
no separate gathering known as the church congregation. The city
assembly, which included all the citizens, was both the basic political
organ in the constitution and the church congregation. The Council
received its authority from the Assembly. By the eve of the Reformation
the village assemblies of the canton were subordinated to the Council
which either appointed or approved the officials who directed their
deliberations. During the Reformation they followed the religious policy
laid down by the Council.

The Council as the city Assembly's representative supervised religious
and political questions in the interest of the common good for the entire
canton. It had in fact already taken on a semi-sacral character and had
gone a long way toward realizing Erasmus' ideal for the reform of the
church before 1519. As the agent of the people, the Council administered the clergy's wealth, compelled it to perform the tasks assigned to
it, and appointed the majority of priests to their prebends. In sum, it
had asserted its authority over the clerical estate and had deprived it of
many of its immunities and much of the power, as well as the independence, that it had previously enjoyed. Before the Reformation, the one
thing the Council never considered doing was to alter the dogma and

cult of the church. It left these questions to the hierarchy because it believed that, regardless of its corruption, the old church was the valid authority in spiritual questions.

During the era of reform, Zwingli's supporters and foes shared the same ideal. They believed that society on earth was a Christian body. Right religion was central to the proper operation of government and its practice was vital for the existence of a Christian society. The traditionalists viewed their church as the source of religious authority. Zwingli and his followers developed a doctrine of scripture illumined by the Holy Spirit that replaced the authority of Rome. Zwingli convinced the magistrates that the scripture, rather than the old church, provided them with the knowledge of God's will. The mandate issued by the Zurich Council late in the fall of 1520 instructed the clergy of the canton to confine their preaching to the scripture. It was the first clear sign that Zwingli's views had found support.

The Council's acceptance of biblical authority was essential to his programme of reform; the rest of the Reformation followed from it. In co-operation with those qualified to interpret the scripture, the Council consolidated its control over the cantonal church and supervised the purification of the church's dogma and cult. Zwingli believed the Council's power also had religious sanction. After the Fall, God established laws of human righteousness to govern the affairs of sinful men, and he appointed rulers to enforce the laws. The administration of the temporal concerns of the church and the supervision of the citizen's outward conformity to the requirements of church membership fell within the ruler's competence.

The two disputations show the magistrates respected the authority of scripture. The Council called the First Disputation because disagreements over the preaching of the Gospel menaced public order. The purpose of the Disputation was to find out whether Zwingli's preaching conformed, not to the dictates of the established church, but to scripture. Zwingli raised no objection to the Council's right to call the Disputation. He accepted the Council as the delegated authority of a Christian people. The magistrates referred theological questions to an authority that Zwingli had convinced them was capable of judging. Once the Council was sure Zwingli's doctrines were founded upon the Bible, it encouraged him to continue his work. He had succeeded in changing the conception of what constituted a valid religious authority.

The Council called the Second Disputation for much the same reason it had summoned the First. The issue of the Mass and the images was causing civil strife. Before taking action on the matter, it was necessary to be sure exactly what scripture required. The Disputation was to discover this, and then the Council had to decide when and how action was to b₂ taken. The way in which Zwingli justified the competence of those assembled at the Disputation to reach a decision proves that he considered the political assembly of the city and the church congregation to be identical. The Zurich Assembly fulfilled the scriptural definition of a local church, i.e., a gathering of believers competent either to act for itself or to delegate others to solve difficult questions for the benefit of all.

The two Disputations put into practice Zwingli's theory of the proper relationship between the secular and spiritual arm. The smooth co-operation between the two would provide orderly government for a Christian city. This co-operation developed quickly at Zurich because of the pressures that the reform produced. If co-operation had not been quickly developed the programme of Christian renewal would have failed.

From 1520 on, Zwingli and his allies had to contend with the hostility of the established church. The Bishop of Constance was goaded into a campaign against the reformer by his vicar, Faber, but Rome's desire to retain Zurich as a recruiting ground for the papal army thwarted the Bishop's efforts during the first stage of the reform. However, he found a willing ally in the Federal Diet. The representatives of the cantons in the Diet were alarmed by the spread of Zwingli's teachings which they believed were Lutheran heresy. They knew he had helped keep Zurich out of the French alliance and was an advocate of Swiss neutrality. His views threatened the basis of Swiss prosperity and power in Europe. The representatives sought to undermine his influence and the Council's control over the canton by encouraging the pro-mercenary party at Zurich to stir up unrest against the government. If it had been willing to go to war before 1523, the Confederacy might have crushed the reform movement, but it hesitated to begin a civil war that might invite foreign intervention. The policy pursued by the Diet in conjunction with the church failed to stop Zwingli. It was the immediate cause of the First Disputation, which led to the consolidation of the reform in the canton and facilitated its spread.

The gravest threat to Zwingli's hopes for a successful Christian renewal at Zurich was posed by the radical faction among his followers. This group probably coalesced late in 1521 or early in 1522 and made its first public appearance in the Lenten fast violation of 1522. Though many scholars disagree on this point, there is good evidence that a direct connection existed between the radical members of Zwingli's supporters and the Baptist movement which emerged in the canton during 1524 and 1525. Conrad Grebel, the future leader of the *Täufer*, can be numbered among the ranks of the radicals by the summer of 1522.

The extremists hoped to induce Zwingli to press for the immediate suppression of the traditional cult and the establishment of a truly reformed church. To achieve this end, they were active in the tithe agitation during the fall of 1522 and the late spring of 1523. They assumed that the abolition of the "spiritual" tenths would deprive the Mass priests of support and stop the performance of the Mass. At some time in the summer of 1523 the radicals proposed the creation of a believer's church, untainted by tithes or by any connection with the old cult. When Zwingli rejected the scheme, they became disenchanted with him and his insistence upon co-operation with the secular arm.

Grebel's friends launched a direct attack upon the Mass and the images in the fall of 1523. Several of them participated in the destruction of crucifixes and statues of saints. Alarmed over these developments, the magistrates summoned the Second Disputation to consider what should be done about the Mass and the images. During this Disputation, the tension between Zwingli and Grebel was revealed, but a complete break did not occur until December, 1523.

The hostility of the Confederacy to Zwingli's teachings and the uncertain state of public opinion in the canton induced the Council to retain the Mass and the images, and Zwingli accepted the Council's decision because the councillors agreed that the Mass and the images should be set aside. The Council then provided for a programme of preaching throughout the canton to prepare the way for this. Zwingli also recognized the need to make concessions to the "weak" in order to win them for the Gospel and to prevent unrest in the city. Renewed agitation in December led him to request the immediate end of the Mass, but even then he qualified his request by presenting several alternatives which he hoped would form the basis for an interim compromise if the Council still wished to delay. The Council remained committed to its original decision that a delay was necessary. It commanded that the outward forms of the ceremony be retained but, because it did not wish to oppose the authority of scripture, it freed the clergy from the obligation to say the Mass and forbade any reference to it as a sacrifice, where the service was continued. As far as conservatives were concerned, the Council's action in fact destroyed the traditional significance of the sacrament. In return for these concessions, which accepted the minimal alternatives he had proposed in lieu of the complete abolition of the Mass, Zwingli agreed to a further delay. Grebel saw his decision as a surrender to the magistracy and a betrayal of the cause of reform. The break between the two men became final.

Zwingli's problem with the radicals was that while, during 1522 and 1523, they shared his aims, they differed with him in their conception of the timing and tactics of reform. Grebel and his friends stirred up discontent at Zurich which played into the hand of Zwingli's domestic opponents. For example, the Zurich monks used the activities of the extremists as an excuse to demand that the reformer be silenced. The behaviour of the enthusiasts also convinced the other cantons that his teachings were a menace to religion and to ordered government; this made the rest of the Confederacy all the more determined to induce the Zurich magistracy to stop supporting him.

Zwingli's aim was to win the entire community for the Gospel and he realized that the support of the magistracy was essential if he were to succeed. In order to gain his object he followed a policy of compromise in the face of all the pressures which were brought to bear upon him. This policy convinced the radicals that he was moving in the direction which they desired and encouraged them to increase their efforts to bring him the rest of the way as soon as possible. When he did not respond, they felt that he had given them false hope and had betrayed them.

Zwingli was willing to compromise with the magistrates because they accepted his doctrine of religious authority based upon the Bible. As long as the government admitted that the requirements for religious reform found in scripture should be carried out, he was content to let the councillors decide when the changes should be made. He recognized that they faced domestic and foreign difficulties that the radicals were often inclined to under-estimate.

The reformer clarified his policy in sermons and treatises repudiating the individualism of the radicals, and he sought to convince the other Confederates that the Gospel was the best support for ordered government. The sermon *On Divine and Human Righteousness*, together with several passages from *Defence of the Sixty-Seven Articles*, printed in the summer of 1523, made explicit what had been implicit in his co-operation with the magistracy from the beginning of his ministry at Zurich. Both works were influenced by the crisis of the tithe agitation and may have been published after he rejected the radicals' plan for a separate church. The sermons provide a full statement of the reformer's beliefs concerning the government of the *corpus christianum*. The division of power between the magistrate and the pastor was based upon his doctrine of divine and human righteousness. The magistrate exercised all secular power and had the right to direct the external affairs of the church. The Christian magistrate, who was a good magistrate, made possible the preaching of the Gospel by the pastor. The knowledge of the Gospel that the pastor proclaimed prevented the ruler from becoming a tyrant and reminded him and his subjects that their righteousness did not make them just before God. It also obliged the magistrate to raise the level of human justice above the bare minimum. Zwingli denied the pastor any part in the exercise of secular power. His task was to preach the Gospel, which summarized God's will for men. When magistrate and pastor performed their tasks, Christian society was properly governed. Zwingli's sermon revealed how much he had been influenced not merely by Erasmus' teaching but also by the corporate theory of society in which he thought and worked. The theory of government he elucidated in the sermons of 1523 stated clearly the basis upon which he had developed his policy from the beginning of his labours at Zurich. The remaining events of that year were consistent with the plan he had followed from 1519.

During the early years of his career as a reformer Zwingli maintained a view of society based upon the assumption that the civic community at Zurich was a unified whole. He recognized no distinction between church and state and believed that together they formed a single society which was best governed when the clergy and the magistracy worked in harmony to realize the will of God. His conception was basically mediaeval and was specifically conditioned by the constitutional traditions of the Swiss city state. Despite all the arguments to the contrary, he retained throughout his career the belief in the balance of power between the prophet, who proclaimed the norms of divine righteousness to society, and the magistrate, who administered human righteousness. It is true that the fullest statement of his ideas appeared towards the end of his life, but this was the natural consequence of his continuing struggle to defend the reform against a host of opponents and of the process of consolidation that took place after he had established himself securely at Zurich.

Two things distinguished his view of Christian society from the ideal held by the men of the middle ages: he denied the clergy the exercise of secular power and rejected the doctrines of papal supremacy over secular princes; he replaced the old church as the source of religious authority, with the scripture, illumined by the Holy Spirit. As Brockelmann has said, his conception of the relationship between the magistracy and the clergy approached the Gelasianism of the early middle ages.

When Zwingli said that the magistrate should raise the standards of his justice toward those of divine righteousness, he demonstrated an optimism and faith in the power of God's Word that set him apart from Luther.

If there was a weakness in Zwingli's theory of government, it lay in his faith in the Christian magistrate. This faith led him to spiritualize the church and to identify the visible church with the outward structure of the community, which distinguishes his view of the church from Calvin's. This fault can be explained both as the natural result of the city's corporate tradition of government and society and as the weakness of an age in which men had lost hope that the clergy could reform itself. In reaction to the corruption of the church Zwingli put too much trust in the Christian magistrate. But there was more to it than that. Above all, Zwingli had faith that the Spirit of God which worked through the preaching of the Word would transform all things. A magistrate who allowed the Word to be proclaimed posed no present or future threat for Zwingli.

The peculiar nature of his conception of the church made his system difficult to spread. Military defeat checked its progress in German Switzerland, and only for a while did it win a strong following in the south German towns whose political structure was similar to Zurich's. It was left to Calvin to evolve an ecclesiology that made the church strong and flexible enough to adapt to various conditions and to maintain itself against the opposition of secular governments. To be sure, if Zwingli's view of the church were separated from the political context within which he developed it, it would provide a model for congregationalism. Whether or not this was ever done must remain a problem that can not be considered here.

Zwingli never tried to set up a system in which God's representative directed the policies of the government, which is what the modern usage of the term "theocracy" would imply. In a far broader sense he did indeed pursue a theocratic goal. He tried to free the clergy from the concerns of worldly wealth and power in order that they might preach the Gospel and not interfere with the Christian magistrate's performance of the duties that God had assigned him. Zwingli assumed that only where the clergy and the secular ruler fulfilled the obligations which they had to a Christian society could the will of God be realized, and he knew no other purpose for the community than to follow the divine will. His view of society and its aim represented a particular version of the theocratic ideal which dominated the political thought of sixteenth-century Europe.

Bibliography

PRIMARY SOURCES

EGLI, EMIL (ed.), *Actensammlung zur Geschichte der Zürcher Reformation in den Jahren 1519–1533* (Zürich: Druck von J. Schabelitz, 1879).
────── (ed.), *Dokumente und Abhandlung zur Geschichte Zwinglis und seiner Zeit* vol. I of *Analecta Reformatoria*, 2 vols. (Zürich: Druck und Verlag von Zürcher & Furrer, 1899).
ERASMUS, DESIDERIUS, *The Complaint of Peace*, ed. J. Hirten (New York: Scholar's Facsimiles and Reprints, 1946).
────── *The Education of a Christian Prince*, trans. Lester K. Born (New York: Columbia University Press, 1936).
────── *The Praise of Folly*, trans. H. H. Hudson (Princeton: Princeton University Press, 1941).
JACKSON, SAMUEL M. (ed.), *The Latin Works of Huldreich Zwingli, Together with Selections from his German Works*, ed. Clarence Nevin Heller, 3 vols. (Philadelphia: The Heidelberg Press, 1912–29).
JEWEL, JOHN, *An Apology of the Church of England*, ed. J. E. Booty (Ithaca: Cornell University Press, 1963).
KÖHLER, WALTHER (ed.), *Das Buch der Reformation Huldrych Zwinglis* (München: Ernst Reinhardt, 1926).
LUTHER, MARTIN, *D. Martin Luther's Werke, Kritische Gesammtausgabe*, ed. Paul Pietsch, 94 vols. (Weimar: Hermann Böhlaus, 1900), vol. XI.
MELANCHTHON, PHILIP, *Philipi Melanthonis Opera Quae Supersunt Omnia*, ed. Carolus Gottlieb Bretschneider, 28 vols. (Halis Saxonum: Apud. C. A. Schwetschke et Filium, 1834–60), vol. I.
VON MURALT, LEONHARD, and Walter Schmid (eds.), *Quellen zur Geschichte der Täufer in der Schwiez* (Zürich: S. Hirzel Verlag, 1952), vol. I.
ROBINSON, HASTINGS (ed.), *The Zürich Letters Comprising the Correspondence of Several English Bishops and Others, with Some of the Helvetian Reformers During the Early Part of the Reign of Queen Elizabeth*, 2 vols. (Cambridge: The University Press, 1842–1845), vol. I.
SPINKA, MATTHEW (ed.), *Advocates of Reform from Wycliff to Erasmus*, vol. XIV of *The Library of Christian Classics*, ed. John Baillie, John T. McNeil, Henry P. Van Dusen (Philadelphia: The Westminster Press, 1953).
The Holy Bible Containing the Old and New Testaments, Authorized King James Version (New York: Thomas Nelson & Sons, 1941).
ZWINGLI, HULDREICH, *Huldreich Zwinglis sämtliche Werke*, ed. Emil Egli, Georg Finsler, 14 vols. (Leipzig und Berlin: Verlag von C. A. Schwetschke und Sohn, 1905–59).

ZWINGLI, ULRICH, *Eine Auswahl aus seinen Schriften auf das vierhundertjährige Jubiläum der Zürcher Reformation*, ed. Georg Finsler, Walther Köhler, D. Arnold Rügg (Zürich: Schulthess & Co., 1918).

SECONDARY SOURCES

BAUR, AUGUST, *Zwingli's Theologie Ihr Werden und Ihr System*, 2 vols. (Halle: Max Niemeyer, 1885–9). vol. I.

BENDER, HAROLD S., *Conrad Grebel 1498–1526 Founder of the Swiss Brethren* (Scottsdale, Pa.: Herald Press, 1950).

BLANKE, FRITZ, *Brüder in Christo, Die Geschichte der ältesten Täufergemeinde (Zollikon, 1525)* (Zürich: Zwingli Verlag, 1955).

BLUNTSCHLI, J. C., *Staats-und Rechtsgeschichte der Stadt und Landschaft Zürich* (Zürich: Druck und Verlag von Orell, Füssli & Compagnie, 1838), bks. 2, 3.

BROCKELMANN, BRIGITTE, *Das Corpus Christianum bei Zwingli*, Heft 5 of *Breslauer historische Forschungen* (Breslau: Prietbatschs Buchhandlung, 1938).

BULLINGER, HEINRICH, *Reformationsgeschichte*, ed. J. J. Hottinger, H. H. Vögeli, 3 vols. (Frauenfeld: Druck und Verlag von Ch. Beyel, 1839), vol. I.

DÄNDLIKER, KARL, *Geschichte der Schweiz mit besonderen Rücksicht auf die Entwicklung des Verfassungs-und Kulturlebens von den ältesten Zeiten bis zur Gegenwart*, 3 vols. (Zürich: Druck und Verlag von Schulthess & Co., 1901), vol. II.

———— *Geschichte der Stadt und des Kanton Zürich*, 3 vols. (Zürich: Druck und Verlag von Schulthess, 1908), vol. II.

EGLI, EMIL, *Schweizerische Reformationsgeschichte umfassend die Jahre 1519–1525* (Zürich: Druck und Verlag von Zürcher & Furrer, 1910).

FARNER, ALFRED, *Die Lehre von Kirche und Staat bei Zwingli* (Tübingen: Verlag von J. C. B. Mohr [Paul Siebeck], 1930).

FARNER, OSKAR, *Huldrych Zwingli*, 4 vols. (Zürich: Zwingli Verlag, 1943–60).

FUETER, EDUARD, *Geschichte des europäischen Staatensystems von 1492–1559*, Abteilung II of the *Handbuch der mittelalterlichen und neueren Geschichte*, Ed. Georg V. Below, F. Meinecke (München und Berlin: Druck und Verlag von R. Oldenbourg, 1919).

FRANZ, GUNTHER, *Der Deutsche Bauernkrieg*, 5, Auflage (Darmstadt: Wissenschaftliche Buchgesellschaft, 1958).

GAGLIARDI, E., *Geschichte der Schweiz von den Anfängen bis zur Gegenwart*, 2 vols. (Zürich: Orell & Füssli Verlag, 1938), vol. II.

GELDNER, FERDINAND, *Die Staatsauffassung und Fürstenlehre des Erasmus von Rotterdam*, Heft 191 of *Historische Studien* (Berlin: Verlag Emil Ebering, 1930).

GERIG, G., *Reisläufer und Pensionenherren in Zürich 1519–1532. Ein Beitrag zur Kenntnis der Kräfte welche die Reformation widerstrebten*, no 12 of *Schweizer Studien zur Geschichtswissenschaft*, Neue Folge (Zürich: Verlag AG Gebr. Leeman & Co., 1947).

GEWIRTH, A., *Marsilius of Padua: The Defender of Peace*, 2 vols. (New York: Columbia University Press, 1951), vol. I.

GIERKE, OTTO VON, *Das Deutsche Genossenschaftsrecht*, 4 vols. (Berlin: Weidmannische Buchhandlung, 1868–1913), vol. III.

GÖTERS, J. F. GERHARD, *Ludwig Hätzer Spiritualist und Antritrinitarier, Eine Randfigur der Frühen Täuferbewegung*, vol. XXV of the *Quellen und Forschungen zur Reformationsgeschichte*, Neue Folge (Gütersloh: C. Bertelsmann Verlag, 1957).

GUGGENBÜHL, G., *Geschichte der Schweizerischen Eidgenossenschaft*, 2 vols. (Erlenbach-Zürich: Eugen Rentsch Verlag, 1947), vol. I.

HEUSLER, ANDREAS, *Schweizerische Verfassungsgeschichte* (Basel: Frobenius AG, 1920).

KÖHLER, WALTHER, *Huldrych Zwingli*, 2nd. ed. (Stuttgart: K. F. Köhler Verlag, 1952).

KRAJEWSKI, E., MANZ, FELIX (ca. 1500–27) Das Leben des Zürcher Täuferführers, Dissertation (Zürich: 1956).

KRESSNER, HELMUT, *Schweizer Ursprünge des anglikanischen Staatskirchentums*, no. 170, Heft 1 of the *Schriften des Vereins für Reformationsgeschichte*, Jahrgang 59 (Gütersloh: C. Bertelsmann Verlag, 1953).

LARGIADÈR, A., *Geschichte von Stadt und Landschaft Zürich*, 2 vols. (Erlenbach-Zürich: Eugen Rentsch Verlag, 1945), vol. I.

LEY, ROGER, *Kirchenzucht bei Zwingli* (Zürich: Zwingli Verlag, 1948).

LOCHER, G. W., *Der Eigentumsbegriff als Problem evangelischer Theologie* (Zürich: Zwingli Verlag, 1954).

LOHMANN, ANNEMARIE, *Zur Geistigen Entwicklung Thomas Müntzers*, vol. XLVII of *Beiträge zur Kulturgeschichte des Mittelalters und der Renaissance*, ed. Walter Götz (Leipzig/Berlin: B. G. Tübner, 1931).

LITTELL, F. H., *The Anabaptist View of the Church*, 2nd. ed. (Boston: Starr King Press, 1958).

MAURER, WILHELM, *Das Verhältnis des Staates zur Kirche nach humanistischer Anschauung, vornehmlich bei Erasmus*, Heft 1 of *Aus der Welt der Religion: Forschungen und Berichte, Problemgeschichtliche Reihe*, ed. H. Frick, R. Otto, E. Fascher, G. Mennsching (Giessen: Verlag von Alfred Töppelmann, 1930).

MCNEIL, JOHN T., *The History and Character of Calvinism*, 2nd printing with corrections (New York: Oxford University Press, 1957).

MURALT, LEONHARD VON, *Stadtgemeinde und Reformation in der Schweiz: Habilitationsschrift der Philosophischen Fakultät in der Universität Zürich* (Zürich: AG Gebr. Leeman & Co., 1930).

MOELLER, BERND, *Reichsstadt und Reformation*, Nr. 180 of the *Schriften des Vereins für Reformationsgeschichte*, Jahrgang 69, (Gütersloh: Gütersloher Verlagshaus Gerd Mohn, 1962).

NABHOLZ, HANS, LEONHARD VON MURALT, RICHARD FELLER, and EMIL DÜRR, *Geschichte der Schweiz von den ältesten Zeiten bis zum Ausgang des sechzehnten Jahrhunderts*, 2 vols. (Zürich: Schulthess & Co., 1932).

OBERMAN, H. A., *The Harvest of Medieval Theology: Gabriel Biel and Late Medieval Nominalism* (Cambridge Mass: Harvard University Press, 1963).

PEACHY, PAUL, *Die Sociale Herkunft der Schweizer Täufer in the Reformationszeit: Eine religionssoziologische Untersuchung*, no. 4 of the *Schriftenreihe des Mennonitischen Geschichtsverein* (Karlsruhe: Buchdruckerei und Verlag Heinrich Schneider, 1954).

PESTALOZZI, THEODOR, *Die Gegner Zwinglis am Grossmünsterstift in Zürich. Der erste Teil einer Arbeit über die katholische Opposition gegen Zwingli in Stadt und Landschaft Zürich, 1519–1531* (Zürich: Druck von AG Gebr. Leeman & Co., 1918).

PREUSCHEN, ERWIN, *Das Altertum*, vol. I of the *Handbuch der Kirchengeschichte für Studierende*, ed. Gustav Krüger, 4 vols. (Tübingen: J. C. B. Mohr, 1911–13), part 1.

ROTHER, SIEGFRIED, *Die religiösen und geistigen Grundlagen der Politik Huldrych Zwinglis. Ein Beitrag zum Problem des christlichen Staates*, no. 7 of the *Erlanger Abhandlungen zur mittleren und neueren Geschichte*, Neue Folge, ed. Heinz Löwe, Ludwig Zimmermann (Erlangen: Verlag von Palm & Enke, 1956).

RICH, ARTHUR, *Die Anfänge der Theologie Huldrych Zwinglis* (Zürich: Zwingli Verlag, 1949).

SCHMID, HEINRICH, *Zwinglis Lehre von der göttlichen und menschlichen Gerechtigkeit*, vol. XII of *Studien zur Dogmengeschichte und systematischen Theologie*, ed. Fritz Blanke, Arthur Rich, Otto Weber (Zürich: Zwingli Verlag, 1959).

SCHMIDT, KURT DIETRICH, *Grundriss der Kirchengeschichte*, 3. Auflage (Göttingen: Vandenhœck & Ruprecht, 1960).

SCHOTTENLOHER, KARL, *Bibliographie zur Deutschen Geschichte im Zeitalter der Glaubensspaltung, 1517–1585*, 6 vols. (Leipzig: K. W. Hiersemann, 1933–39).

SEEBERG, REINHOLD, *Lehrbuch der Dogmengeschichte*, 6th ed., 4 vols. (Darmstadt: Wissenschaftliche Buchgesellschaft, 1959), vol. III.

SPITZ, LEWIS W., *Conrad Celtis, The German Arch-Humanist* (Cambridge: Harvard University Press, 1957).

—— *The Religious Renaissance of the German Humanists* (Cambridge: Harvard University Press, 1963).

STAEHELIN, RUDOLPH, *Huldreich Zwingli. Sein Leben und Werken nach den Quellen dargestellt*, 2 vols. (Basel: Benno Schwabe Verlagsbuchhandlung, 1895).

STEFFEN-ZEHNDER, JOSY-MARIA, *Das Verhältnis von Staat und Kirche im spätmittelalterlichen Zürich* (Immensee, Schwyz: Calendaria A. G., 1935).

STEINEMANN, HANS, *Geschichte der Dorfverfassung im Kanton Zürich* (Affoltern a. A.: Buchdruckerei Dr. J. Weiss, 1932).

TAVARD, GEORGE H., *Holy Writ or Holy Church: The Crisis of the Protestant Reformation* (New York: Harper and Brothers, 1959).

TELLENBACH, GERD, *Church, State and Christian Society at the Time of the Investiture Contest*, trans. by R. F. Bennett (Oxford: Basil Blackwell, 1948).

WACKERNAGEL, RUDOLPH, *Geschichte der Stadt Basel*, 2 vols. (Basel: Verlag von Helbing & Lichtenhahn, 1916), vol. II, part 2.

YODER, JOHN H., *Täufertum und Reformation in der Schweiz: I. Die Gespräche zwischen Täufern und Reformation 1523–1528*, Nr. 6 of *Schriftenreihe des Mennonitischen Geschichts-Verein* (Karlsruhe: Buchdruckerei und Verlag H. Schneider, 1962).

ARTICLES AND PERIODICALS

BAINTON, R. H., "Religious Liberty and the Parable of the Tares," *Early and Medieval Christianity*, series 1 of *The Collected Papers in Church History*, 3 vols. (Boston: Beacon Press, 1962).

BIRNBAUM, "The Zwinglian Reformation in Zürich," Archives de Sociologie des Religions, vol. IV, 15–30.

BOEHMER, P., O.F.M., "Ockham's Political Ideas," *Collected Articles on Ockham*, ed. E. M. Buytaert, no. 12 of *The Philosophy Series*, Franciscan Institute Publications (St. Bonaventure, N.Y.: The Franciscan Institute, 1958).

BORN, LESTER K., "Some Notes of the Political Theories of Erasmus," *Journal of Modern History*, II (1930), 226–36.

BORNKAMM, H., "Das Ringen der Motive in den Anfängen der reformatorischen Kirchenverfassung," *Das Jahrhundert der Reformation Gestalten und Kräfte* (Göttingen: Vanderhœck & Ruprecht, 1961).

DÄNDLIKER, KARL, Die Berichterstattungen und Anfragen der Züricher Regierung an die Landschaft in der Zeit vor der Reformation," *Jahrbuch für Schweizerische Geschichte*, XXI (1896), 37–61.

EGLI, EMIL, "Die Zürcherische Kirchenpolitik von Waldmann bis Zwingli," *Jahrbuch für Schweizerische Geschichte*, XXI (1896), 1–31.

ENTHOVEN, LUDWIG, "Uber die Institutio principis Christiani des Erasmus. Ein Beitrag zur Theorie der Fürstenerziehung," *Neue Jahrbücher für das klassische Altertum, Geschichte und Deutsche Literatur und für Pädagogik*, XIV (1909), 312–29.

FIFE, ROBERT, "Humanistic Currents in the Reformation Era," *The Germanic Review*, XII, no. 2 (April, 1937), 75–94.

HILLERBRAND, HANS, "The Origin of Sixteenth-Century Anabaptism: Another Look," Archiv für Reformationsgeschichte, vol. 53 (1962), 152–80.
——— "The 'Turning Point' of the Zwinglian Reformation: Review and Discussion," *The Mennonite Quarterly Review*, XXXIX (1965), 309–12.

KÖHLER, WALTHER, "Huldrych Zwinglis Bibliothek," *Neujahrsblatt zum Besten des Waisenhauses in Zürich für 1921*, LXXXIV (1921), 1–33.

LIECHTENHAN, RUDOLPH, "Die politische Hoffnung des Erasmus und ihr Zusammenbruch," *Gedenkschrift zum 400. Todestage des Erasmus von Rotterdam* (Basel: Verlag Braus-Riggenbach, 1936).

LOCHER, G., "Die evangelishe Stellung der Reformatoren zum öffentlichen Leben," *Kirchliche Zeitfragen*, Heft 26 (1950).
———"Staat und Politik in der Lehre der Reformatoren," *Reformatio*, Vol. I (1952), 202–13.

MURALT, L. VON, "Zum Problem: Reformation und Täufertum," *Zwingliana*, VI (1934), 65–85.

OECHSLI, WILHELM, "Zwingli als Staatsmann," *Ulrich Zwingli 1519–1919*. *Zum Gedächtnis der Zürcher Reformation 1519–1919* (Zürich: Gedruckt und verlegt von der Buchdruckerei Berichthaus, 1919).

OBERMANN, H., "The Virgin Mary in Evangelical Perspective," *Journal of Ecumenical Studies*, I (1964), 271–98.

POLLET, J. V. M., "Zwinglianisme," *Dictionnaire de Théologie Catholique*, ed. A. Vacant, E. Mangenot, E. Amann (Paris: Librarie Letouzey et Ané, 1926–50), 3745–927.

ROHRER, FRANZ, "Das sogenannte Waldmannische Koncordat," *Jahrbuch für Schweizerische Geschichte*, IV (1879), 1–33.

SCHULTZE, ALFRED, "Stadtgemeinde und Kirche im Mittelalter," *Festgabe für Rudolph Sohm* (München & Leipzig: Duncker Verlag, 1914).

——— "Stadtgemeinde und Reformation," *Recht und Staat in Geschichte und Gegenwart. Eine Sammlung von Vorträgen und Schriften aus dem Gebiet der gesamten Staatswissenschaft* (Tübingen: Verlag von J. C. B. Mohr, 1918).

USTERI, MARTIN, "Initia Zwingliana. Beiträge zur Geschichte der Studien und der Geistesentwicklung Zwinglis in der Zeit von Beginn der Reformatorischen Tätigkeit," *Theologische Studien und Kritiken. Eine Zeitschrift für das gesamte Gebiet der Theologie*, LVIII, I (1885), 607–71.

——— "Initia Zwingliana," *Theologische Studien und Kritiken*, LIX (1886), 95–159.

VASELLA, OSKAR, "Kleine Beiträge zur Geschichte der Täuferbewegung in der Scheiz," *Zeitschrift für Schweizerische Kirchengeschichte*, XLVIII, Heft II–III (1954), 179–86.

WHITNEY, E. A., "Erastianism and Divine Right," *Huntington Library Quarterly*, II, no. 4 (July, 1939).

WOLF, ERIK, "Die Sozialtheologie Zwinglis," *Festschrift Guido Kisch Rechtshistorische Forschungen*, ed. friends, colleagues, and students (Stuttgart: W. Kohlhammer Verlag, 1955).

YODER, JOHN H., "The Turning Point in the Zwinglian Reformation," *Mennonite Quarterly Review*, XXXII (April, 1958), 128–40.

——— "A Review and Discussion," *Mennonite Quarterly Review*, XXXV, no. 1 (January, 1961), 79–88.

OTHER SOURCES

GÖTZE, ALFRED, *Frühneuhochdeutsches Glossar*, no. 101 of *Kleine Texte für Vorlesungen und Übungen*, ed. Kurt Aland, 6. Auflage (Berlin: Walter De Gruyter & Co., 1960).

Index

Abbot of Kappel, 197
Abbot of Wettingen, 92, 144; complains to the Diet about Stumpf, 92; complains to the Council, 142
Aberli, Heini, 61, 63, 64, 147n, 179; violates the fast and demands communion in both kinds, 60; request for communion in both kinds represents desires of the radicals, 145; see also Baptists, Grebel, Zwingli and the Baptists, Zwingli and the enthusiasts, Zwingli and the extremists, Zwingli and Grebel, Zwingli and the radicals
abolition of the Mass: a question of timing divided Zwingli from Grebel and Stumpf, 190; see also Mass, Zwingli and Grebel, Zwingli and the Mass, Zwingli and the radicals, Zwingli and the sacraments
Abraham, 213
Acts, 150, 151
adiaphoron, 78
adiaphora, 87
Admonition to Schwyz, 104, 128; general argument, 105–6; as an early specimen of Zwingli's political theory, 105; purpose, 106; successful effect short-lived, 106–7
Affoltern, 99
Against the Wiles of the Anabaptist (1527), 150; indicates discussions of separate church before issue of infant baptism, 152
Albisrieden, 178
allgemein versamlung der Christen, 82; see also Zwingli and the church
Ammann, Rudolph: placed under the ban of the church, 91; letter to the Council, 91n; later career, 91n
Anabaptism, 60, 66, 67; raises issue of role of Christian religion in society, 84; see also Baptist, Zwingli and Baptists, Zwingli and Grebel
Anabaptists, 67n

Anfrage, 54n; see also Volksanfrage
Anglican polity, xi
anti-French party, 54n; see also pro-French party
anti-mercenary party: had popular support, 56; see also pro-mercenary party, Zwingli and the mercenary system
Antioch, 185
anti-tithe agitation: see tithes, Zwingli and individualism, Zwingli and the radicals
Apologeticus Archeteles (1522), 36, 90, 128, 135, 149n; the argument of, 115–26; sanctioned by the Council, 114, 115; bears out assertion that Zwingli's views remained consistent, 115; coherent justification for reform carried out under leadership of Council, 125
Apology, 177
apostles, 58
appeal of moderates: attempt to conciliate the men who sided with Grebel, 198; see also Grebel, Zwingli and radicals
Appenzell, 139, 140, 194; congregation of fulfils requirement for a valid church, 191; assembly of had worldly as well as spiritual responsibilities, 192
Archduke Ferdinand, 139
Arian heresy, 117
Arians, 117
artisan: support for Constafel, 52
assemblies of canton: subordinated to the Council, 220; see also Council
assembly of Christian people: composition, 74; see also church, Zwingli and the church, Zwingli and society
assembly of Christians, 83; a proper assembly, 136; see also church, Zwingli and the church, Zwingli and society
Augustine, 22, 42, 117n

pands circle of admirers, 58; zealous followers, 71; demands right to speak before the Council, 72; threat to kidnap him, 74, 75; attempts to murder him, 88, 95, 103; concept of Christian freedom, 76, 77, 83, 84; requirements of Christian love, 78; use of Old Testament prophets, 79; concept of essentials and non-essentials (adiaphora), 80, 85, 87, 195; definition of good works, 80, 81; response to Bishop's commission, 82; twofold conception of law, 83; debate with Fattlin, 84, 85, 86; protected by policy of Holy See, 89; shifts emphasis of preaching, 93, 94; and monks, 93, 94, 95; debate with Lambert, 94; oath as People's Priest, 94; accused of radicalism, 98, 110, 111; and his followers heretics, 101; followers lampoon Faber, 139; and his followers, 149; answer to Vadian, 102; delays answer to Bishop's letter, 104; distinguished between Hugo and Faber's faction, 104; writes *Godly Admonition*, 104; and image of God, 105; role prophetic, 106; hopes dashed, 107; threatens to exercise right of self-help, 113; support for him in canton, 114; affirms he is no radical, 114; use of case of Paul and Timothy, 117, 187; argument for abolition of ceremonies, 120; and man's nature, 128; family fears his radicalism, 129; proposal to the Pope, 130; resigns as People's Priest, 131, 142; freed from priestly functions, 132; open to criticism, 133; belief that Disputation will conform to beliefs of other Christians, 135–6; reply to Faber, 135–8; burned in effigy, 139; impact of preaching, 141; reply to Bishop's letter, 149n; question of usury, 160–1; significance of discussion of abolition of ceremonials not tithes at end of *On Divine and Human Righteousness*, 166–7; concept of the just, 167; and Jud preach against images, 178; and Jud results of sermons, 179; satisfied with course

of events, 182; sharp response to Konrad Schmid, 187–8; proposal does not bear out Yoder's contention, 202; accusation that he betrayed his original position, 207; right in context of time, 208; theological vision, 208; forced to alter his views, 209; part in founding the synod, 209; views (1528–1531) a rationalization for the creation of a theocracy, 214; influences upon his programme, 219

aim of reform of, ix, 29, 40, 85, 130; win Confederacy, 51; reform church from within, 58; salvation for whole of society, 79; win Bishop, 89; convert people of Schwyz, 104; attitude consistent with plan for Christian renewal, 104; serve well-being of all Christians, 112; prepare men for citizenship in the Heavenly City, 115; put religion on theocentric basis, 121; "spiritualization" of religious affairs, 122; to win all for Christ, 200; proper co-operation of ruler and priest, 218; win all Europe, 220; win entire community for Gospel, 224; see also policy of reform

and baptism: magistrate to control ban and baptism, 167; place of baptism in Church Universal, 171; twofold nature of baptism and Eucharist, 171, 212; spoke of baptism as an outward sign before *Täufer* raised the question of rebaptism, 171; infant baptism and confirmation, 171; did not reject infant baptism, 172; unbaptized children not damned, 172; infant baptism external sign of membership in a Christian society, 172; see also Zwingli and the sacraments

and the Baptists: concept of patience for the weak applied to Baptists, 78; unlike Baptists did not call for a return to norms of early church, 113; testimony in 1525, 150; account of origin of movement, 150–1; rebaptism a sign of "tumultuous men," 151; Baptists made contradictory demands, 152, 153;

cause difficulty over externals, 205;
criticism of Baptists, 212, 213; see
also Baptists, Grebel, radicals,
Zwingli and Grebel, Zwingli and
the radicals
and Blarer, 188, 209n, 214–16
and celibacy: married, 107; marriage
kept secret, 109; seeks end to
clerical celibacy, 110, 112; promises married clergy won't make
prebends hereditary, 114; celibate
life, 127
and the church, 79, 129; rebirth of
the church, 45, 46; desire to maintain unity of church, 46; concept
of Kingdom of God, 77, 78;
Christ's kingdom, 122, 123; a generally assembled church, 81, 82,
83; trust in a Christian assembly,
84; church's relationship to magistrate, 86; views on church and
magistrate consistent, 115; left
exercise of secular authority to
guardians of kingdom of this
world, 123; doctrine excludes idea
of believer's church, 86, 106;
preaching of Word constitutive element in forming church, 110;
called for a return to traditions of
church drawn from proper sources,
113; proper definition of church
and bishops, 117; Christ rock upon
which church is built, 118; sure
salvation, 122; weakness in idea
of the church, 122; belief in Christ
not membership in institutional
church the ground of salvation,
123; church born in Christ's blood,
123; church of the wicked, 123;
spiritual *versus* institutional church,
123; no secular power for true
church, 123; requirements for
membership in the church, 124;
view of relationship between church
and government not fully clarified,
124; Christ's church soul of community, 125; church and magistracy, 128; policy and ecclesiology
consistent, 131; lack of clarity concerning structure of the reformed
church, 137; never mentioned
church in sermon, 167; discussion
of the ban, 174–5; doctrine of
church explains division with radi-

cals, 216; doctrine of church pre-
condition for success, 216; doctrine of church made it difficult
to spread, 226; congregation autonomy, 4, 24–25, 55, 174, 175, 226;
Church Universal, 174; and Gospel, 117, 124; under God, 123,
124; free, 125; mystical body, 125;
defined, 170–1; and local churches,
172; members known only to God,
212; definition of the church, 40,
86, 87, 122, 136, 137, 170, 183–4,
191, 193, 216; charges that he
compromised, 193; local gatherings
of the church, 85; definition provides rational for "provincial
church" to undertake reform, 134–
5, 136; mixed bodies, 152, 172,
210, 212; biblical requirements for,
183; infallible, 184; visible church
identified with political assembly,
55, 87, 122, 123, 124, 129, 137,
170, 172, 184, 185, 213; *curiata
comitia* an adequate consensus of
the church, 215; see also church,
Zwingli and society
and the old church: continues to
attack corruption of the church,
57; maintains campaign, 103;
answer to the Bishop, 114; bishops
fail to fulfil requirements of office,
115; old church failed to meet
needs of Swiss, 115; questions
sacramental function of bishops,
115–16; Bishop placed Gospel
under authority of an institution
founded upon precepts of men,
118; attacks misuse of excommunication, 118; abuse of pope's and
bishop's office, 118; his programme
served interests of commonwealth
better than bishop's, 120; anger at
greed of hierarchy, 120; unreliability of man-made religious decisions, 122; reasons for rejecting
institutions of old church, 125;
attitude toward tradition, 127;
criticism of theologians and the
church, 128; criticism of higher
clergy, 135, 135n; attacks clergy's
status, 182
and the clergy: function of the
clergy, ix, x, xx, 79, 81, 83, 109,
110, 116, 117, 122, 123, 136, 170,